JMEWS ◆ Journal of
Middle East Women's Studies

Volume 12 • Number 2 • July 2016

Everyday Intimacies of the Middle East

SERTAÇ SEHLIKOGLU and ASLI ZENGIN, Special Issue Editors

Tribute to Assia Djebar (1936–2015)

The Writing Subjects: Halide Edip and Assia Djebar •
DIDEM HAVLIOĞLU

Languaging Space in Assia Djebar's *L'amour, la fantasia* •
RACHEL ROTHENDLER

Everyday Intimacies of the Middle East

✧ ✧

ASLI ZENGIN and SERTAÇ SEHLIKOGLU

In the last decade the question of intimacy in the Middle East has received renewed scholarly attention in its relation to love, sentimentality, sexuality, gender, and erotics (Mahdavi 2009; Najmabadi 2005; Ozyegin 2015; Peirce 2010; Pursley 2012). This research has greatly contributed to understanding the role of distinctive historical and social processes and transformations in constructing the realms of intimacy. We suggest that the question of intimacy and its relation to the everyday domains of life requires further attention. How people, bodies, and objects meet and touch—and the zones of contact that they create (Pratt and Rosner 2006, 17) in the everyday life of publics, institutions, and families—are critical issues to further examine.

This special issue aims to contribute to studies of intimacy first from an area studies perspective and second from a theoretical standpoint. Regarding the first goal, the authors in this volume explore how multiple domains and forms of intimacies are defined, shaped, constructed, and transformed across the cultural and social worlds of the Middle East. Two historians, Afsaneh Najmabadi (2005) and Dror Ze'evi (2006), have made key theoretical contributions to the notion of intimacy in the Middle East. Their work has inspired this special issue in two ways. First, they trace links between the overarching structural conditions that individuals operate in (religion, state, family, kinship) and the historical trajectories of norms and their regulation. Second, Najmabadi's and Ze'evi's works emphasize the interactive and intersubjective registers of intimacies in the Middle East. They do so by carefully examining and emphasizing that cross gender dynamics in different parts of the region and at different historical moments of change. How should we calibrate these changes in a time of rapid transition? Focusing on everyday definitions, circulations, constructions, and transformations of intimacies in Egypt, Turkey, and Israel, the articles in this issue engage with this question.

The second goal of this special issue is to explore and interrogate the analytic, theoretical, and political work intimacy does and promises as a concept. What do we mean by intimacy; what does it hold for our individual and social lives; and what kinds of social, political, and economic possibilities does intimacy create? In seeking to address these questions, this issue discusses intimacy as a concept that is multiple in its formation, circulation, and organization. We suggest that intimacy is integral to the formation of what is called "the human"—selves, subjectivities, communities, publics, collectives, and socialities. We also examine the close relationship between intimacy and power, violence, sex, sexuality, gender, domesticity, embodiment, relatedness, commodification, and spatial production and organization. These domains and their related social actors construct, privilege, and deconstruct specific intimate worlds and intimacies.

Intimacy, as an analytic concept, interrogates and transgresses established understandings of private and public domains, highlighting how such notions nurture intimacy itself. For us, the private is always "mediated by publics" (Berlant and Warner 1998, 547), and therefore notions, languages, and constructs of intimacy are always already public. Discourses and practices of intimacy are important means of mediating between the private and the public but even more broadly between different socialities, spaces, and geographies. This volume takes up the idea of intimacy as a form of mediation and investigates what forms of intimacy may be identified in relation to and beyond the domains of sex, sexuality, domesticity, and familiarity.

This collection engages with scholarship on the exercise and organization of intimate state power (Aretxaga 2003; Hoodfar 1997; Joseph 1993; Mir-Hosseini 1993; Povinelli 2006; Stoler 2002). The primary domains of this (political) socialization range from regulations related to marriage, childbearing and child rearing, and reproductive health and sexual life to assumptions and expectations about gender identity and its related behaviors and embodiments. With the implementation of legal strategies and regulatory practices, the so-called sphere of the private emerges as a locus of evolving forms of state power that determines the intimacies (sexual, domestic, and family relations) that are legitimate (Kandiyoti 1991; Parla 2001). Referring to these discussions, we analyze the forms of state power that operate through the establishment of intimate and sexual links to the lives and bodies of its individual citizens.

Without question, intimacies are also formed beyond local and national contexts. As we stress in this issue, the role of transnational processes in shaping existing forms of intimacy and producing new ones necessitates special attention. The dramatic increase in the extent of connectedness between people through communication technologies, economic exchanges, and forms of mobility calls for a transnational perspective to understand the novel forms intimacy takes.

Overall, each piece in this collection presents a context-specific discussion of how legal, economic, and political regulations and practices promote a social environment in which certain intimate bonds are stigmatized, sanctioned, or dissolved while others are encouraged. We hope this volume will trigger further discussion on theoretical formulations and regional understandings of intimacy.

ASLI ZENGIN is an anthropologist and postdoctoral fellow in the Women's, Gender, and Sexuality Studies Program at Brandeis University. Zengin has widely published in peer-reviewed journals, including *Anthropologica* and *Transgender Studies Quarterly*, and edited volumes. Contact: a.zengin@gmail.com.

SERTAÇ SEHLIKOGLU is a social anthropologist at the University of Cambridge. Her work has been published in edited collections and in such peer-reviewed journals as the *Cambridge Journal of Anthropology, Feminist Media Studies*, the *Journal of Middle East Women's Studies*, and *Leisure Studies*. Contact: ss935@cam.ac.uk.

Acknowledgments
We would like to thank the Division of Social Anthropology at the University of Cambridge and Newnham College of Cambridge for their financial support of the workshop on intimacy that we organized with Marlene Schäfers at the University of Cambridge in May 2014. This special issue is composed of the papers selected for and discussed during this workshop.

References
Aretxaga, Begona. 2003. "Maddening States." *Annual Review of Anthropology* 32: 393–410.

Berlant, Lauren, and Michael Warner. 1998. "Sex in Public." *Critical Inquiry* 24, no. 2: 547–66.

Hoodfar, Homa. 1997. *Between Marriage and the Market: Intimate Politics and Survival in Cairo.* Berkeley: University of California Press.

Joseph, Suad. 1993. "Connectivity and Patriarchy among Urban Working-class Arab Families in Lebanon." *Ethos* 21, no. 4: 452–84.

Kandiyoti, Deniz. 1991. *Women, Islam, and the State*. Philadelphia: Macmillan.

Mahdavi, Pardis. 2009. *Passionate Uprisings: Iran's Sexual Revolution*. Stanford, CA: Stanford University Press.

Mir-Hosseini, Ziba. 1993. *Marriage on Trial: A Study of Islamic Family Law in Iran and Morocco.* London: Tauris.

Najmabadi, Afsaneh. 2005. *Women with Mustaches and Men without Beards: Gender and Sexual Anxieties of Iranian Modernity*. Berkeley: University of California Press.

Ozyegin, Gul. 2015. *New Desires, New Selves: Sex, Love, and Piety among Turkish Youth*. New York: New York University Press.

Parla, Ayse. 2001. "The 'Honor' of the State: Virginity Examinations in Turkey." *Feminist Studies* 27, no. 1: 65–88.

Peirce, Leslie. 2010. "Domesticating Sexuality: Harem Culture in Ottoman Imperial Law." In *Harem Histories: Envisioning Places and Living Spaces*, edited by Marilyn Booth, 104–35. Durham, NC: Duke University Press.

Povinelli, Elizabeth. 2006. *The Empire of Love: Toward a Theory of Intimacy, Genealogy, and Carnality.* Durham, NC: Duke University Press.

Pratt, Geraldine, and Victoria Rosner. 2006. "Introduction: The Global and the Intimate." *Women's Studies Quarterly* 34, nos. 1–2: 13–24.

Pursley, Sara. 2012. "Daughters of the Right Path: Family Law, Homosocial Publics, and the Ethics of Intimacy in the Works of Shi'i Revivalist Bint Al-Huda." *Journal of Middle East Women's Studies* 8, no. 2: 51–77.

Stoler, Ann Laura. 2002. *Carnal Knowledge and Imperial Power: Race and the Intimate in Colonial Rule.* Berkeley: University of California Press.

Ze'evi, Dror. 2006. *Producing Desire: Changing Sexual Discourse in the Ottoman Middle East, 1500–1900.* Berkeley: University of California Press.

Exercising in Comfort

Islamicate Culture of *Mahremiyet* in Everyday Istanbul

◊ ◊

SERTAÇ SEHLIKOGLU

ABSTRACT Women's control of their bodily movements, especially in the Islamicate contexts of the Middle East, constitutes a multilayered process of building privacy, heterosexuality, and intimacy. Physical exercise, however, with the extensive body movements it requires, problematizes women's ability to control their public sexualities. Drawing on ethnographic fieldwork conducted in 2011 and 2012 in Istanbul, this article explores the everyday concerns of Istanbulite women who seek *rahatlık* (comfort) during exercise. The interviewees frequently used the word *rahatlık* when referring to women-only spaces in the culture of *mahremiyet* (intimacy, privacy). This article furthers the scholarship on Muslim sexualities by examining the diversity of women's concerns regarding their public sexualities and the boundary-making dynamics in the culture of *mahremiyet*. I argue that *mahremiyet* operates as an institution of intimacy that provides a metacultural intelligibility for heteronormativity based on sexual scripts, normative spaces, and gendered acts.

KEYWORDS intimacy, sexuality, Turkey, public sphere, Islam

Referring to the choice of women-only gyms, the diverse body of interlocutors I met during my ethnographic fieldwork in 2011 and 2012 in Istanbul cited exercising in a *rahat* (comfortable) environment as the central concern. Depending on the context, *rahat* may refer to a place where men do not disturb women (*rahatsız etmek*) or a state in which women feel comfortable (*rahat hissetmek*) and do not fear being perceived as *rahat kadın* (lit. "comfortable woman," a Turkish expression referring to a seductive or promiscuous woman). The women I interviewed achieved *rahatlık* (comfort), which is directly linked to their ideas of self-control of their public sexualities, through multiple techniques in everyday life: gender segregation, the company of female friend(s), controlling bodily movements

JMEWS • Journal of Middle East Women's Studies • 12:2 • July 2016
DOI 10.1215/15525864-3507606 • © 2016 by the Association for Middle East Women's Studies

in public, and avoiding anything that makes them feel *rahatsız* (uncomfortable). Physical exercise in public spaces presents a challenge to women's pursuit of comfort by making their bodily movements visible. Sibel, one of my interlocutors, articulated the possible immodesty and sexualization of the movements involved in aerobics, for example, as "bedroom movements" (interview, January 27, 2012). What are the specificities of exercise that trouble women's concerns about their modesty in public?

This article is concerned with women's recurrent use of the word *rahat* to describe their feelings behind their choices of men-free environments in which to exercise. As this article suggests, women's demand for segregated exercise is linked to their control of (unruly) public sexuality, and their concerns are best explored in relation to the larger institution of intimacy and sexuality that I refer to as the culture of *mahremiyet* in Turkey. *Mahremiyet* is the Islamic notion of privacy and intimacy and acts as a boundary-making mechanism. I explore the culture of *mahremiyet* that is constituted through cultural scripts, normative spaces, and gendered acts in the Islamicate contexts of the Middle East. In their edited volume *Islamicate Sexualities*, Kathryn Babayan and Afsaneh Najmabadi (2008, ix) suggest the term *Islamicate* "to highlight a complex of attitudes and practices that pertain to cultures and societies that live by various versions of the religion Islam." When studying the culture of *mahremiyet*, understanding Istanbul as an Islamicate context fits well with the diverse Muslimhoods of my interlocutors.

This article is based on ten months of ethnographic fieldwork involving interviews with forty-two exercising Istanbulite women and participant observations in which women, including many who did not become interviewees, shared moments of joy, excitement, and frustration with me as we sweated side by side. These women were from upper-, middle-, and lower-class backgrounds and were between the ages of eighteen and sixty-two during the time of this research (2011–12).[1] Some of them were devout Kemalists, while a few others were Islamist activists.[2] However, they all shared similar concerns about public sexuality that led them to seek modesty and women-only spaces in which to exercise.[3] I further investigated the daily techniques women used to meet certain social expectations in relation to public sexuality and institutions of intimacy that are overshadowed by contemporary political debates on the head scarf.

I use the term *public sexuality* not to designate an act of sex in public but to refer to the making and remaking of (hetero)sexed bodies of women and men in public (and inevitably in private). The daily techniques I refer to are embedded not only in gender relations and gender constructions but also in the multiple ways women implement their subjectivities. Such an approach seeks to address the broad question of which mechanisms enable, define, and differentiate particular forms of "comfort" in homosocial settings for women and the particularities of what these women mean by "comfort" when explaining their choices of women-only gyms.

What is particular about segregation in an Islamicate context from the perspective of women? How do women shape, reshape, and negotiate with the culture of *mahremiyet* in their everyday lives when they exercise? These questions also compel me to ask how the historical, cultural, religious, and linguistic particularities of Turkey, as well as global visual interactions enabled by media tools, influence and shape women's privacy, specifically, the interaction between women's bodies and public space. In this perspective and analysis, it is crucial to disentangle women's dynamic and multiple gendered subjectivities. By "multiple," among other dimensions of subjecthood, I refer to the work of Asma Afsaruddin (1999, 4–5) and her call to "re-examine the notion of one grand paradigm of gender relations and gender exclusivity in cultures dominated by what are generally perceived to be Islamic/ate values."

To address the proposed questions, it is crucial to pay attention to language, history, and culture as constructing forces of sex and sexuality (Moore 1994). The analysis of *mahremiyet* revolves around women's own conceptualization and imagination. Therefore it may not necessarily involve a theological or legal analysis per se. In other words, instead of centralizing the rules that contemporary popular figures of Sunni Islamic jurisprudence in Turkey (Islamic clerics such as Mustafa İslamoğlu, Nihat Hatipoğlu, or Hayrettin Karaman) explain or which the Quran and the Hadith lay out, I pay attention to how Islamic/ate culture informs the everyday lives of individuals. I aim to understand the relational mechanisms used to maintain the limits and boundaries between gendered bodies, construct femininity and womanhood through space making, and regulate the relationship between the sexes. I argue that the "discomfort" women refer to leads them to choose segregation and to use multiple strategies to establish distance from the opposite sex. This is related not only to normality and (hetero)sexuality in Turkey as an Islamicate context but also to the ways women need to deal with the fragility of their privacy in public in an era when the institution of intimacy (Berlant 1998) is undergoing change.[4]

Mahremiyet as an Institution of Intimacy

Intimacy, in this article, is not necessarily tied to romantic coupling but involves boundaries and borders of the gendered female body and the ways female heterosexuality and femininity are built and rebuilt, made and remade in everyday life, producing gendered knowledge and meaning (Moore 1988; Strathern 1990; Yanagisako and Collier 1987). I consider the culture of *mahremiyet* an institution of intimacy (Berlant and Warner 1998). Lauren Berlant and Michael Warner (ibid., 553) discuss sex and sexuality as always "mediated by publics" and argue that heterosexual culture creates privacy to preserve its own coherency: "Heterosexual culture achieves much of its metacultural intelligibility through the ideologies and institutions of intimacy." Berlant (1998, 286, 288) defines the institution of intimacy as something "created to stabilize" and "normalize particular forms of knowledge and practice and to create compliant subjects." Such an approach illuminates the roles of unspoken assumptions, techniques, expectations, and nonverbal cues drawing the lines of intimacy observed in the multiple heterosocial and homosocial settings in which women engage in an activity—such as exercise—loaded with sexual appeal, as explained in the following pages. In other words, in this framework segregation and the culture of *mahremiyet* are inherently public.

The word *mahremiyet* is not translatable into English. It suggests multiple words, including privacy, secrecy, and domesticity. Derived from the Arabic root *h-r-m*, *mahremiyet* literally refers to forbiddenness and sacredness simultaneously. *Mahremiyet* relates to a notion of privacy and confidentiality, which the insider is expected to preserve and an outsider is expected not to violate. This insider-outsider dichotomy, however, is complex and multilayered. It does not neatly fit into the public-private dichotomy (Göle 1996). *Mahremiyet* is a mechanism that creates boundaries between spaces and individuals and within the body of the individual. The question of *mahremiyet* and the prerogatives to infringe such boundaries is the focal point of this article.

Mahremiyet, as a boundary-making mechanism, marks *mahrems* ("forbidden," such as same-sex individuals and opposite-sex relatives) as *insiders* and non-*mahrems* as *outsiders*. The regulatory and boundary-making nature of *mahremiyet* is embedded in Islamic jurisprudence that regulates marital relationships, a core part of culture entangled in everyday life. According to Islamic marital law, it is forbidden for two relatives of the opposite sex to marry, and the word *mahrem* refers to this ban on an intimate heterosexual relationship. The proximity of these two individuals of the opposite sex is formed either by blood (i.e., father and daughter), by marriage (father-in-law and daughter-in-law), or by breast-feeding or milk (i.e., a woman and a man breast-fed by the same woman).[5] Although they are forbidden to marry, they are *mahrems* to each other and thus have fewer boundaries. In other words, forbiddenness denotes and creates proximity and a familial intimacy.

In this vein, two non-*mahrems* of opposite sexes are expected to establish distance and follow codes of invisible boundaries, such as segregation, veiling, a limited gaze, and controlled behavior. By delineating basic principles of marriage, *mahremiyet* creates heterosexual barriers and regulates proximity and gendered intimacy at multiple levels. In this way, Islamicate sexualities are created and normalized in the everyday lives of individuals, including nonobservant Muslims (Sehlikoglu 2015c).

Gazing Produces Sexual Scripts

The boundaries created in the culture of *mahremiyet* are signified primarily by regulating *seeing*, or who can see whom and how.[6] In their everyday lives, women become aware of their sexed bodies in relation to different types of gazes: the male gaze, the female gaze, the foreign (non-*mahrem* or *namahrem*) gaze, the gaze of envy, and so on. *Mahrem* boundaries are regulated in order not to attract a foreign gaze, which produces sexual scripts in public settings.

The gaze as a producer of a sexual script is an expansion of the psychoanalytic approach that considers gaze a love object, which Sigmund Freud first argued and Jacques Lacan (1981) later expanded. To Freud's list of partial objects (breast, face, phallus) Lacan adds two other objects: voice and gaze. It is therefore by no means accidental that gaze and voice are love objects par excellence — not in the sense that we fall in love with a voice or a gaze but rather in the sense that they are a medium, a catalyst that sets off love.[7]

In the culture of *mahremiyet*, however, the gaze produces a sexual script that is more than a mere medium. As the term *sexual script* suggests (Simon and Gagnon 1986), gazing is entangled with larger cultural meanings enabled by historical makings and maintained by intersubjective displays. Furthermore, the gaze has a clear and almost physical embodiment in the everyday life of the Middle East. In Turkey the gaze has nonhuman agency with the capacity to bring misfortune or illness through *nazar* (strong eye), which is able to touch people (*nazar değmesi*).[8] The significance of the gaze we witness here is not fully reflected in Western theories, such as Lacanian *le regard* (translated into English as "gaze" almost exclusively). Lacanian *le regard* refers to looking or staring, often with desire, yet it does not encapsulate the physicality of gaze in this particular context. In the following pages I revisit the ways my interlocutors negotiate different types of gazing in various spaces in daily life. Since gaze is imagined to be physical and concrete, powerful and ambient rules, emotions, and beliefs are created around it.[9] As such, in everyday life the sensation of the gaze is experienced as tactile rather than visual.

In a culture that envisages (and regulates) gaze as a physical object, the one who is looked at feels a "discomfort," since the *mahrem* boundaries have been crossed, violated, and even *penetrated*. Looking, in this context, embodies more than curiosity, as it becomes an active, masculine, penetrating act against the passive, feminine, and penetrated position, as Dror Ze'evi (2006) lays out when he points out the duality embedded in the heterosexual culture of Ottoman society. The curious, penetrating gaze is therefore an intrapsychic reflection of the heterosexual active male. Aside from the sensorial dimension of intimacy, as I discuss below, the female is also positioned as penetrable, marking women's privacies with fragility.

Harem: A *Mahrem* Space for Leisure

The culture of *mahremiyet* has adapted to new habits as particular leisure practices have become established in Turkey. To stay within the boundaries of the complex social rules regarding the gaze that *mahremiyet* demands, various space regulations emerged and were adapted as the solution to that complexity. Although androgenic fantasies predominantly stimulated colonial interest in the harem (Alloula 1986; Yeğenoğlu 1998), it has in fact been one of the main ways of regulating *mahrem* boundaries.

As opposed to the common misunderstanding, the harem is a socialization zone of the *mahrems*, of those who remain inside the borders created by the culture of *mahremiyet*. Thus if the place in question is a household, the insiders who have access to the harem are not only women (as the common stereotype suggests) but also male relatives, such as fathers, sons, and brothers. The households with harems were predominantly of the upper and ruling classes during Ottoman rule (Booth 2010; Brown 2011; Peirce 1993), and the uses of those spaces were aimed at regulating the gaze (Lad 2010). A harem was often situated where one could see other parts of the house (garden, main room) or outside but outsiders could not see inside. In sum, as Marilyn Booth (2010) brilliantly points out, the idea of the harem was in fact the *result* of a border-making mechanism that still exists in Islamicate contexts.

I agree with the call in Booth's edited collection for closer attention to the ways those borders are established, maintained, and threatened. "Islamic" rules are not enough to understand the culture of *mahremiyet* fully, as its historical, temporal, spatial, and sociable dimensions complicate individuals' (and in this case women's) relationships with it. Moreover, even when individuals have the interest and ability to apply particular Islamic interpretations regarding *mahremiyet* and its regulations, there are times they choose to ignore them. For instance, it is permissible for women to breast-feed in the presence of women and male relatives (i.e., brothers or fathers), yet it is a highly unusual practice. On the contrary, despite the prohibition against women seeing other women's genitalia, this does often occur, as when women visit a waxing salon. The ways women regulate their bodies cannot be understood outside the culture of *mahremiyet*, since their sexed bodies have been constructed through it. However, there are ways they also negotiate these regulations, as I demonstrate in the following.

The Living Borders of *Mahremiyet*

> Do you know what *mahrem* is? It is a secret and a seal. It is private.
> —Feray, interview, May 22, 2012

Sibel was a single woman in her late twenties who was working toward a doctoral degree in dentistry during the time of this research. As a young single woman with a respectable job in higher education who lived in a suburban area of Istanbul (Beşyüzevler), she considered herself a more *aydın* (enlightened) woman compared to her family members and her neighbors. Indeed, Sibel was the "perfect" modern Turkish woman: she was tall and skinny with natural-looking blonde hair, often wore tight pants and miniskirts, and had an academic career. She was by no means a traditional or religious woman, according to her own accounts and circulating stereotypes in Istanbul.

The way Sibel explained her choice of a women-only space for her aerobics-fitness class is worth examining as a whole:

> Well, in the end, you stretch your legs, spread your legs, lie down, and raise your feet. Your body may be revealed. In the end, you would be surrounded by people you don't know, which is discomforting in my opinion. I mean, I wouldn't feel comfortable. For instance, your trainer tells you to spread your legs, and I wouldn't want to do that, I would be uncomfortable. Or, for instance, you wear sweatpants and do the cycling movement with your feet up and you will have to worry about your T-shirt coming off, and you will have to worry about your sweatpants coming off, and you will try to stuff it into your socks. Why should I have to have all these concerns? . . . I don't feel comfortable at all. I don't want to do aerobics movements when I am with people I don't know. . . . Why would I do such bedroom movements? I don't want to. (interview, January 27, 2012)

Sibel's example elaborates on the shared aspect of the culture of *mahremiyet*. Her words reflect three layers of *mahremiyet*. The first, most obvious level corresponds with the bodily movements she avoids in the presence of foreign (non-*mahrem*) men. Her concern is not about all men or just any men but about men that she does not know. What she refers to as "bedroom movements" is the resemblance between the body movements of a woman during an act of sexual intercourse and those of a woman exercising. Her lack of desire to exercise with people she does not know is based on this resemblance and the way it may appear to a foreign man. She wants to be safe from anyone imagining or fantasizing about her body; therefore, to avoid the heteroerotics of the movements, she avoids exercising in public.

On another level she depicts aerobics as "bedroom movements." She does not directly say that the movements are sexual. Instead, she refers to the closed-door space of the bedroom in which such movements should or could occur. She uses what Najmabadi (1993, 489) calls an "invisible metaphoric veiled" language of the "newly produced woman" of modernity. Unlike the cases Najmabadi shares in her work, however, Sibel is not trying to establish a physically removed veil with her language. Instead, she uses a legitimized symbolic language to refer to the heteroerotics of her body through which she maintains everyday control of her public sexuality.

Sibel reveals a third *mahrem* layer when she explains, very vividly, that what pushes the boundaries of sexuality is not limited to the content of the bodily movement. Despite proper clothing, through movement the outfit can become less controllable and reveal the body. Sibel complains about her uncontrollable sweatpants. This third layer highlights the possibility of losing control through movement, which for Sibel is exemplified through clothing, and she explains how in exercise loss of control of clothing could expose sexualized body parts.

Gül, another interlocutor, also provided a detailed description of controlling her outfit when exercising and how women-only gyms saved her from having to make these calculations. She was a forty-one-year-old married woman with two children who worked as a manager in an international corporation. Gül was a member of two gyms, a women-only one and a mixed one. In the gated community where she lived at the time, she had access to a gym (Yeşilvadi, YV) with separate hours for women and men. During the hours YV was open for men only, Gül went to a mixed gym not far from her home. When I asked her to compare the two gyms, she first compared their services, such as towel provision and swimsuit drying machines. She then described levels of "comfort" and discomfort:

> There is an advantage here [YV], which, of course, is a disadvantage for some others: men and women are segregated. You are more comfortable. For instance, when you need to exercise, you don't go all, "Oh, have my underpants gone between my hips? Oh, has my underwear appeared over the top [of my sweatpants]? Oh, did the neck of my top show my breasts when I bent over?" You have to check each and every one of these things [in a mixed gym]. "Oh I'm sweating, is my shirt sticking to my body too much?" So yes, you need to have a certain level of *mahremiyet* between men and women. You don't have to worry about these when there aren't any men around. (interview, December 21, 2011)

Gül did not wear a head scarf, and, as part of her professional life, she usually preferred sleeveless shirts under jackets and skirt lengths just above her knees. Yet her body's movements during exercise made her clothing uncontrollable and thus uncomfortable. She then felt obliged to pay attention to whether her bunched-up T-shirt exposed her back and tummy.

Neither Gül nor Sibel wore a head scarf; both considered themselves modern, secular Turkish women. Yet the culture of *mahremiyet* goes beyond covering and segregation. It is, more broadly, a multilayered boundary-making mechanism of privacy and sexuality that women live through and in and with which they negotiate. Women in several Euro-American contexts may have similar concerns. However, the particularity of the Istanbul context is not only about the different ways the link between the public and the intimate is constructed through sociality and relationality but also about the significance of the *gaze*. What both Gül and Sibel avoid is *frikik*, referring to the "free kick" movement in football, a highly masculine zone. In football a free kick allows the player the chance to score directly. But when a woman performs the movement, she loses control of her outfit and reveals parts of her body that she normally tries to keep concealed (i.e., her legs). She also loses control of her (guarded) sexuality, leaving her with a feeling of shame, of unwanted public nudity. This movement allows a potential (foreign, non-*mahrem*) male gaze to see something he was not supposed to see. So, figuratively, he "scores" against the woman who was trying to guard (part of) her body. By avoiding this movement, both Gül and Sibel disallow victory to the opposite sex. While Sibel wears knee-length skirts often and is not necessarily concerned with men seeing her legs, the avoidance of these kinds of movements in non-sex-segregated exercise spaces causes her to worry about control.

During this research my informants were often unable to describe their discomfort. In fact, unlike Gül and Sibel, very few women were able to describe how they control their sexuality in public. Thirty-year-old Elif had taken her Islamic head scarf off four years prior to our interviews after wearing it for more than a decade. This experience allowed her to compare her concerns during her head scarf-wearing years with her subsequent concerns. She said: "Many women, veiled or not, already prefer to cover their private parts and protect them from men's eyes. When you are running, you do not want your tits to be jumping around in front of men. This is also a cultural thing" (interview, September 16, 2011). Because it is a "cultural thing," the content of the "comfort" was often inexplicable for many of the women I interviewed. This sense of comfort is so deeply embedded in their lives that explaining their discomfort often sounded unnecessary to them. Seval was another nonscarved young career woman. She was in her early thirties and single. She came from, in her words, "a traditional family" (interview, January 8, 2012), reflecting the way traditional discourse is tied to religion and rural culture, and referred to herself as "progressive modern" (*çağdaş modern*). "It's something you learn from your family, and on the streets," she said about her discomfort in exposing herself through certain bodily movements and dressing in a particular way in the presence of men. Seval's reference to "the streets" concerns highly intersubjective relations in the public sphere, where interactions are built through multiple means but overwhelmingly through the gaze. This is what Alev Çınar (2005, 34) terms the "public gaze," arguing that since public space is loaded with meanings, interactions, debates, contestations, identities, and subjectivities, the public gaze dominates that sphere at multiple levels of encroachment.

I asked Seval to explain her discomfort in relation to gaze:

Sertaç: Do you restrain yourself because men look at you? Or because you are used to it?

Seval: That can be a reason too. I mean we are raised to behave properly as women and girls in the presence of men, like subconsciously. It doesn't really matter if you look *açık* [open, uncovered] and comfortable, you are careful because it's engrained in your culture. That's why I am content to exercise with women. (interview, January 8, 2012)

Head scarf-wearing women in Turkey are sometimes called *kapalı*, which signifies both covered and closed. *Kapalı* also refers to being modest or closed to flirtation and seduction. Women who do not wear a head scarf are called *açık*, meaning both uncovered and open. Seval does not say "if you are *açık*," she says "if you look *açık*," because she does not believe that she is made less modest by not wearing a head scarf.

Seval's awareness of regulating her sexuality in public echoes Najmabadi's (1993, 513) analysis of the transformation of Iranian women from all-female homosocial to heterosocial spaces. During Reza Shah Pahlavi's mandate for compulsory unveiling in 1930, women began to develop strategies to discipline their sexuality by other means to maintain cross sex barriers. Najmabadi (ibid.) provides the example of "walk[ing] to work facing the walls" as one of these strategies. Thus she argues that "in its movement from a homosocial female-bounded world into a heterosocial public space, the female body was itself transformed," including women's voluntary adaptation of an "invisible metaphoric veil, *hijab-i'iffat* [veil of chastity], not as some object, a piece of cloth, external to the female body, but . . . a disciplined modern body that obscured the woman's sexuality, obliterated its bodily presence" (ibid., 489).

Unveiled and yet pure, the new Turkish women of the early republican period were also expected to be "modern" in appearance and intellect but were still required to preserve the "traditional" virtue of chastity and to affirm it constantly (Durakbaşa 1988; Parla 2001). Seval's everyday negotiations and strategies reflect how she maneuvers through the demands of patriarchal mechanisms. She states that despite her looks, she in fact maintains the norms of public sexuality.

Other women, regardless of whether or not they wore a head scarf, echoed Seval's concern. This suggests that in Turkey's cultural expectations of public sexuality, women need to learn how not to look accessible or, in their words, *açık* or *rahat*. The following example is from Mübeccel, a head scarf–wearing woman who was single and a freshman at a local university. I met Mübeccel at the municipally run Hamza Yerlikaya Sports Center. She was one of the many respondents who shared long lists of details regarding how they regulated their bodies and attitudes *dışarıda* (out in public). During our conversation Mübeccel pointed out these limits:

Mübeccel: In the end, I am covered [head scarved] and should know where to draw the line. . . .

Sertaç: So how do you know where to draw your line? How do you do that?

Mübeccel: With my attitudes and behaviors. . . . Sure, I do everything when I'm with women. I mean, everything, like I wear low necklines and do this and that. But when I go out, I pay attention to my behavior, for instance. When I walk or talk, for instance, I don't laugh *dışarıda*. There's this thing, like my character. I am never too close to men for instance. [*Thinks for a moment.*] Actually, I have a tough character *dışarıda*, did you know that? People who see me *dışarıda* usually think "what a tough girl" about me. (interview, December 30, 2011)

Dışarıda refers to the nondomestic sphere that is both nonfamilial and heterosocial. *Dışarıda* indicates mixed-gender public spheres, such as streets, public transportation, and school campuses, perhaps with the exception of special occasions, such as weddings, where people are known and familiar to a certain extent.

Mübeccel was from a lower-class background, and *dışarıda* refers to the neighborhoods of her class, where she encountered, in various proximities, foreign males all the time. Her experience differed from that of women I talked to from the upper-middle and upper classes. Mübeccel took public transportation to school and walked on the streets in lower-class suburbs of Istanbul, while women from the upper-middle and upper classes told me that they walked only in "sterilized" public spaces, such as upper-class neighborhoods or shopping malls. Thus to rebuild the boundaries she needs in a heterosocial public space (of predominantly lower-middle-class people), Mübeccel has developed a body language and a series of attitudes. Her *dışarıda* lines are invisible boundaries. She avoids looking easy or *rahat* and expresses a "tough" look. These lines are there to prevent complications. She explained: "I am not tough in my real life. . . . I need to appear as serious [*ciddi*], that's how it's supposed to be. Time and environment are corrupted [referring to rising sexual harassment]. I mean, what would they think if I laugh? They could derive multiple meanings from that laughter" (interview, December 30, 2011). Mübeccel knows not only what kind of message she needs to give through her public appearance and performance but also how to manifest it. Mübeccel's control of her behavior in public is shaped with reference to an imagined gaze that not only monitors but also judges, evaluates, criticizes, and approves. It is also worth mentioning that Mübeccel's head scarf, or her *kapalı* look, does not save her from any of these calculations.[10] She still calculates the effects of her acts and her looks, which demands that she continuously and self-consciously evaluate her appropriateness and potential threats or misunderstandings. Thus the culture of *mahremiyet* works almost exclusively against women's privacies. Therefore women feel obliged to ensure that their boundaries are not broken.

Morning Exercises in the Parks: Public by Nature, Private by Culture

Even if a ten-week gym membership at ten Turkish liras (less than US$3.50) was financially feasible, open-air exercise with no fee was still compelling for several women I talked to both for financial reasons and because they enjoyed outdoor exercise. If women's privacies were so fragile, then what sort of strategies did they use to guard their boundaries and to establish *comfort* while they exercised in a public park, I wondered. How does the culture of *mahremiyet* take shape in mixed and public spaces?

Middle-aged and senior women walking in sneakers and exercising in outdoor gyms in public parks in the early hours of the day are a familiar scene to most residents and even visitors in Istanbul. The trend has become mainstream.

Figure 1. Women walking in a public park in loose outfits.
Photo: Sertaç Sehlikoglu

Sports Inc., a subsidiary of the Istanbul Metropolitan Municipality established to "strengthen the physical and mental health of Istanbulites" through outdoor exercise in public parks, has initiated early bird training sessions.[11] The (immediate) difference between women's outdoor exercise in North America, the United Kingdom, or Continental Europe and that in Istanbul is in appearance. Rather than tight-fitting athletic clothing, women in Istanbul exercising outdoors often dress in casual, loose-fitting clothing and sometimes wear robes or even black veils that cover the whole body and sneakers (fig. 1). But there are less visible differences as well.

Sports Inc.'s early bird training sessions are part of a project called Morning Sports in thirty-one locations across the city, with multiple sessions for some of these spots. For instance, in Fatih, a majority-Islamic neighborhood of Istanbul, there are two outdoor exercise sessions — at 7:00 a.m. and at 8:00 a.m. — due to high demand from women (Selim Terzi, interview, July 22, 2011). Sports Inc. employs and sends (predominantly female) trainers who are graduates of sports academies to sports centers in various neighborhoods. Terzi, vice president of Sports Inc., told me that the sessions were offered "upon demand" (interview, May 18, 2012).

The early bird exercise sessions require bodily movements that immediately trigger issues related to heteroerotics. These movements include running that involves the movement of hips and breasts, stretching that may emphasize the contour of the body, and leg movements that draw attention to the genitalia. As such, my informants often considered them highly sexual, even erotic. The eroticization of exercising female bodies can be observed in Turkish popular culture. Women's volleyball has long been perceived as a "leg show," for example. In the 1970s all-male audiences regularly harassed female volleyball players on national teams (Harani 2001; Sehlikoglu 2015a). In the early 1990s, when private television broadcasting emerged, the nighttime erotic show by Yasemin Evcim was popularly referred to as *gece jimnastiği* (night gymnastics). Even today the Turkish pilates guru Ebru Şallı's videos on YouTube are subject to the sexualized comments of male viewers. Indeed, in Sultançiftliği, where I conducted my ethnography, at the request

Figure 2. Women using outdoor gym equipment in Cumhuriyet Park. Faces are not exposed to honor their request. Photo: Sertaç Sehlikoglu

of women participants, morning exercise sessions were eventually moved to an indoor facility due to the gazes of men. In other words, the discomfort caused by the foreign male gaze resulted in a demand for a segregated indoor space.[12] Given Mübeccel's everyday calculations in a nearby (equally lower-middle-class) neighborhood, women's demands for indoor spaces for exercise come as no surprise.[13]

Besides the sessions Sports Inc. offers, women walk and do light exercise in small groups in public parks. This is an emergent trend and not a privately initiated project. The practice has become so popular in recent years that municipal governments have redesigned many public parks, installing walking paths and outdoor gym equipment (fig. 2).

Outdoor gym equipment in these public parks include cross trainers; leg, shoulder, and chest presses; benches; and equipment to work arms and shoulders, like hand bikes and shoulder wheels.[14] In a park near the Hamza Yerlikaya Sports Center, women almost take over the park as early as sunrise — the time of morning prayer — until 9:00 or 10:00 a.m., depending on the season. By "taking over," I mean that they not only outnumber men but also that they determine the ways male patrons of the park behave during that time.

Even though women avoid "bedroom movements" during their exercise in public and do not stretch, run, or (for the most part) dress in tight clothes, they can still be targets of harassing oglers, albeit in limited numbers. Responding to an imagined (if not actual) foreign male gaze in public, women's sexuality is rebuilt and internalized daily to reproduce normative boundaries.

Figen, a woman in her forties who regularly exercised in this park, revealed in an interview that in her mind the looks of "everyone" and "men" were in fact interconnected:

Sertaç: What bothers you in a mixed [gender] environment?

Figen: [*Slightly surprised with the question, almost finding it irrelevant and the answer too obvious.*] To be out in the open [*öyle açıkta olmak*]! I don't know, I would be spreading my legs and raising my arms while men are passing by, out in public [*dışarıda*], in the middle of the street [*sokak ortasında*]. Everyone would turn and look at you. It would bother me if everybody were to look at me!

Sertaç: When you say "everybody," do you mean men?

Figen: Yes, men. (interview, February 13, 2012)

Figen's few sentences are haunted by boundaries, outsiders, discomfort, and openness. Her reference to "everybody" as a source of discomforting gazes is not hollow. On the contrary, when Figen says "everybody," she refers to the possibility of a male gaze evaluating her public acts. Evaluation and judgment of this kind are independent from the gender of the looker, as it marks Figen as a woman. In other words, the gaze, whether by a man or a woman, places judgment on the person who is its object, making her a woman who exercises in the (potential) presence of an actual foreign male gaze. Like Mübeccel, she refers to the opinions and judgments about herself that lie behind the gaze. Figen feels *uncomfortable* exercising outside of her *mahrem* zone, in her words, "out in the public, in the middle of the street," sites loaded with unpredictable, foreign, and violating interventions.

Likewise, Kamile, a thirty-six-year-old lower-class housewife and mother of two, decided to become a member of a women-only gym a couple of weeks after she began to exercise in her neighborhood. She lived in Cumhuriyet Mahallesi, a suburban part of Istanbul that is home to primarily middle- and lower-income families, most of whom are first-generation migrants from other parts of Turkey. The park there is very small, about twenty square meters, with five outdoor exercise machines. It has no trees and no rubber walking paths, so Kamile needed to walk on the streets circling the park and use the equipment where any passerby could see her. In Kamile's experience, she was visible in public and therefore more vulnerable. She complained about the actual male gaze staring at her moving body.

Kamile: We used to start and continue for one or two months and then take a break. And maybe we would start again. One naturally hesitates when there's no one else [to accompany her when she exercises]. Also, Sultançiftliği [her old neighborhood] is more rural [*kırsal*, referring to the area's mostly rural immigrant population] compared to here [Cumhuriyet Mahallesi].

Sertaç: How so?

Kamile: You go out to exercise alone in the morning and everybody gawks at you like a moron [*bön bön bakmak*], men and all. You cannot do it alone. There's nobody [doing sports] there. It's not like here.

Sertaç: Yes, you are right, you need to have someone to accompany you.

Kamile: Exactly!

I asked her to further describe her discomfort:

At the beginning, I did not feel comfortable while I was walking in the park. Your hips move, and there are men around you. I especially cannot be free with the equipment where you should open and close your legs [referring to the inner-legs trainer]. Men look especially when we are on the trainers in the park. I hate them! Women have to argue with men who sit on purpose right across women to watch women. Actually, security deals with them, but they return again after an hour. (interview, January 10, 2012)

The aforementioned segregation draws a boundary between women's bodies and male strangers and regulates verbal and nonverbal (i.e., the gaze) cues. These same limits also turn women's bodies into strange objects in the public sphere. Particular types of exercises—in Kamile's case, opening and closing legs in the sitting position—include bodily movements that cannot be performed without concern in the presence of the non-*mahrem* male gaze, as these movements resemble acts of sexual intimacy. The "penetrating" aspect of the gaze is a result of a combination of factors, including the looker's attitude and the tactility of the gaze. Therefore the discomfort caused by the penetrating foreign male gaze parallels the feeling of harassment. Moreover, this gaze, unlike physical or verbal harassment, is not a concrete act of violence and cannot be prevented, stopped, or reported despite the disturbance it causes. So Kamile needed to develop strategies to negotiate it.

Kamile's discomfort and initial impotence in the face of street harassment (by gazing) exposes how easily and randomly women's bodies can be turned into public matters and the fragility of their privacies. Because of the power dynamics embedded in the very fabric of heterosexual duality in Turkey, women's privacies are always more fragile than men's (Sehlikoglu 2013, 2015c). For women, the fact that at any moment their bodies can be made public is experienced as risk. This in fact is the nexus of the problem for women when it comes to exercising in public. Whether they are followers of the Islamic faith or are veiled or not, self-identify as modern or traditional does not necessarily change this experience of risk. This problem cannot be reduced to being subjected to the male gaze or patriarchal control. While these may be aspects of the larger felt problem, what women really worry about on a day-to-day basis is the instability of what may occur at any moment during exercise because of the fragility of their privacies. A woman can be at any moment caught by that instability and troubled by it through violation of her privacy. A word, an insistent gaze that touches, or in some cases a physical touch leaves room for potential instability and thus harm.

Like those of Elif, Seval, and Sibel, Kamile's experience also draws attention to the bodily movements or *bedroom* movements. But due to her limited financial income and the fees at a women-only gym, Kamile exercises outdoors from time to time, and her "bedroom movements" encounter the (non-*mahrem*) male gaze in the public, heterosocial sphere. A man sits across from Kamile to watch her as she opens and closes her legs. She performs a *mahrem* act, meant to be private, and the man takes advantage of its public performance. As Kamile described this incident, all three adult women present had a clear idea about the look in the harasser's eyes. Kamile mimicked the erotic pleasure of his gaze. "When it first happened, I felt so angry.... I was ashamed. I couldn't do anything," she explained. She initially tried to confront the situation by calling security, yet this did not seem to provide a solution. She shrugged her shoulders and added: "Then I learned to ignore it.... Now, I think that we do not know each other, so never mind!" (interview, January 10, 2012).

These words reveal a process in which she agentively unlearns the *mahrem* borders and the feeling of privacy that comes with them. Instead of maintaining and guarding her *mahrem* borders, she begins to ignore them. In the culture of *mahremiyet*—which situates males as active and penetrating, females as passive and penetrated—ignoring this penetrating foreign male gaze is not a simple act, but the ability to do so enables the woman to steal the power of penetration away from her harasser (Sehlikoglu 2015b).

Kamile underwent a personal transformation evinced by her ability to ignore a significant and powerful male gaze. As she moved from Sultançiftliği, a more suburban (rural, in her words) neighborhood, to a less suburban, more city-like and "progressive" neighborhood, she changed her attitudes, her body movements, and her exercise routine. By using the gaze as a gauge, she evaluated her new environment and coordinated her body accordingly. She was aware of the pedagogic aspect of her environment but also the stakes of the "ethico-aesthetics of a body's capacity for becoming" (Gregg and Seigworth 2010, 14). What I would like to highlight here is not how she evaluates the conditions in her new neighborhood or how she negotiates them. Rather, what is important here is her creative use of all of the possibilities and options as part of her transformation and her self-formation without *directly* challenging the culture of *mahremiyet* and while indirectly blurring the borders within it.

Figure 3. Women's exercise often begins with a fast walk followed by a workout on the equipment. There are only two men in this photo: one is walking against the stream (Zeki, in the front, facing away from the camera), and another comes with his spouse. Cumhuriyet Park. Photo: Sertaç Sehlikoglu

Exercising in Public Parks

When women take over a park, however, the situation changes, and the culture of *mahremiyet* starts acting against male patrons, who thereby feel obliged to control their own public sexualities. They start worrying about how they will be perceived if they visit the park, ordinarily a heterosocial space. In Cumhuriyet Park, for example, which two of my interlocutors frequented during in the summer because it was financially difficult to access an indoor gym, a curious spectacle took place. The photo in figure 3 was taken in the Cumhuriyet Park in Sultanciftliği. As it illustrates, very few male patrons come to the park simply to watch women's moving bodies or to meet women. More often, men come to exercise either with their wives or by themselves, but this is also quite rare. Thus it is easy to spot men who are there for gazing, a frequent subject of women's disdainful conversations. As such, there is a public consensus about the "intentions" of male patrons present in the park early in the morning. Women refer to the males who are in the park only to exercise — not to watch or harass women — as those with "pure, untainted intentions [*saf, temiz niyet*]" (Sinem, Feray, and Esra, focus group interview, May 11, 2012). Yet those with "untainted intentions" need to demonstrate this in a public manner. I observed two strategies that a small number of men use to display their "untainted intentions," that they are in the park solely to exercise and not to watch women's moving bodies. In the photo, the gentleman with the cap walking with the lady in black has come to the park with a female relative, and Zeki, facing away from the camera, walks against the stream so that women can see where he is looking. That is to say, Zeki feels obliged to prove that he is not there to stare at women's moving bodies (from behind), and to do so he has adopted this practice of facing them. In a way, he proves that women are "safe" from his gaze. One aspect of performing proper public Islamicate sexuality necessitates limiting the *mahrem* body. Another, however, necessitates limiting the penetrating gaze. This is what Zeki, a retired high school teacher, was doing in Cumhuriyet Park.

Conclusion

The daily techniques women use to build boundaries between themselves and the "foreign" opposite sex are pivotal elements of public sexuality and its culture of segregation. The call for a feminist investigation of women's daily gendered negotiations with respect to cross sex relations fits nicely into Afsaruddin's attention to the gap in feminist studies. Afsaruddin (1999, 14) calls for a more diligent study, "a dispassionate, nuanced look" that does not overfocus on women's attire, which inevitably overlooks the ways women "appropriate public space and assert their presence." Afsaruddin's call for a nonessentialist gender analysis is partly influenced by Lois McNay's (1992, 64) interrogation of Foucauldian theory and feminism's nondifferentiated remarks that neglect cultural, historical, temporal, and geographic shades, leaving women's experiences "either not understood in their full complexity, . . . devalued or . . . obscured altogether." This problem exists in scholarship on Turkey, which includes an impressive number of studies on the issue of veiling, the head scarf, and visible Islam. Although there are significant and groundbreaking works among them, this dominant interest and obsession has obfuscated alternative probes on Islamicate gender practices in the public sphere and women's appropriation of public space.

Multiple factors lie behind the ways women organize their bodily movements in multiple spaces, which constitutes a multilayered process of building privacy, heterosexuality, and intimacy. These layers are established through cultural scripts (heteroerotics), structural fixations (class and religion), normative spaces, and gendered acts (Ze'evi 2006). Through analyzing women's management of their bodies in relation to public sexuality and public visibility, I have aimed to shed light on the ways selfhood, gender, and body are linked in Islamicate contexts.

I have connected women's strict management of their bodies to larger schemes, such as the culture of *mahremiyet* as it operates in various aspects of life. Women's relationships with this culture, as *mahrem* bodies in it, involves several layers of calculation and risk due to the instability and fragility of women's privacies. In this context of "approachability," women employ various techniques to avoid the instability of *mahrem* zones, often also avoiding the foreign male gaze altogether and sometimes intervening with confrontation. Thus women reimagine, re-create, and negotiate their privacies through everyday forms of contestation. In any moment their privacy risks becoming public, which can result in a feeling of violation. Sexual harassment is just one of the many moments that signify this risk of private becoming public. In other words, the culture of *mahremiyet* concerns the very fabric that produces normalcy, or "comfort," defining the boundaries between private and public and illustrating the penetrability of those borders.

However, women are far from docile objects in the culture of *mahremiyet*, no matter how fragile their privacy is in that culture. As Kamile's case demonstrates, by taking arbitrary risks women exhibit agentive responses and often create ruptures in this culture. The rupture is even more visible in the case of Cumhuriyet Park, where women have reversed the power dynamics of *mahremiyet* by "taking over" the park. As such, *mahremiyet* operates in their favor. While women may not be taking bold risks or directly challenging or resisting existing systems as they avoid random violations of their privacies, they nevertheless test the limits of the culture of *mahremiyet* and negotiate these boundaries.[15] They indirectly change the dynamics when they ignore the power of the male gaze or take over a park.[16]

This article has also examined Istanbulite women's control of their bodily movements in public spaces, analyzing these movements as parts of a multilayered process of building privacy, heterosexuality, and intimacy. I have argued that the demand for privacy (*mahremiyet*) has created regulated spaces and institutions of intimacy. At one level, Istanbulite women's concerns and demands for segregation shed light on discussions in social studies about Muslim women's visibilities, modesty concerns, dress codes, and public sexuality. Different forms of modesty are established in the community through various techniques (Antoun 1968; Werbner 2007), including veiling, segregation, language, and behaviors such as body language, sitting, walking, laughing appropriately, and posture. These techniques are related to the ways *mahremiyet* is defined, made, and remade in daily life as part of what Berlant (1998, 281) terms "institutions of intimacy." Such perspective is particularly crucial in developing conceptual tools to identify the ways normalcies are created and reinforced through institutions of intimacy, which extend beyond female bodied persons (Zengin 2011) and may also include young or gay men (Korkman 2015; Özbay 2010). It also contributes to an important recognition of similarities with other, non-Islamicate institutions of intimacy (Agathangelou 2004; Lazaridis 1995).

SERTAÇ SEHLIKOGLU is a social anthropologist at the University of Cambridge. Her work has been published in edited collections and in such peer-reviewed journals as the *Cambridge Journal of Anthropology*, *Feminist Media Studies*, the *Journal of Middle East Women's Studies*, and *Leisure Studies*. Contact: ss935@cam.ac.uk.

Acknowledgments

This article is part of a larger study that has benefited from a William-Wyse Fieldwork Grant from the University of Cambridge, the Abdullah Mubarak British Institute of Middle Eastern Studies Scholarship, and a research grant from the British Institute at Ankara. I would like to thank Henrietta L. Moore and Afsaneh Najmabadi for their invaluable comments on earlier versions of this article. I would also like to thank Rüstem Ertuğ Altınay and Giulia Liberatore for their thorough reading of and feedback on this article.

Notes

1. None of my interlocutors was living below poverty. Class differences are not as sharp in Turkey as they are in the United Kingdom, for instance. I define class based on income, occupation, and lifestyle. Lower-class refers to blue-collar workers and their wives. Middle-class refers to owners of small and medium enterprises and to white-collar workers, including doctors and engineers, and their wives. Upper-class refers to the employers of white-collar workers and their wives. For an extensive study on class formation in Turkey, see Keyder 1987.

2. Kemalism is the official secular and nationalist ideology of Turkey promoting the principles of Mustafa Kemal Atatürk, the founder of the republic.

3. Muslim women-only spaces have both parallels with and differences from women-only gyms and leisure spaces in the non-Muslim world. As I elaborate in this article, women-only gyms are spaces freed from the male gaze—suggesting the centrality of the gaze to privacy concerns—which is not necessarily the case in Western gyms, where there are male janitors, trainers, or security guards.

4. For other work examining changing forms of sexuality in Islamicate contexts, see Ozyegin 2009; Smith-Hefner 2006.

5. For further information and anthropological analysis of forms of milk kinship and *mahrem* relationships in Muslim societies, see Altorki 1986; Clarke 2007; Parkes 2005; and vom Bruck 1997.

6. The regulations on seeing in relation to sexuality in Islamicate contexts mostly discuss illicit gazing at beardless boys by adult men (see Babayan 2008, 266–67; Najmabadi 2005, 17–19; Ze'evi 2006, 97).

7. In a similar vein, a feminist literature of performance studies examines the relationship between sexual pleasure and the gaze (Mulvey 1975).

8. *Nazar* is often misunderstood and mistranslated into English as the "evil eye." In fact, it refers to a strong look conveying envy as well as love.

9. The Middle Eastern and eastern Mediterranean concept *nazar* originates from Arabic but also exists in Turkish, Urdu, and Farsi and their wider cultures. The rituals surrounding it have only minor variations in different ethnic and geographic contexts. According to Timothy Mitchell (1991), in Egypt *nazar* refers to a certain kind of power that makes the object of the gaze more vulnerable. This belief system is referred to as "superstition" in early sociological and ethnographic works (Johnson 1924). In one of the earliest works that connects beliefs about the eye and gazing and the eye's power, a psychologist suggests that the overall evil eye culture stems from particular cultural behaviors regarding staring and gazing (Coss 1974). After the mid-1980s closer examinations of *nazar* emerged in ethnographic works (Brav 1992).

10. Several women who donned a head scarf told me that they needed to be more careful, as they are still exposed to the gaze even with a headscarf, which, they highlighted, was not the case twenty years ago. Recent work suggests that the culture of sexuality in Turkey is changing (Ozyegin 2015; Sehlikoglu 2015b), and this change should be considered when evaluating women's everyday worries.

11. Istanbul'da Sabah Sporları, www.sporas.com.tr/media/286354/sabah-sporlari-raporu/html (accessed June 3, 2013).

12. For a good overview of sexual harassment in Turkey, see Ilkkaracan 2000.

13. In some Istanbul neighborhoods where more privileged residents live (i.e., Caddebostan, Bebek), both women and men exercise regularly and often in typical sports outfits.

14. Different from indoor gym equipment, these machines are heavier, water-resistant, and less sophisticated. These spaces look like playgrounds for adults, seesaws and swing sets replaced by adult-size exercise equipment.

15. Although my informants were not activist feminists, their everyday negotiations with the fragility of their privacies spoke to the frequent antiharassment campaigns. One example is the recent dispute over *müsait* (available), translated in the official Turkish-language dictionary as "[the woman] who readily goes out or flirts."

16. A similar transformative power is observed in women-only parks in Iran, which Nazanin Shahrokni (2014) has analyzed.

References

Afsaruddin, Asma. 1999. Introduction to *Hermeneutics and Honor: Negotiating Female Public Space in Islamic/ate Societies*, edited by Asma Afsaruddin, 1–28. Cambridge, MA: Harvard University, Center for Middle Eastern Studies.

Agathangelou, Anna M. 2004. *The Global Political Economy of Sex: Desire, Violence, and Insecurity in Mediterranean Nation States*. New York: Palgrave Macmillan.

Alloula, Malek. 1986. *The Colonial Harem*. Minneapolis: University of Minnesota Press.

Altorki, Soraya. 1986. *Women in Saudi Arabia: Ideology and Behavior among the Elite*. New York: Columbia University Press.

Antoun, Richard T. 1968. "On the Modesty of Women in Arab Muslim Villages: A Study in the Accommodation of Traditions." *American Anthropologist* 70, no. 4: 671–97.

Babayan, Kathryn. 2008. "'In Spirit We Ate Each Other's Sorrow': Female Companionship in Seventeenth-Century Safavi Iran." In *Islamicate Sexualities: Translations across Temporal Geographies of Desire*, edited by Kathryn Babayan and Afsaneh Najmabadi, 239–74. Cambridge, MA: Harvard University, Center for Middle Eastern Studies.

Babayan, Kathryn, and Afsaneh Najmabadi. 2008. Preface to *Islamicate Sexualities: Translations across Temporal Geographies of Desire*, edited by Kathryn Babayan and Afsaneh Najmabadi, vii–xiv. Cambridge, MA: Harvard University, Center for Middle Eastern Studies.

Berlant, Lauren. 1998. "Intimacy: A Special Issue." *Critical Inquiry* 24, no. 2: 281–88.

Berlant, Lauren, and Michael Warner. 1998. "Sex in Public." *Critical Inquiry* 24, no. 2: 547–66.

Booth, Marilyn, ed. 2010. *Harem Histories: Envisioning Places and Living Spaces*. Durham, NC: Duke University Press.

Brav, Aaron. 1992. "The Evil Eye among the Hebrews." In *The Evil Eye: A Casebook*, edited by Alan Dundes, 44–54. Madison: University of Wisconsin Press.

Brown, Joanna. 2011. "The Athenian Harem: Orientalism and the Historiography of Athenian Women in the Nineteenth Century." *New Voices in Classical Reception Studies*, no. 6: 1–12.

Çınar, Alev. 2005. *Modernity, Secularism, and Islam in Turkey: Bodies, Places, and Time*. Minneapolis: University of Minnesota Press.

Clarke, Morgan. 2007. "The Modernity of Milk Kinship." *Social Anthropology* 15, no. 3: 287–304.

Coss, Richard G. 1974. "Reflections on the Evil Eye." *Human Behavior* 3, no. 10: 16–22.

Durakbaşa, Ayşe. 1988. "Cumhuriyet Döneminde Kadın Kimliğinin Oluşumu" ("Construction of Women's Identity during Republican Time"). *Tarih ve Toplum (History and Society)* 51: 37–48.

◇ ◇ ◇ ◇ ◇ ◇ ◇ ◇

Göle, Nilüfer. 1996. *The Forbidden Modern: Civilization and Veiling*. Ann Arbor: University of Michigan Press.

Gregg, Melissa, and Gregory J. Seigworth. 2010. "An Inventory of Shimmers." In *The Affect Theory Reader*, edited by Melissa Gregg and Gregory J. Seigworth, 1–28. Durham, NC: Duke University Press.

Harani, Yavuz. 2001. "Türk Kadınının Sporla İmtihanı" ("The Challenge of Women with Sports"). *Hürriyetim*, January 13. webarsiv.hurriyet.com.tr/2001/01/13/282581.asp.

Ilkkaracan, Pinar, ed. 2000. *Women and Sexuality in Muslim Societies*. Istanbul: Women for Women's Human Rights.

Johnson, Clarence Richard. 1924. "The Evil Eye and Other Superstitions in Turkey." *Journal of Applied Sociology* 9: 259–68.

Keyder, Caglar. 1987. *State and Class in Turkey: A Study in Capitalist Development*. London: Verso.

Korkman, Zeynep Kurtulus. 2015. "Feeling Labor: Commercial Divination and Commodified Intimacy in Turkey." *Gender and Society* 29, no. 2: 195–218.

Lacan, Jacques. 1981. *The Four Fundamental Concepts of Psychoanalysis*, edited by Jacques-Alain Miller, translated by Alan Sheridan. New York: Norton.

Lad, Jateen. 2010. "Panoptic Bodies: Black Eunuchs as Guardians of the Topkapı Harem." In *Harem Histories: Envisioning Places and Living Spaces*, edited by Marilyn Booth, 136–76. Durham, NC: Duke University Press.

Lazaridis, Gabriella. 1995. "Sexuality and Its Cultural Construction in Rural Greece." *Journal of Gender Studies* 4, no. 3: 281–95.

McNay, Lois. 1992. *Foucault and Feminism*. Cambridge: Polity.

Mitchell, Timothy. 1991. *Colonising Egypt*. Berkeley: University of California Press.

Moore, Henrietta L. 1988. *Feminism and Anthropology*. Cambridge: Polity.

———. 1994. *A Passion for Difference: Essays in Anthropology and Gender*. Cambridge: Polity.

Mulvey, Laura. 1975. "Visual Pleasure and Narrative Cinema." *Media and Cultural Studies* 16, no. 3: 6–18.

Najmabadi, Afsaneh. 1993. "Veiled Discourse—Unveiled Bodies." *Feminist Studies* 19, no. 3: 487–518.

———. 2005. *Women with Mustaches and Men without Beards: Gender and Sexual Anxieties of Iranian Modernity*. Berkeley, CA.

Özbay, Cenk. 2010. "Nocturnal Queers: Rent Boys' Masculinity in Istanbul." *Sexualities* 13, no. 5: 645–63.

Ozyegin, Gul. 2009. "Virginal Facades: Sexual Freedom and Guilt among Young Turkish Women." *European Journal of Women's Studies* 16, no. 2: 103–23.

———, ed. 2015. *Gender and Sexuality in Muslim Cultures*. Burlington, VT: Ashgate.

Parkes, Peter. 2005. "Milk Kinship in Islam: Substance, Structure, History." *Social Anthropology* 13, no. 3: 307–29.

Parla, Ayse. 2001. "The 'Honor' of the State: Virginity Examinations in Turkey." *Feminist Studies* 27, no. 1: 65–88.

Peirce, Leslie P. 1993. *The Imperial Harem: Women and Sovereignty in the Ottoman Empire*. New York: Oxford University Press.

Sehlikoglu, Sertaç. 2013. "Vaginal Obsessions in Turkey: An Islamic Perspective." *Open Democracy*, February 18. www.opendemocracy.net/5050/serta%C3%A7-sehliko%C4%9Flu/vaginal-obsessions-in-turkey-islamic-perspective.

———. 2015a. "Contestation and Dichotomies concerning Women's Bodies and Sports in Turkey: From Aysun Özbek to Neslihan Darnel." In *Sport in Islam and in Muslim Communities*, edited by Alberto Testa and Mahfoud Amara, 187–202. London: Routledge.

———. 2015b. "The Daring *Mahrem*: Changing Dynamics of Public Sexuality in Turkey." In *Gender and Sexuality in Muslim Cultures*, edited by Gul Ozyegin, 235–52. Burlington, VT: Ashgate.

———. 2015c. "Intimate Publics, Public Intimacies: Natural Limits, Creation, and the Culture of *Mahremiyet* in Turkey." *Cambridge Journal of Anthropology* 33, no. 2: 77–89.

Shahrokni, Nazanin. 2014. "The Mothers' Paradise: Women-Only Parks and the Dynamics of State Power in Iran." *Journal of Middle East Women's Studies* 10, no. 3: 87–108.

Simon, William, and John H. Gagnon. 1986. "Sexual Scripts: Permanence and Change." *Archives of Sexual Behavior* 15, no. 2: 97–120.

Smith-Hefner, Nancy J. 2006. "Reproducing Respectability: Sex and Sexuality among Muslim Javanese Youth." *Review of Indonesian and Malaysian Affairs* 40, no. 1: 143–72.

Strathern, Marilyn. 1990. *The Gender of the Gift: Problems with Women and Problems with Society in Melanesia*. Berkeley: University of California Press.

vom Bruck, Gabriele. 1997. "Elusive Bodies: The Politics of Aesthetics among Yemeni Elite Women." *Signs* 23, no. 1: 175–214.

Werbner, Pnina. 2007. "Veiled Interventions in Pure Space: Honour, Shame, and Embodied Struggles among Muslims in Britain and France." *Theory, Culture, and Society* 24, no. 2: 161–86.

Yanagisako, Sylvia Junko, and Jane Fishburne Collier. 1987. "Toward a Unified Analysis of Gender and Kinship." In *Gender and Kinship: Essays toward a Unified Analysis*, edited by Jane Fishburne Collier and Sylvia Junko Yanagisako, 14–50. Stanford, CA: Stanford University Press.

Yeğenoğlu, Meyda. 1998. *Colonial Fantasies: Towards a Feminist Reading of Orientalism*. Cambridge: Cambridge University Press.

Ze'evi, Dror. 2006. *Producing Desire: Changing Sexual Discourse in the Ottoman Middle East, 1500–1900*. Berkeley: University of California Press.

Zengin, Aslı. 2011. *İktidarın mahremiyeti: İstanbul'da hayat kadınları, seks işçiliği ve şiddet* (*Intimacy of Power: Prostitution, Sex Work, and Violence in Istanbul*). Istanbul: Metis.

Territories of Desire

A Geography of Competing Intimacies in Cairo

ABSTRACT This article addresses multiple paths of desire in Egypt. To date, research has mainly focused on the family as the realm of intimacy. To understand desire, it is important to take into account other contexts that contribute to shaping experience. Conversations about sex among men in coffee shops are contrasted with family discourses as a symbolic locus for alternative modes shaping intimacy in homosocial circles. The hierarchy of truth whereby confessions are supposed to give insight into subjects' core feelings are reassessed, allowing the sketching of a geography of competing intimacies that outline the coordinates of masculine desire.

KEYWORDS Egypt, intimacy, desire, family, coffee shops

In early 2015, at the opening of a small repair shop for computers and mobile phones in Sayyida Zaiynab, a popular neighborhood of Cairo, I am sitting with three men in their early thirties. The two waiters take orders and bring us drinks and hookahs. Loudspeakers in front of the shop broadcast Quranic recitations until one of the men switches to Egyptian pop music. Our conversations tackle various topics, but one seems particularly enjoyable to my friends: sex. One of the waiters with a hole in his trousers explains that it is "to let the girl play with 'it.'" Minutes later he simulates copulation with a client talking on the phone. Another friend speaks of the ways mangoes can be eaten and teases him, hinting at the sexual connotations. This same friend then comments, "This guy, tell him anything dirty, it makes him happy!" Shortly after, another acquaintance joins us. He is teased by all three — he should marry a Russian girl working in a cabaret in Cairo — he would get a good amount of money just for helping her obtain Egyptian residence while also not interfering in

JMEWS • Journal of Middle East Women's Studies • 12:2 • July 2016
DOI 10.1215/15525864-3507617 • © 2016 by the Association for Middle East Women's Studies

166

her job. This friend loudly expresses his reluctance to become a pimp. They laugh at his seriousness. The conversation then turns to the owner of the new repair shop. At another repair shop where he formerly worked, he was told to take advantage of the opportunity to have affairs with married women encountered on the Internet. According to him and his friends, he invited women to the shop's mezzanine to have intercourse with them. His friends ask him how he will proceed in his new shop, which has no mezzanine. He has no answer so far. During the course of this conversation, girls pass by the coffee shop, and the men look at them discretely. One of them concludes, "This is how the popular neighborhoods are."

Similar conversations take place in these kinds of gatherings in coffee shops all around the city. Access to most of them is reserved for men. Their settings vary widely, from large rooms to counters where tea is prepared with a few hookahs, chairs, and tables. Often owners install a television screen on a wall to attract viewers during football games. The smell of tobacco blended with molasses, the loud ordering of drinks, the gentle bubbling of the water in the hookahs, and the conversations of men create a specific atmosphere. Some men spend hours at coffee shops, smoking, watching television, and, most of all, chatting with the waiters, other clients, and friends.

In this article I argue that coffee shops play a central role in alternative forms of intimacy for men outside the family. Current work on intimacy and sexuality in Egypt is centered on family and marriage. Surprisingly, coffee shops in Egypt have been of marginal interest to anthropologists. *Baladi* (local) coffee shops, frequented by men, are especially understudied, even though they are central places of sociability. Anouk de Koning (2009) devotes a large part of her research to coffee shops. However, she focuses on classy ones frequented equally by women and men. Farha Ghannam (2002, 109–11; 2011, 749) also writes on coffee shops in her seminal texts on the poor neighborhood of al-Zawiyya al-Hamra. But she describes them as places outside the realm of respectability, where young people waste their time and money, meet bad people, and are at constant risk of being arrested by police. This perspective of coffee shops as places of idleness and danger gives only a partial appraisal of them shaped by the point of view of the family context. It is probably women's unease in hanging around in such places for lengthy periods that lies behind these assumptions about coffee shops, a difficulty that Ghannam (2013, 24) acknowledges. Nevertheless, as Peter Loizos (1994, 79) states, it is important to recognize that we only have access to "particular distorting mirrors" of manly performance that depend on the context in which it is studied. It is thus important not to consider masculinity as discussed in the family context as the complete picture but to take into account other situations, such as coffee shops.

Families and coffee shops should not be reduced to dyads, because different modes of intimacy can occur in both. However, both act as landmarks for reterritorializing desire, orienting it around definite paths that need to be explored. Thus it is possible to sketch a geography of intimacies in Egypt by contrasting the home and the coffeehouse as complementary assemblages of desire, conveying conflicting notions of closeness with porous borders.[1] Susan Gal (2002) has underscored that to grasp the public-private distinction analytically, it is necessary to understand its indexical and fractal character. As she explains, public and private are semantic categories that cannot be understood out of their specific contexts. Further, the borders between the two are always shifting — a public setting having privacy and vice versa. The home, when compared to the street, is considered private. Inside the house, the living room is the public realm, especially when guests are present. But even in formal settings, side conversations and specific body postures allow the creation of a sense of privacy. Whispering, leaning in toward one's interlocutor, or catching a gaze can help build a sense of proximity that places a conversation to one side. These shifts and subdivisions make the divide fractal. Gal also claims that the basis of the public-private distinction is located in the body and the distance from or proximity to it. Intimacy, as Lauren Berlant (1998, 285) puts it, is about creating closeness through an "aesthetic of attachment" found in a family, couple, or friendship.

Words create the privacy of an intimate setting, and specific registers of talk are intended to convey closeness. Personal confidences, for instance, perform a bond of trust through the disclosure of confessions deemed shameful or dangerous for the speaker. Expression of hidden feelings seems to be the key element. This idea of conceptions of truth as lying in some deep layer of emotional subjectivity where past sufferings are concealed has been criticized as far too restrictive and Eurocentric (Hafez 2011, 12; Joseph 2005, 81), but it is one that is also shared by counselors and psychologists in Egypt. The trust established through the act of confessing is the mark of a strong tie. But it is crucial not to confuse the existence of these different levels of speech with a naturalized opposition of "inner truth" to "superficiality." Michel Foucault (1976) made his readers aware of the traps of subjectification as a technique of power, contesting the very idea of a preexistent "inner truth" to be discovered through discursive means. Another means of creating intimacy that is less addressed by the literature is collusion as expressed through jokes or anecdotes, a shared understanding creating closeness through mutual enjoyment. The situation of a man never speaking his problems out loud would be difficult to bear for the loneliness it seems to imply, but at the same time a context where people talk without relief of their inner feelings appears equally difficult. It is less a matter of truth than of the context of expression.

Hence, to explore the geography of intimacies as revealed by sex talk, I contrast the promotion of the nuclear family, notably by state institutions, and of intimacies inside the family realm with the intimacy of men in coffee shops in moments of fun, where connivance is based on a shared demonstration of self-confidence. I then describe the entanglements and reciprocal annexation between these two modes of closeness, for instance, in exchanges in a mode of confidence with special friends, called *intim*. Finally, I develop a reading of the relationship between family and coffee shop inspired by Gilles Deleuze and Félix Guattari (1972, 1980, 1991; see also Sauvagnargues 2004). In this theoretical frame, family and coffee shops are considered as pertaining to the main coordinates of Cairene masculinities.

This contribution draws on ethnographic research into the ways to speak of love and sex in Cairo (Kreil 2012a). The main fieldwork was carried out between 2007 and 2011, in the final period of the Hosni Mubarak era. It focused on coffee shop conversations and a counseling center. As a young man in his late twenties speaking Egyptian Arabic, I had easy access to coffee shop conversations. A problem for me was timidity, as most of the time I was shy about asking direct questions about the topic, but it turned out that this apparent flaw had its advantages. As I did not initiate the talk about these topics, I could observe its spontaneous emergence. At that time I was conducting fieldwork in parallel with the work of Lucile Gruntz, a French anthropologist, who gave me insights into the similar conversations among women during meetings at their homes. Later I had surprisingly easy access to the counseling center I studied, even though it was exclusively a gathering of women. I even participated in sex education classes and group therapy sessions. The fact that the teaching was presented as pertaining to the realm of scientific neutrality probably contributed to making it appear sufficiently gender neutral for these women to have a man in their midst. In this context, the presence of a foreign researcher could even be seen as a pledge of legitimacy. This article is based on observations at these two main settings and thirty interviews with counselors, psychologists, and sexologists.[2]

Territory of Intimacy 1: The Family

To understand the position of coffee shops in Egypt's geography of intimacies, it is important to see how they relate to another important space of social closeness, the family, particularly the nucleus of parents and their children. Historical and anthropological research shows that the Egyptian elite has actively promoted a specific model of intimacy based around companionate marriage since the end of the nineteenth century (Abu-Lughod 1998; El Sadda 2007). French law and family theory were particularly influential in shaping the conception of a modern family (Cuno 2015). Justifications for the education of women often emphasized the need for knowledgeable nurturing of children and providing partners for Egyptian men whose company is pleasant at home (Kholoussy 2010, 99–122). Later, in the Gamal Abdel Nasser era, the nuclear family was promoted energetically. Demographic concerns entered the picture as demographic transition theory made its way into Egypt, associating relative status equality to partners with fewer children (Bier 2011, 130–32; El Shakry 2007, 145–222), though, for reformers, equality in this context

most often meant not interchangeability between husband and wife but complementarity based on difference. Thus general trends to emulate the West in the name
of progress have been influential in defining modern and happy marriages as shaped
by mutual feelings.

In the prevailing development paradigm in Egypt, with its opposition between
"backwardness" and "progress," the latter is clearly associated with an ongoing
renewal of love through the use of sweet words and declarations of affection.
Egyptians distinguish between "traditional marriage" and "love marriage." The first
implies a strong parental role in partner choice and goes along with conceptions of
"true love" as only emerging after the wedding, through a complicity based on silent
coexistence. The second considers love as the root of marriage, with an urge to
express one's feelings continuously to keep them alive. Naturally, this dichotomy is
relative, and rather than a strict opposition, a continuum should be seen between
love marriages and those determined by parents (Springborg 1982, 29–30). Many
couples meet at work or at education venues, feel attracted to each other, and later
ask for their parents' blessings.[3]

In discussions at the counseling center that I studied, expressive love was seen
as a necessary condition for individual fulfillment. Family is the realm in which it is
best felt. Expressing feelings strengthens confidence, giving parents a means to
monitor the behaviors of younger members. It can also improve the quality of sexual
relations in couples through an ongoing dialogue between husband and wife about
emotions and desires. Speaking about feelings is seen as a means of overcoming
misunderstandings about desire. Among the main issues at stake in the debates of
the participants was the balance between the quest for stability and the need for
affective fulfillment. One day, during a lesson on codependency, the women of the
counseling center vehemently debated the case of a woman who was dedicated to
her husband even though he mishandled her and their children. An older woman
praised this way of "conserving her family." She faced a storm of contrary opinions
stating that it had nothing to do with true love either for her husband or her children
and pathologizing her refusal to seek divorce as stemming from a fear of being alone.
Partner choice was seen to be influenced by criteria external to affection, such as
social status, an aspect emphasized during the discussions at the center. In regard
to these constraints around choosing a partner, expressive love is meant to permit conciliatory stability and affection, allowing better understanding and solving
problems these constraints can provoke.

The injunction to express loving feelings inside marriage finds its way even
into some Salafi sermons, as this excerpt of a lesson by the famous Salafi preacher
Muhammad Hassan illustrates:

> You have to know that you will possess the heart of your spouse or wife only thanks to
> love. Don't imagine that money will make it possible. Even if you cover her with gold,

you won't get her heart. You have to show her that you love and esteem her. I gave you an example: I've told you that if a brother, impressed by these words and willing to apply them, would take his portable Satan — I mean, his portable phone — and call his wife to tell her: "*Salam 'alaykum*, how are you, my beloved one?"...the woman would first look at her phone. [*The sheikh pauses and looks at the palm of his hand; laughter in the audience*] . . . I swear by God, she would first look at her phone and tell to herself: "It's really his number!" Then she would answer: "You want to announce to me a catastrophe. . . ." [*laughter in the audience*] "You have married a second wife? Tell me everything! You are acting!" She hasn't heard these words before. She is not used to it. You are a decent man — a Si Sayyid . . . who says, "It's blameworthy to say to my wife that I love her!"[4] Who told you that? The wife begs for sweet words and a shared smile. With others you are perfect, and the most appropriate person for these words is your wife. Let her hear them, my brother! These words will make a mountain of ice melt, filling from its start to its end marriage with a great amount of problems! Let her hear sweet words! Do it by observing the orders of the Messenger of God! [*The audience*: God's prayer and peace be upon him.] (Belker 2012; my translation)

By contrast, the comparison between men and women that can occur in homosocial talks is explicitly condemned. For example, in the short manual *Awwal Layla min Layali Shahr al-'Asal: Mustasharuka al-jinsi fi layla al-zifaf* (*The First Night of the Honeymoon: Your Sexual Counselor for the Wedding Night*), Ayman al-Husayni (1994, 36) explains to the readers that "we sometimes hear from the spouses that they could hardly leave their homes during their honeymoon, as if they had freed themselves of all obligations to focus on sex only! Consequently, some complained that they could only have sex once a day with their wife despite being newly-wed!" (my translation). He tries to reassure readers that the quality of sexual relations is more important than their quantity. The sexologist Hiba Qutb also shows utter contempt for the conversations about sex that take place between female friends. In her eyes, their advice is misleading and indecent. The topic of sex should be restricted to the close family circle, particularly to the marriage partner, or to experts. For instance, answering a woman who wrote to her asking about discussions she had about her sex life with "parents and friends," Qutb (2006, 42) states that "these discussions are definitely forbidden by Islam because every individual has different potential in matters of sex and comparison could provoke resentment" (my translation). All of the counselors I encountered and whose texts I have read shared this opinion. The only sound way to speak about sex seems in the close family realm, ideally in the couple, or with specialists.

In response to this challenge, introducing sex education classes in schools is a shared project among counselors. The limits of what is deemed decent are quickly reached, however. To be seen as acceptable, sexual issues have to be addressed as health problems, as family matters, or as burdens for the development of the country. The fast withdrawal in 2010 of a sex education project in schools backed by the United Nations Children's Emergency Fund (UNICEF) after protests by Muslim Brotherhood deputies in parliament is one example of the difficulties encountered in building an official discourse on sexuality. The struggle with the Islamist party for power has played a role in labeling sexual issues as a domain to avoid (Farag 1994); respectability does not allow a discourse on desire at the public level. Counselors often complained of the difficulties they faced trying to speak of sexual issues at schools not because of the reactions of the pupils but because of the fear expressed by administrative staff and teachers. As a result, when studying the issue of sex in Egypt, one encounters the discourse that sexuality is a taboo for Egyptians (Kreil 2015). This sounds paradoxical when contrasted with the common — and also often very detailed — evocations of sex in conversations, jokes, insults, and so on, not to mention questions directed to preachers about sexuality or the publicity given to erectile dysfunction pills.

Territory of Intimacy 2: The Coffee Shops

The gap between the ideals of intimacy shown above and the meeting of men at coffee shops makes it obvious that the latter are a crucial place of inquiry if someone wants to understand desire in Egypt. Of course, there are tacit rules underlying encounters at coffee shops. Yet the main aim for sitting together is most often to enjoy the moment. Like hashish and alcohol, sex, even the realm of prostitution, is open for discussion even by those who portray Salafism as the correct interpretation of Islam if asked. Religion can thus be compartmentalized either to other contexts or to specific persons, such as sheikhs and priests (Kreil 2012b; see also Haenni 2005, 55–56).

Coffee shops have other functions. They can serve as topographical landmarks in neighborhoods, furnish meeting places for strangers and friends when your home is too small or you wish to avoid the scrutiny of your family, or help in job hunting (Depaule 2007). People go to coffee shops to watch films or football games. Clients learn the names of the owners and waiters and are sure to meet at least someone they know. In return, they demand privileged service from the staff. Thus the informal networks of friends called *shilla* favor a coffee shop where they meet on a regular basis. These gatherings sometimes play a role in the informal networking (*wasta*) that is important in many areas of life in Egypt. Coffee shops mix all possible registers of action, from the commercial to the political, yet always stay below the level of an explicit institutionalization, as Omar Carlier (1990, 995) notes for the apparently similar context of Algeria.

Coffee shops are not the only places where men have fun. They can meet on the street for a wedding party, at their apartments, or at a shop owned by a friend. Indeed, some of the most telling examples of festive transgression that I encountered took place at private homes. Consumption of alcohol or watching pornographic movies happened most of the time at someone's home, although weddings are also known as moments of transgressions, when people block a small street for nights of dancing and in many cases enjoy the spectacle of scantily clad belly dancers and consume hashish. Nevertheless, for the geography of intimacies, coffee shops remain symbolic of fun. They earn this reputation due to their open and public character, making them an easy target, while weddings could at best be reformed due to their necessary character in the opinion of a majority of Egyptians.[5] Coffee shops shape a form of manly leisure, giving a specific style to meetings that often involves a mutual teasing that sometimes gets out of hand (Depaule 2007, 259–60) but also builds a specific form of intimacy on which trust and confidences can grow.

Women are not alone in complaining about coffee shops. Official discourses largely condemn them. Their clients are depicted as lazy; they should be worshipping God and working hard (Bayat 2007, 435–36). For Salafis, coffee shop clients are avoiding their responsibilities to their religion, society, and families. Various attempts to forbid the hookah are probably a result of this view rather than the health concerns raised by the huge amount of tobacco consumed. However, asceticism and self-restraint in terms of pleasure have little chance of becoming a dominant pattern of conduct, as testified by attempts to forbid coffee shops and tries by Salafis in the 1990s and early 2000s to impose their rules of conduct (Haenni 1999; Hattox 1985; Kreil 2012b; Schielke 2009). Despite criticisms, there are coffee shops everywhere around the city.

One can hear wonderful stories at coffee shops. A man in his forties related his experiences in Geneva to a group. On the shores of the lake waiters bring you joints on silver plates while you watch girls swimming in bikinis. If you drive for just half an hour, he added, you get to a mountain covered in snow but can still see the girls below swimming in bikinis. The story is not checked for its factual truth value, which is irrelevant in this context (Veyne 1988). What counts here is the enjoyment it offers the group.

When the talk comes more directly to the topic of sex, celebration of masculine potency prevails. Distinctions can be observed between unmarried and married men in how the topic is addressed, the latter speaking more easily of practical issues, exchanging advice on chemical and natural aphrodisiacs, including pills, shrimps, and nutmeg. In coffee shops a lot of talk equates pleasure with male sociability, explicitly opposing it to married life, portrayed as dull and disappointing. It appears through jokes about wives and their untruthfulness and constant kidding about "the government" or "the police"—that is, the spouse — putting pressure on men to come home early. Beside this portrayal of a domestic tyrant or equating marriage to prison, stories at coffee shops often portray women as sexual prey through boasts about past prowess or remarks addressed to women passing by. Homophobic insults are also widely spread in this context, sometimes as a kind of teasing.

The complicity between men is not devoid of power stakes. For instance, many of the interactions described in the opening section can be read as tests of masculinity, contributing decisively to the shaping of hegemonic models of behavior. The exclusion of women shows hierarchies at play, and although the mocking exchanges seem unidirectional in this situation, this is not always the case: the waiter and the older and less educated client of the group are teased the most. But even if the teasing was sometimes cruel, the general tone of these exchanges never contradicted the principle aim of creating a pleasurable atmosphere for common enjoyment. Collusion created by these jokes strengthens the friends' network.

The sense of intimacy shaped around the coffee shop has a deep impact on imaginaries of manhood and provides an important path for desire. It should be noted that women also have access to other realms of intimacy than the family circle. They often meet with neighbors, and the conversations on sex they have during these chats (Hoodfar 1999, 250–56) often share men's assumptions about pleasure and strength in coffee shop conversations. This partially explains the success of models of manhood that could be deemed oppressive among certain women; they are seen as most able to provide pleasurable moments. It is a common subject among married women to prize the strength of their husbands when they are gathered and sometimes even to celebrate violent behavior.

Entangled Intimacies

Coffee shop conversations avoid weaknesses, doubts, and feelings revealing men's frailty. That does not mean that their existence is not acknowledged. The lyrics performed by such singers as Umm Kalthum and Muhammad 'Abd al-Wahhab and the more recent 'Amru Dyab and Shereen evoke them constantly and are often the musical background in coffee shops. Such feelings are simply out of place in this context, because they would ruin the atmosphere of fun.

Despite the promotion of the family models based on mutual understanding, even public agents of the state can occasionally mobilize macho registers. Since the political intervention of the military in 2013, glorifications of the new president, 'Abd al-Fattah al-Sisi, often emphasize his manhood in ways reminiscent of coffee shop conversations about sexual prowess. Evoking al-Sisi as a "male," while sometimes making an arm movement signifying the erect penis (one arm with fist clenched held from below by the hand of the other arm) and praising how attractive he is for women, has been very common since 2013, even on television. Likewise, coffee shop customers can be described as authentic Egyptians, "sons of the country" who define its real roots (El-Messiri 1978). They become bearers of imaginaries of the nation based on masculine strength (Ghannam 2012).

In other situations, though, also sometimes in coffee shops, expressions of doubt and weakness are welcome proof of trust and of the strength of mutual bonds. As in Gal's examples, even in such settings moments of privacy can occur, and multiple kinds of entanglements can occur. In an example from women's gatherings, the impact of sexual counseling programs became apparent through the efforts of a Nubian woman in a low-income neighborhood to speak with her husband about their feelings to resolve lack of arousal. She was explicitly quoting TV shows as an inspiration. At the same time, the woman told this story to her female neighbors, parents, and friends with explicit details about their sexual relations, from the ways they were having intercourse to the size of his penis, in a manner that is explicitly condemned by counselors. In 2009 I assisted a discussion among young men on how to distinguish sexual harassment from other ways of picking up girls, a topic that became highly debated in Egyptian media in about 2006 (Kreil 2012a, 187–206). One of the young men, the future mobile-phone repairer from the opening scene, explained to me that harassment was an issue of education, as some people, even when willing to say nice words, came out with insults. Just afterward he added jokingly that love is everywhere in Egypt and that "a beautiful girl couldn't enter a street without having ten men following her." Thus, in front of the audience of his friends, he mingled arguments for reforming ways of expressing feelings toward woman influenced by campaigns for public awareness with the macho repertory of seduction as a matter of jokes and complicity among men.

Therefore not all conversations involving love and sex put one's worth as a man on trial. Less than the topic itself, the mode of addressing it indicates if it pertains to the realm of confidences. The use of aphrodisiacs, sexual problems, or longing for women can be presented as laughable, the humor of an inverted domination confirming at the same time its basic tenets. Body language is very important in making the switch to a more sensitive register: a lowered voice, a torso and head leant forward, or tearful eyes point to the speaker's vulnerability. For instance, Wassim, a man in his early twenties working as an accountant, liked to boast in front of his male friends of his female conquests, depicting himself as a victim of his own success. He spoke endlessly of his adventures with girls he dated on the Internet and in real life. But he was also very prone to confidences, alternating these two styles of speaking of his life and creating bonds with men. In these moments his favorite topic was one unfortunate love affair with an English teacher at the University of Cairo, a woman he described as of a higher status than him. During such confidences, he presented all his other relationships as mere substitutes. The frustration resulting in the impossibility of marrying the beloved woman because of parental refusal was among the most common topics of confidences that I heard. Impossible love is also a central subject in the sad songs at coffee shops.

The larger the group, the more likely boasting about sex will come up. In large gatherings the people present are often loosely acquainted with each other. More sensitive conversations unfold in a close circle of friends. They rely on trust and are at the same time constitutive of it. A word derived from European languages, *intim*, designates a very close friend. He or she is the one with whom a friend "can empty himself" of all his burdens. Contrary to the conversations described above, the *intim* can be either a man or a woman—it does not make a difference. *Intim* bears an analogy with romantic love as an expressive kind of friendship, but emotional subjectivity here seems to be at least partly gender neutral.

Redrawing the Coordinates of Desire

As a key for understanding the interplay between family and coffee shop as competing territories of intimacy, I propose to deal with two aspects of Deleuze and Guattari's philosophy that seem particularly interesting for analyzing desire in Cairo. First, Deleuze and Guattari put forward the creative energy of desire and refuse to consider it as the result of a want (Deleuze 2003, 112–22). Hence an approach inspired by Deleuze and Guattari allows moving beyond perspectives on "men in crisis" (Amar 2011, 36–39) in the Middle East whose focus on the alleged frustration of young men denies them any genuine enjoyment of life. The discourse on frustration, which is often evoked by the actors themselves, as discussed earlier (see also, for the Egyptian rural context, Schielke 2015, 27–46), refers to a similarly univocal definition of desire anchored in the sexual intimate coupling of a man and a women. This equates to the "familialism" denounced by Deleuze and Guattari (1972, 63–165) as a serious limitation of scope, entrapping all modes of desire in the stiff frame of the nuclear family. The strength of the experienced homosocial bond and the alternative paths of desire it provides call into doubt the universal validity of this familialist perspective.

Second, Deleuze and Guattari (1980) hint at the flexibility and mobility of intimate geographies. They describe moving landscapes of desire open to multiple actualizations. These territories constitute hierarchized spaces. In this sense, coffee shops can be read as the territory of a minor mode of sex talk when compared to the family, instituted as the sole legitimate domain of intimacy. However, depending on context, hierarchies can be reversed, as I have showed. Contrasting these adjacent territories establishes the expressive milieus of Cairene masculinities with their competing experiences of respectability and pleasure. Rather than strict opposites, then, these territories appear as the coordinates of a symbiotic assemblage along whose lines desire moves.

Samuli Schielke theorizes the inconsistency of moral ideals, always bound to particular situations in the efforts of persons to do right. He evokes ideals about religion and love as orientation for ethical commitments, stating that "much of life is not characterized by moral concerns, and sometimes people quite consciously avoid considering a possible moral aspect of their action" (Schielke 2015, 56). According to Schielke, actors compartmentalize their ethical standards according to situations. Putting the argument further, I hint at the danger of hierarchizing univocally the importance they take for actors. The flows of desire can be more important than moral norms for inhabiting the world, because people do not behave only out of a sense of goodness. Understanding this allows one to take into account all the ambivalences and entanglements that make an experience happen. Sets of desire can seem to last forever or for just the time span of a laugh. All these moments convey their own senses of truth set in particular historical conjunctures, where they simultaneously contribute to shaping the experience of being a man.

Conclusion

In Egypt men have access to competing contexts of intimacy. Each of these places is shown as allowing a different quality of bond; a couple's confidences do not equate with the homosocial complicity between men based on saucy jokes. As discussed, most people compartmentalize different settings and adapt their discourses accordingly. An individual can defend the preeminence of intimacy in the realm of the family or the importance of strictly abiding to religious injunctions and then put this principle aside for a conversation with friends in a coffee shop. Drawing shifting territories of intimacy avoids a conception of one kind of intimacy from the past and another from the present. It allows thinking about the coexistence of different paths of desire.

Authors working on intimacy in Cairo have neglected fun as a shaping factor. An exception is Asef Bayat (2007), who has underscored its importance at the political level. Here the focus has been on desire. An emphasis on the couple and the family as a locus of intimacy has meant the neglect of other paths of desire that can be equally or sometimes even more important in Egyptians' experiences. While it is crucial to recognize the power of such institutions as the family (Hasso 2011), research should not reproduce their discourses by asserting authoritatively which parts of experience are significant. The poietic virtualities of life cannot be reduced to a simple formula. More research should be done on interactions in coffee shops, because it is clear that to understand gender roles, it is necessary to look beyond the state and the family and to take into account these informal areas where men discuss their pleasures and fantasies together. The map should not be confused with the territory, as entanglements of modes of intimacy prove. Nevertheless, these places, by sketching the coordinates of a shifting geography of intimacy, provide a partial but indispensable way to highlight the territories of desire in Egypt.

AYMON KREIL works at the University of Zürich and at the Geneva University of Art and Design. His main research interests are religious authority, gender, and the definitions of the political in Egypt. Contact: aymon.kreil@uzh.ch.

Acknowledgments

I would like to thank Sertaç Sehlikoglu, Valerio Simoni, Aslı Zengin, and the anonymous reviewers for their work, as well as miriam cooke for the English editing.

Notes

1. Ghannam (2002, 88–115), for instance, precisely details variations during the lifetimes of places in a neighborhood deemed respectable for a man or a woman.

2. Recently, the turmoil of 2011–13 enabled expressions of stances on love and sex that would not have been possible under the authoritarian rule of Mubarak. The case of Alya Mahdy's nude pictures, much mediated in the West, is one particularly famous example, but the electropunk band the Wetrobots could also be included. However, the comeback of the authoritarian state in its former shape after 2013 has prompted the resurgence of crackdowns on same-sex relationships and atheists, reinstating a consensus forcibly imposed by institutions. It hints at a return to the practices of the Mubarak era at all levels. Hence most of the conclusions drawn at that time seem only marginally affected by the political changes, as far as I can see.

3. Likewise, conceptions of progress are socially debated. What some see as backwardness others read as cultural authenticity. On the contrary, progress can also be equated with alienation.

4. Si Sayyid, a character in Naguib Mahfuz's trilogy of novels, symbolizes the figure of the traditional patriarch.

5. This function, providing pleasure to customers, has been attested to since the sixteenth century at least, prompting some craftspeople and ulemas worried about their respectability to avoid them (Hattox 1985; Tuchscherer 1997).

References

Abu-Lughod, Lila. 1998. "The Marriage of Feminism and Islamism in Egypt: Selective Repudiation as a Dynamic of Postcolonial Cultural Politics." In *Remaking Women: Feminism and Modernity in the Middle East*, edited by Lila Abu-Lughod, 243–69. Princeton, NJ: Princeton University Press.

Amar, Paul. 2011. "Middle East Masculinity Studies: Discourses of 'Men in Crisis,' Industries of Gender in Revolution." *Journal of Middle East Women's Studies* 7, no. 3: 36–70.

Bayat, Asef. 2007. "Islamism and the Politics of Fun." *Public Culture* 19, no. 3: 433–59.

Belker, Absher. 2012. "Al-shaykh Muhammad Hassan yansah al-shabab al-muqbilin 'ala al-zawaj" ("The Sheykh Muhammad Hassan Gives Advice to Young People before Marriage"), January 17. www .youtube.com/watch?v=GwywEp9Avig.

Berlant, Lauren. 1998. "Intimacy: A Special Issue." *Critical Inquiry* 24, no. 2: 281–88.

Bier, Laura. 2011. *Revolutionary Womanhood: Feminisms, Modernity, and the State in Nasser's Egypt.* Stanford, CA: Stanford University Press.

Carlier, Omar. 1990. "Le café maure: Sociabilité masculine et effervescence citoyenne (Algérie, XVIIe–XXe siècles)." *Annales: Économies, sociétés, civilisations* 45, no. 4: 975–1003.

Cuno, Kenneth M. 2015. *Modernizing Marriage: Family, Ideology, and Law in Nineteenth- and Early Twentieth-Century Egypt.* Syracuse, NY: Syracuse University Press.

Deleuze, Gilles. 2003. *Deux régimes de fous: Textes et entretiens, 1975–1995.* Paris: Minuit.

Deleuze, Gilles, and Félix Guattari. 1972. *Capitalisme et schizophrénie.* Vol. 1, *L'anti-Œdipe.* Paris: Minuit.

——. 1980. *Capitalisme et schizophrénie.* Vol. 2, *Mille plateaux.* Paris: Minuit.

——. 1991. *Qu'est-ce que la philosophie?* Paris: Minuit.

Depaule, Jean-Charles. 2007. "Les établissements de café du Caire." *Études rurales*, no. 180: 254–62.

Farag, Iman. 1994. "Identité, natalité ou les avatars d'une conférence internationale." *Égypte/Monde arabe* 1, no. 20: 43–66.

Foucault, Michel. 1976. *Histoire de la sexualité.* Vol. 1, *La volonté de savoir.* Paris: Gallimard.

Gal, Susan. 2002. "A Semiotic of the Public/Private Distinction." *differences* 13, no. 1: 77–95.

Ghannam, Farha. 2002. *Remaking the Modern: Space, Relocation, and the Politics of Identity in a Global Cairo.* Berkeley: University of California Press.

———. 2011. "Mobility, Liminality, and Embodiment in Urban Egypt." *American Ethnologist* 38, no. 4: 790–800.

———. 2012. "Meanings and Feelings: Local Interpretations of the Use of Violence in the Egyptian Revolution." *American Ethnologist* 39, no. 1: 32–36.

———. 2013. *To Live and Die like a Man: Gender Dynamics in Urban Egypt*. Stanford, CA: Stanford University Press.

Haenni, Patrick. 1999. "Ils n'en ont pas fini avec l'Orient: De quelques islamisations non islamistes." *Revue du monde musulman et de la Méditerranée*, nos. 85–86: 121–47.

———. 2005. *L'ordre des caïds: Conjurer la dissidence urbaine au Caire*. Paris: Karthala.

Hafez, Sherine. 2011. *An Islam of Her Own: Reconsidering Religion and Secularism in Women's Islamic Movements*. New York: New York University Press.

Hasso, Frances. 2011. *Consuming Desires: Family Crisis and the State in the Middle East*. Stanford, CA: Stanford University Press.

Hattox, Ralph. 1985. *Coffee and Coffeehouses: The Origins of a Social Beverage in the Medieval Near East*. Seattle: University of Washington Press.

Hoodfar, Homa. 1999. *Between Marriage and the Market: Intimate Politics and Survival in Cairo*. Cairo: American University in Cairo Press.

Al-Husayni, Ayman. 1994. *Awwal Layla min Layali shahr al-ʾAsal: Mustasharuka al-jinsi fi layla al-zifaf* (*The First Night of the Honeymoon: Your Sexual Counselor for the Wedding Night*). Cairo: Ibn Sina.

Joseph, Suad. 2005. "Learning Desire: Relational Pedagogies and the Desiring Female Subject in Lebanon." *Journal of Middle East Women's Studies* 1, no. 1: 79–109.

Kholoussy, Hanan. 2010. *For Better, for Worse: The Marriage Crisis That Made Modern Egypt*. Stanford, CA: Stanford University Press.

Koning, Anouk de. 2009. *Global Dreams: Class, Gender, and Public Space in Cosmopolitan Cairo*. Cairo: American University in Cairo Press.

Kreil, Aymon. 2012a. "Du rapport au dire: Amour, sexe et discours d'expertise au Caire." PhD diss., École des Hautes Études en Sciences Sociales and University of Neuchâtel.

———. 2012b. "Salafis as Shaykhs: Othering the Pious in Cairo." In *Ethnographies of Islam*, edited by Baudouin Dupret, Thomas Pierret, Paulo G. Pinto, and Kathryn Spellman-Poots, 135–43. Edinburgh: Edinburgh University Press.

———. 2015. "Pudeur des corps, impudeurs des mots en Égypte: Formes et usages de la rhétorique du 'bris de silence' sur la sexualité." In *Voile, corps féminin et pudeur, entre Islam et Occident: Approches historiques et anthropologiques*, edited by Yasmina Foehr-Janssens, Silvia Naef, and Aline Schlaepfer, 155–70. Geneva: Labor et Fides.

Loizos, Peter. 1994. "A Broken Mirror: Masculine Sexuality in Greek Ethnography." In *Dislocating Masculinity: Comparative Ethnographies*, edited by Andrea Cornwall and Nancy Lindisfarne, 66–81. London: Routledge.

El-Messiri, Sawsan. 1978. *Ibn al-Balad: A Concept of Egyptian Identity*. Leiden: Brill.

Qutb, Hiba. 2006. *Li-l-kubar faqat: Asʾila wa ajwiba 2* (*For Adults Only: Questions and Answers 2*). Giza: Hala.

El Sadda, Hoda. 2007. "Imagining the 'New Man': Gender and Nation in Arab Literary Narratives in the Early Twentieth Century." *Journal of Middle East Women's Studies* 3, no. 2: 31–55.

Sauvagnargues, Anne. 2004. "Deleuze: De l'animal à l'art." In *La philosophie de Deleuze*, edited by François Zourabichvili, Anne Sauvagnargues, and Paola Marrati, 117–227. Paris: Presses Universitaires de France.

Schielke, Samuli. 2009. "Ambivalent Commitment: Troubles of Morality, Religiosity, and Aspiration among Young Egyptians." *Journal of Religion in Africa* 39, no. 2: 158–85.

———. 2015. *Egypt in the Future Tense: Hope, Frustration, and Ambivalence before and after 2011.* Bloomington: Indiana University Press.

El Shakry, Omnia. 2007. *The Great Social Laboratory: Subjects of Knowledge on Colonial and Postcolonial Egypt.* Stanford, CA: Stanford University Press.

Springborg, Robert. 1982. *Family, Power, and Politics in Egypt: Sayed Bey Marei—His Clan, Clients, and Cohorts.* Philadelphia: University of Pennsylvania Press.

Tuchscherer, Michel. 1997. "Les cafés dans l'Égypte ottoman (XVIe–XVIIIe siècles)." In *Cafés d'Orient revisités,* edited by Hélène Desmet-Grégoire and François Georgeon, 91–112. Paris: Centre National de la Recherche Scientifique.

Veyne, Paul. 1988. *Did the Greeks Believe in Their Myths? An Essay on the Constitutive Imagination,* translated by Paula Wissing. Chicago: University of Chicago Press.

Grooming Istanbul

Intimate Encounters and Concerns in Turkish Beauty Salons

◇ ◇

CLAUDIA LIEBELT

ABSTRACT Based on research in Istanbul in 2013–14, the article describes a changing urban geography of beauty, which has multiple repercussions on women's spatialized notions of femininity, intimate bodily grooming, and aesthetics. Beauty salons in two neighborhoods typically placed on different ends of both the social and the Islamist-secularist axes highlight the similarities and differences of intimate concerns and encounters. Urban beauty salons are where publicly debated ideals of femininity and sexuality are visibly manufactured, and those involved have to negotiate new styles of bodily appearance and forms of intimate relations. Beauty salon customers and workers create strategies to deal with (bodily) intimacy and test the moral, social, and religious boundaries of what is attractive, respectable, or permissible. Defying common assumptions, upwardly mobile pious women display a willingness to establish intimate relationships and negotiate the boundaries of moral permissiveness and bodily well-being.

KEYWORDS intimate labor, beauty work, femininity, Islam, Turkey

stanbul, like other major cities worldwide, has seen a boom in commercialized beauty services closely tied to the development of an increasingly global, neoliberalized consumer economy since the 1980s and to the feminization of the workforce in an expanding urban service sector. Amid a rich landscape of beauty that includes private beauty schools, municipally run classes on bodily grooming and beauty, online discussion forums on the topic, beauty fairs, and makeover reality television series, in 2014 over seven thousand hair and beauty salons were listed in the Istanbul Chamber for Women Hairdressers and Manicurists.[1] While these

JMEWS • Journal of Middle East Women's Studies • 12:2 • July 2016
DOI 10.1215/15525864-3507628 • © 2016 by the Association for Middle East Women's Studies

generally offer noninvasive aesthetic treatments, it is noteworthy that in 2013, among the countries worldwide with the highest number of plastic surgeons per capita, Turkey ranked ninth (ISAPS 2014). Most of Turkey's plastic surgeons reside in Istanbul. Unisex or women's hair and beauty salons, which first opened in the European quarter of Pera (now Beyoğlu) in the 1920s, are now found all over the city, even in the most staunchly conservative Muslim neighborhoods. Drawing on my research in beauty salons in different parts of the city in 2013–14, this article analyzes the intimate encounters between beauty salon workers and their customers and the concerns the encounters trigger. Not least, there is a place-specific dynamic in the relationship between female bodywork and intimacy in present-day Istanbul that relates to both the historical role of women's intimate social spaces for bodily grooming in the city and an urban geography that can no longer be neatly divided into poor Islamic and well-off secular neighborhoods (see Turam 2013).

I draw on an ethnographic analysis of the negotiations of femininity, class, religion, and beauty work in two urban neighborhoods that are commonly seen as being on opposite ends of an imagined Islamist-secularist axis, namely, the conservative working-class neighborhood of Fatih and the central upper-middle-class neighborhood of Nişantaşı. I examine the similarities and differences as well as the paradoxes and ironies at play. The commercialization of beauty services requires that beauty salon workers and customers alike negotiate the complex and affective dimension of intimacy in their encounters, and the ways they deal with intimacy varies considerably across the city and cannot be routinely anticipated. The past decades have seen the rise of a new Islamic middle class in urban Turkey, and in this process many (young) women have adopted the veil or embraced Islam out of a conscious, virtuous choice (Sandıkçı and Ger 2010; White 2013). These women often strikingly reconcile their imaginings of themselves with public notions of appropriateness and Islamic piety. In contrast, driven by the fear of losing cultural hegemony, the beauty work and performance of an older, self-proclaimed cosmopolitan secularist elite assumes elements of social exclusivity and political anxiety.

This article seeks to contribute to the research on gender, sexuality, faith, and body politics in Istanbul and the wider Middle East by engaging with the current debate on intimacy and "intimate labor" (Boris and Parreñas 2010; Kang 2010; Zelizer 2005, 2010). In her book on Korean nail salons in New York City, Miliann Kang (2010, 35) describes the boom in intimate services that were formerly considered the preserve of families, friends, and communities as "the surreptitious but revolutionary reorganization of social life in the late twentieth century." In this process intimate daily activities that are regarded as "private," such as caring for children or the elderly, housework, sex, gardening, and caring for the body, are subject to a pervasive commercialization and are increasingly outsourced to paid service workers, typically migrant women or those from the lower social strata of society. Among these commercialized services, those directed at the upkeep and appearance of the body have been expanding globally, with a large array of (new) professionals providing haircuts and massages, dietary advice, manicures and pedicures, makeup, aesthetic surgery, and various noninvasive aesthetic procedures for purposes of "rejuvenation" or to lose weight. In their influential volume *Intimate Labors*, Eileen Boris and Rhacel Salazar Parreñas (2010, 1) likewise emphasize the "heightened commodification of intimacy that pervades social life" in contemporary global capitalism. For them, intimate labor "entails touch, whether of children or customers; bodily or emotional closeness or personal familiarity, such as sexual intercourse and bathing another; or close observation of another and knowledge of personal information, such as watching elderly people or advising trainees" (ibid., 2). As the following will show, aspects such as touch, trust, familiarity with and attentiveness to particular bodies, and people all play a central role in the intimate bodywork in Istanbul's beauty salons. However, as I argue, the meaning of intimacy and indeed its permissibility may vary considerably for those involved and across the city. Whereas beauty salons may cultivate vastly different styles of intimacy, the interpretation and handling of intimate labor requires negotiation between beauty salon workers and their customers. I will therefore challenge the implicit assumption in the literature that, in the process of commercialization and "professionalization," the relationships of intimate bodily care have become the same around the globe.

Intimacy can be translated into Turkish using the concepts of *samimiyet* and *mahremiyet*, with each term touching on different semantic fields. While *samimiyet* describes the quality of a relationship and implies a sense of integrity, *mahremiyet* refers more to the context of the encounter (see Sehlikoglu 2015). Accordingly, interlocutors spoke about intimacy mostly in terms of *samimiyet*, emphasizing a physical and emotional closeness that comes out of everyday practice rather than kinship relations. The intimacy created in all-female salons that prohibit entry for men or that may be seen as lacking in salons that cater to both men and women suggests the concept of intimacy implied in the term *mahremiyet*, that is, a social and topographical space protected in a social and moral sense as well as one that is confined and possibly confining. As the description of online religious forum discussions will show, some forms of beauty work and some parts of the body may be interpreted as too intimate (*haram*) to be delegated or presented to others. In contrast to Debra L. Gimlin's (2002) concept of bodywork as women's participation in shaping their own bodies in a form of self-work, I understand bodywork or beauty work as a social relationship between a person who performs this kind of work, whether paid or unpaid, and the recipient of this work. The relationship between them is permeated by affects and informed by cultural, moral, and social notions of gender, beauty, bodily care, and well-being.

Analyzing US public discourses after the conservative "Reagan revolution," Lauren Berlant (1997) argues that the American political public sphere has become an *intimate* public sphere in which matters of sexuality, morality, and family values have all become key publicly debated issues. For Turkey, Esra Özyürek (2006, 6) has described a similar process of the privatization of politics in the early 2000s, where "the controversy between Islamism and secularism ma[d]e privacy and intimacy vital to politics and citizenship in a particular way." More than ten years after Özyürek (ibid.) studied Turkish secularists' creation and display of "novel privacies and intimacies in order to represent freely internalized, and hence voluntary and legitimate, political positions," intimate matters have become vital to debates on national identity and the definition of how citizens, especially women, should look and act. After the third electoral success of the conservative, pro-Islamic Justice and Development Party (Adalet ve Kalkınma Partisi) in 2011, the government's repeated interference with women's intimate lives, such as the draft proposal for a ban on abortion in 2012 and the incentives provided to families with three children or more, intensified feminist struggles and sparked street protests and online activism that have been interpreted by some as a prelude to the far-reaching Gezi Park protests of spring and summer 2013 (Tekay and Ustun 2013).

From the perspectives of the feminist and lesbian, gay, bisexual, and transgender movements, the Gezi Park protests can be seen as a (temporary) reclaiming of a public space by women and transgender people that, before the eruption of the protests, had become infamous for rampant sexual harassment and (police) violence (Korkman and Acıksöz 2013). Research for this article took place in the wake of these protests and hence in an atmosphere of political polarization and ongoing public conflict about intimate issues, such as the debate on coed university housing in November 2013 (Arango 2013) and the declaration of Turkey's deputy prime minister, Bülent Arınc, in July 2014 that women should not laugh out loud and should remain chaste in public at all times (see Kandiyoti 2014). In this climate beauty salons assumed a central role as places where publicly debated ideals of femininity and sexuality are visibly manufactured and hence become real.

Against this background of intimate politics that turn "women's bodies and practices" into a "battleground" for secular and Islamic ideologies (Gökarıksel 2012, 15) and "taste wars" among the Turkish urban middle classes (Sandıkçı and Ger 2010, 29), the article describes a changing urban geography of beauty that has multiple repercussions on women's highly spatialized notions of femininity, intimate bodily grooming, and aesthetics. In what follows I provide a short outline of the discussion on gender, bodily grooming, and space in Istanbul, then I present my methodology and ethnographic data. Finally, I discuss intimate encounters and concerns comparatively in two urban salons and neighborhoods.

Gender, Bodily Grooming, and Space in Istanbul

Beginning in the 1960s processes of social and economic transformation, mass migration, and urban restructuring transformed and, in some parts of Istanbul, eroded the urban *mahalle* (neighborhood) that for centuries had characterized everyday life in the city (see Behar 2003; Duben and Behar 2002, 29–35). This had tremendous effects on the intimate lives of the city's residents, including practices of beautification, bodily grooming, and sociality. Defined by neighboring practices that create "networks of support" between neighbors and resident-owned shops and businesses, writes Amy Mills (2007, 335), "the mahalle is the space of intimate daily life in the Turkish urban context, and narratives of and ways of life in the mahalle articulate competing notions of what it means to be a woman in Turkey."

In the neighborhood collective rituals of washing, grooming, and bathing formed a major foundation of sociability for women in public, gender-segregated baths or *hamams* and later in private homes. Indeed, because of the lack of bathrooms in private homes and female seclusion, for many urban women in Ottoman times and beyond a regular visit to the bath was one of the few legitimate social occasions outside private homes in the immediate neighborhood (see Akşit 2011, 279; Cichocki 2005, 99; Özkoçak 2007; Semerdjian 2013, 655). Public baths may be considered antecedents of today's beauty salons, spaces for bodily grooming, intimacy, and sociality for women. Similar to spaces of sociality that catered to adult males in Ottoman times, such as the *boza* (fermented malt drink) house, the tavern, the mosque, and, since early modern times, the coffeehouse, public baths were attended by all social classes and, at least to some extent, encouraged social leveling (Yashar 2003, 86). The immense role of public (neighborhood) baths before the installation of running water and washrooms in private homes has to be seen not only in terms of their practical, aesthetic, and social uses but also their ritual use (ibid.; Akşit 2011).

Once the urban social structures that included the rituals of collective bathing had been dissolved, in the middle-class imagination public baths became spaces of pollution rather than purity, infested with all kinds of fungal diseases and reserved for the lower social classes, whose private homes did not allow for a decent bath (Cichocki 2005, 101, 105–6).[2] In her analysis of continuity and change in Istanbul's public bathing culture, Nina Cichocki (2005, 101) describes a process beginning in mid-nineteenth-century Istanbul in which public spaces like theaters, parks, and cinemas came to be frequented by the urban elite, meaning that "the bathhouses were not the most chic places any more." In this process the Beyoğlu district (historically known as Pera), with its long boulevard, La Grande Rue de Pera, later renamed İstiklal Street, and its modern Taksim Square, assumed a central role as a "European" and cosmopolitan secular space of entertainment and commerce. There non-Muslim Istanbulites opened the first women's hair and beauty salons in the early republican era. Until at least the 1970s all but a few salons in the city that catered to women were located in Beyoğlu and the nearby residential neighborhoods of the secular elite, such as Nişantaşı, Şişli, Levent, and Etiler. In these neighborhoods hair and beauty salons for women became part of a "secular space," that is, "urban public sites that are associated with secular ways of life, nonreligious activities and symbols" (Turam 2013, 410n1). This changed dramatically when, during the global boom in the beauty industry in the 1990s (Jones 2010), places directed at bodily grooming, hygiene, and beautification, such as fitness centers, hair and beauty salons, spas, and nail bars, mushroomed all over the city and increasingly across not only the social but also the secular-religious divisions that characterized the urban space.

Numerous studies have pointed out that women's bodies are the center of attention in processes of nation building and modernization, as has certainly been the case in Turkey (Göle 1997; Özyürek 2006, 29–64; Shissler 2004; White 2013). As elsewhere, in Turkey imaginations of bodily aesthetics are historically produced and tie a specific bodily appearance to imaginations of modernity, morality, and citizenship. In her analysis of beauty contests in early republican Turkey, for example, A. Holly Shissler (2004, 117) shows the pivotal role of the public presentation of feminine, bodily beauty in republicans' attempts to project images of a modern and "civilized" nation while also redefining patriarchal concepts of honor and shame to "secularize Islam and to normalize the female body." Amid the politicization of the head scarf in the 1990s, a number of studies focused on the continued role of women's bodies as a battleground between modernity and tradition, secularism and Islamism, and the role of Islamic dress and sartorial styles in creating new Islamic (elite) lifestyles (Çınar 2005; Gökarıksel 2009, 2012; Gökarıksel and Secor 2009, 2010; Navaro-Yashin 2002, 78–113; Secor 2001; White 2002, 29–55, 212–41). In focusing on the manufacturing of beautiful, feminine, and more generally proper bodies in diverse urban neighborhoods, I seek to contribute to this large body of literature. Similar to what Banu Gökarıksel (2012) has argued in regard to an emerging veiling fashion industry, in analyzing the intimate and commercialized encounters between women in beauty salons across the city, I argue that the dissolution of the boundaries between Islamic and secular neighborhoods is more than topographic; it is embodied and gendered. The focus on intimate bodywork in beauty salons and clinics, however, draws attention to the fact that the fashioning of female identities clearly goes beneath the dress and even beneath the skin, being produced in a social encounter and as such being affectively laden, often painful and sensual at the same time.

Methodology

This article is part of an ongoing research project on femininity, beauty work, and aesthetic body modification in Istanbul that draws on fifteen months of field research, including five short field trips since 2011 and an uninterrupted period of fieldwork in 2013 and 2014. I conducted some one hundred ethnographic guideline interviews, most scheduled and recorded, with customers and patients of hair and beauty salons and clinics; beauty salon owners and workers; aesthetic surgeons and other experts, among them tattoo artists; activists in various feminist organizations; a fashion photographer; and an Islamic scholar who rules on the permissibility of beauty treatments. Moreover, the project employs media analysis, including the systematic analysis of newspaper archives, online forums (Kadınlar Kulübü and Fetva Meclisi), and so-called makeover shows on private television. In 2013 and 2014 I attended the annual Istanbul Beauty and Care Fair[3] and distributed questionnaires among its visitors. I also distributed questionnaires among participants in two municipal training courses on makeup and facial care.

I used multisited ethnography to follow beauty practices in different hair and beauty salons and clinics in the city, with a focus on residential and commercial sites in socially and politically diverse urban neighborhoods, namely, Başakşehir, Fatih, Nişantaşı, Beyoğlu, Moda/Kadıköy, and Etiler. I selected one or two hair and beauty salons or clinics in each of these neighborhoods in which to observe participants during regular ongoing visits. I strategically chose the neighborhoods as highly contested urban areas for various reasons. In the popular imagination, Fatih and Nişantaşı, the two neighborhoods described in greater detail below, are at different ends of the Islamist-secularist axis, with Nişantaşı being a well-off secular neighborhood and Fatih being a rather conservative working-class neighborhood. By choosing these neighborhoods, I wish to illustrate the similarities and differences in intimate encounters and concerns in the city and point out that processes like the commercialization and professionalization of beauty work affect both neighborhoods even though aesthetic norms and the spatial performance of beauty vary considerably. Hence the sites and persons selected for presentation are neither representative of nor at the extreme ends of a continuum, but they do draw attention to the urban diversity involved and to some common themes and issues with regard to bodily grooming and intimate encounters.

Following the feminist and anthropological focus on everyday spaces, on quotidian and seemingly mundane practices, I argue that beauty practices and beauty salons are excellent research themes and sites in which to study the relationships between gender, bodily intimacy, space, and consumption. Female beauty salons have been described as intimate social spaces in a number of academic studies (see Black 2004; Furman 1997; Ossman 2002). Indeed, whereas male-dominated spaces such as the coffeehouse or the (black) barbershop have often been theorized as crucial for forging a public sphere (Habermas 1989, 36; Özkoçak 2007) and political subjectivities (Harris-Lacewell 2004), female beauty salons have typically been associated with female care and sharing. For example, Frida Kerner Furman's (1997) ethnographic study of a specific beauty salon catering to elderly Jewish women in New York emphasizes the comfort, caring, even friendship that women find in this space, while Paula Black (2004) similarly describes the beauty salon as a highly feminized and therapeutic space where notions of beauty are not as important as heteronormative notions of femininity and well-being and an increasing aestheticization of women's workplaces. Moreover, the emergence of professional beauty salons may also be interpreted as an alienating process in which bodily grooming, according to bell hooks (2007), turns from a ritual of bonding between women into an expensive, isolating, and commercialized experience.

In her "linked comparison" between beauty salons in Paris, Cairo, and Casablanca, Susan Ossman (2002) makes the distinction between three kinds of hair and beauty salons, which helps us differentiate among salons where particular kinds of femininities and intimacies come into play. These are (a) the neighborhood or proximate salon, a kind of "cocoon" that "nurture[s] bodies in formation" and is a space of female solidarity set off for feminine concerns (ibid., 101); (b) the "fast-cut" salon, which is more impersonal and often centrally located, with a clear hierarchy from owner to hairdresser to assistant; and (c) the "special salon," which, located in central or upmarket shopping districts, centers around "famous products, hairdressers, and clients" (ibid., 121). Drawing from the insights of this literature and contextualizing different beauty salons in their respective settings in a specific street, neighborhood, and urban space, I intend to go beyond their analysis of intimate spaces per se or spaces lacking intimacy due to commercialization to examine the transforming intimate encounters in their particular urban, social, and political complexities.

A Tale of Two Salons

The Nur Hair and Beauty Salon in Fatih

Fatih, a well-known working-class neighborhood within the old city walls, has been described as "the paradigmatic Muslim mahalle" (Gökarıksel 2012, 9) in terms of its historical spatial organization and demographics.[4] Its main street, Fevzi Paşa Boulevard, with its small cafés and restaurants, clothing stores selling modest fashions, Islamic financial institutions, and tourist agencies specializing in the hajj (Islamic pilgrimage), points to the conservative character of the neighborhood. Diverse styles of Islamic dress dominate the streets of Fatih, and prominent pictures of beautifully arranged and decorated head scarves in the windows of its numerous hair and beauty salons advertise the styling of head scarves (*türban tasarım* in Turkish) alongside the usual services. The Nur hair and beauty salon is on a little side street just off Fevzi Paşa Boulevard. Sibel, a trained hairdresser-beautician and former midwife, opened Nur in 2000, and it is one of the oldest salons in the neighborhood that cater to women exclusively.

Thus, following the principle of Muslim gender segregation like an increasing number of salons in Fatih and other conservative neighborhoods, the Nur salon prohibits entry to men and is protected from the public view by a white foil covering its windows on the inside. Amid notices of special deals and posters of beautiful women, all covered, a large sign at the entrance announces that men are not permitted entry unless by prior appointment. A veil behind the entrance protects those inside from the gazes of passersby even when the front door stands open, which commonly happens on hot summer or busy weekend days.

Sibel is an energetic, tall, self-confident, and somewhat extravagant woman in her forties who takes great care of her appearance and loves flashy fashion jewels and glittery shirts and boots. The daughter of migrants from the Black Sea, Sibel grew up in Fatih and lives with her teenage son and her second husband in the adjacent neighborhood of Çarşamba, known as one of the most conservative parts of the city. Like many Çarşamba residents, Sibel became *çarşaflı* a couple of years ago; that is, in public she hides her hair and body shape under a long black coat. In the salon she works alongside her two "girls," Azra and Feride, who are in their midtwenties and midthirties, respectively, and who do not cover their hair or dress modestly. Sibel's twenty-one-year-old daughter helps in the salon, applying makeup, performing depilation, and, until her recent marriage, offering private classes in *oryantal*, the Turkish belly dance. Several times a week two middle-aged beauticians offer skin treatments, permanent makeup, eyelash extensions, eyelash perms, various treatments for losing weight and rejuvenation, and intense pulsed light (IPL) laser treatments for permanent body hair removal. Both beauticians describe themselves as secular and live outside Fatih. More recently, amid a growing number of refugees in the neighborhood, Sibel added two young Syrian women as apprentices. Except for the apprentices, all the women working in the salon have known each other for many years and describe each other as "like family," preparing meals together and, when business is slack, often drinking tea together or sharing food.

The Nur salon is on three floors, with the main hair salon on the ground floor; rooms for the beauticians and depilation on the upper floor; and a kitchen, a toilet and shower, Sibel's office, a prayer room, and a little gym in the basement. On entry, the customer finds herself in the main hair salon, decorated in white and purple, with three hairdressing chairs and large round mirrors on one side and a waiting area with a black leather sofa and armchairs on the other. As in most hair salons, the wall behind the counter beside the entrance displays the owner's and her employees' framed diplomas in such diverse qualifications as "hairdressing," "eyelash extension," "IPL laser depilation," and "Japanese manicure." A white ornamental folding screen separates the front of the room, reserved for makeup and hairstyling, from the back, where manicures and pedicures are provided in a special chair. The TV above the entrance is usually set to the popular music channel KralPop and plays Turkish pop music at full volume. When the salon is busy, the sound of the music mixes with that of the hairdryers and the lively chatter between the customers and the hairdressers. Those waiting can choose between various promotional flyers, the conservative women's magazine *Ala*, and catalogs of hairstyles, including bridal hair, on the coffee table next to the sofa. Most important, the basement extends into the "garden," a large tent in the building's backyard. With an airy atmosphere, a large dining table, comfortable armchairs, and a stereo, this is a prominent place of sociality for workers and customers alike and is one of the salon's greatest assets.

Thus in the mornings before the salon gets busy, Sibel, her daughter, and the hairdressers have breakfast in the garden, sometimes joined by an early customer. At night the space may be rented for a celebration after someone has given birth or for a henna night, the women-only celebration shortly before a wedding. On some nights during Ramadan, the women break their fasts there, inviting friends and customers to join them. In summer 2014, when Israel launched Operation Protective Edge, a corner of the garden was devoted to the commemoration of Palestinian children killed during Israeli bombardments of the Gaza Strip. Some of the customers come to the garden to smoke a cigarette or have a chat before or after their treatments, and sometimes Sibel or her daughter serves tea and homemade pastries. While their hair is still wrapped in aluminum foil or their nail polish is drying, women's conversations and gossip revolve around children, common acquaintances, food, cooking, or beauty. Sibel, a clever businesswoman and a great mentor, frequently comments that a customer's skin or hair is desperately in need of a special treatment, one that—what a coincidence—is on offer only this week. Sibel contributes her knowledge of childbirth, alternative healing, or infertility and its cures, and when she still practiced midwifery she delivered the children of a few of the regulars. Other customers come not only for beauty but also for business, promoting their own services and products, including during my visits a saleswoman for a Japanese firm selling magnet therapy products, a woman from Chechnya on a visit from Cairo who performs *hacamat* (cupping) treatments, and a travel agent who with her husband organizes travel to the Arab Middle East, including pilgrimages to Mecca and Jerusalem. Many of the more regular customers are housewives who live nearby, some of whom arrive with children who play in the garden while their mothers are treated. Younger women, often in pairs or in groups, arrive for a quick eyebrow shape or a blow-dry in the middle of a day of shopping on Fevzi Paşa Boulevard.

In the Nur salon the intimacy (*samimiyet*) that Sibel strives to create and that her employees and customers cherish is linked to the sociality of the garden and the sharing of tea, food, and cigarettes. The association between intimacy and the sharing of food or tea is not peculiar to this salon or even related to its location in a conservative working-class neighborhood. Thus the owner of another beauty salon in the secular, (upper-) middle-class neighborhood of Suadiye on the Asian side of the city, telling us about the intimate nature of her relations with her employees and customers, laughingly and proudly recounted how some of her customers enter the salon asking, "What's the soup of the day?"[5]

Nevertheless, there are intimate concerns that are more clearly linked to the location of the beauty salon and to the piety of its owner and clientele. Sibel recounted in an interview that she entered the beauty sector rather reluctantly out of economic necessity as a recently divorced mother of two forced to leave her profession when the state, adjusting to European Union regulations, withdrew the license for her independent birthing center. Before opening her beauty salon, Sibel solicited *fetvas* (legal rulings) from three well-known Islamic scholars on the permissibility of the salon and its treatments to meet her own and prospective customers' scruples. While the rulings were concerned with the gender-segregated nature of the salon and prohibited eyebrow shaping,[6] the scholars did not oppose the idea of a salon in principle. The beauty salon nevertheless met fierce resistance from some of Sibel's neighbors, and shortly after its opening a group of women attacked her home, smashing windows and defacing a wall. For months she was abused verbally by a group of *çarşaflı* women who followed her between her home and the beauty salon. For even longer anonymous people called Sibel or sent her text messages attacking her for opening a beauty salon, which they regarded as sinful, a place of vanity and creation of sexual allure that was misplaced in a respectable neighborhood. Sibel remained steadfast, and after she sought the mediating support of an influential Islamic scholar (and, one might add, after she married again), the hostility subsided. Today she counts many of her pious neighbors among her customers.

One aspect of beauty work, however, continued to trouble Sibel in spite of the *fetvas*, namely, pubic hair removal. Rationalized as a matter of cleanliness (*temizlik*) rather than beauty (*güzellik*), the removal of body hair, including pubic hair, is widespread (cf. Delaney 1994, 164). As a trained midwife, Sibel of course was accustomed to working with the bodies of female strangers, including touching their genital areas. However, the presentation, not to mention touching, of another woman's "private part" (*avret bölgesi* in Turkish)[7] for other than medical reasons was considered sinful and was prohibited by religious scholars. Initially, she refused to perform this service in spite of her customers' requests. In an interview she explained:

> I received serious reactions when I told my customers in *tesettür* and *çarşaf* [Islamic styles of pious dressing] who wanted to have it [pubic hair removal] done that I wouldn't do it. Because I thought it was forbidden [*haram*]. But on the other hand—this is about health, too! I also helped them give birth, after all. Nevertheless, I thought that hair removal [*ağda*] was different from midwifery, because the removal of hair in that area is optional and in a sense arbitrary. [On the other hand,] I also do professional massages. An Islamic legal ruling allows performing massages . . . , saying that it is allowed [*helal*] because it relates to health. . . . So there's a treatment aspect [to pubic hair removal], too. So never mind if it's *helal* or *haram*—I have already started to perform it! [*She laughs.*][8]

This quotation underlines both Sibel's uncertainty about how to categorize and make a judgment about the treatment and the pragmatism of her approach. In a situation in which neither social conventions nor religious rulings are fully worked out, Sibel and her customers managed to negotiate a procedure that eventually came to satisfy both sides. It is noteworthy that, in their desire to meet standards of beauty and cleanliness, even Sibel's most pious customers were ready to interpret their faith self-consciously and make Sibel overcome her reluctance to perform intimate bodywork that she had initially perceived as *haram*. This applied to other procedures as well, and while Sibel's beauticians observed that in the beginning it was hard to find customers for procedures that may have been problematic from an Islamic point of view, such as eyebrow shaping, nail polishing, or permanent makeup,[9] in recent years requests for these services have increased even among Nur's conservative clientele. Likewise, while Sibel initially delegated many of these tasks to her "open," that is, uncovered, beauticians and criticized the hypocrisy of her customers who publicly supported radical Islamic ideas but secretly engaged in many of these "problematic" practices, by the time we met in 2011 she had worked out a rather pragmatic approach. Thus more than a decade after the salon's opening in Fatih, the services demanded and provided resembled those of all-female salons elsewhere, including in Nişantaşı, considered one of the urban centers of beauty. These findings resonate with those of other studies on the veiling fashion industry in Turkey, namely, that there is an increasing concern with aesthetics among the new Islamic middle class and that, while piety and (the creation of) bodily beauty have an ambivalent relationship, women adapt Islamic norms creatively (cf. Gökarıksel and Secor 2009, 2012; Sandıkçı and Ger 2010). In this process hitherto unthinkable intimate relationships emerge, and intimate concerns once considered morally problematic become routinized.

The American Nail Bar in Nişantaşı

Built in the mid-nineteenth century for a new European bourgeoisie and still inhabited mostly by affluent and secular residents, Nişantaşı is considered one of the city's most exclusive neighborhoods. In contrast to Fatih's domestic products, in Nişantaşı international brands are dominant in advertisements; in clothing stores; and indeed in the clothes, shoes, and handbags seen in the neighborhood streets and cafés. The American nail bar is in the basement of a commercial building on Vali-konağı Avenue, a busy shopping area that hosts art galleries, designer workshops, and upmarket cafés and restaurants along with numerous international products. Stacey, a US college graduate in economics and a US native married to a Turk, opened the American-style nail bar in 2006. She explained in an interview[10] that American *style* means that if a group of four or five women walks in without appointments, the women can be sure of being served right away. Accordingly, out of a total of eight manicurists, at least five are present at any given time during the day, seven days a week, from at least ten in the morning to eight at night. Stacey herself does not perform treatments but comes in several times a week, mostly sticking to her small office in the back of the salon. Treatments include a long list of manicures and pedicures, facials, body hair removal, and aromatherapies and massages.

On entry, the visitor is greeted by a receptionist, a stylish young woman in a skirt and high heels, who works behind a counter and in front of a wall of framed diplomas and pictures of the founder of the Turkish republic, Kemal Atatürk. She makes or checks appointments, assigning a manicurist to each customer. The manicurists, all rather young and stylishly dressed, wait on a bench next to the entrance. They lead their customers into the main room and ask them to relax in one of the six large manicure and pedicure chairs with beige leather covers. Another female employee, the *çaycı*, who is also responsible for generally assisting the manicurists, serves tea or Turkish coffee. As the salon's website states, a visit is intended to be much more than a manicure or a pedicure: "Sink yourself into a reclining chair surrounded by a forest of organza drapery, sip a green tea while soothing New Age music washes over you, close your eyes and inhale the soothing scent of 100% pure and organic essential oils, now surrender yourself to the simultaneous pampering of your hands and feet, including Thai-inspired massage and [a] seemingly endless choice of nail polishes!"[11] In its evocation of a "forest," where one may forget about the noise, stress, and traffic outside on Valikonağı Avenue and find peace and quiet while being served and "pampered," the nail bar becomes an experience of sensual care and well-being. Signal words, such as *organic* and *green tea*, announce a specific type of upper-middle-class cosmopolitanism that, in the urban geography of Istanbul, is rather well placed in this particular neighborhood.

In Ossman's (2002) taxonomy of beauty salons, the American nail bar comes closest to a special salon. It is in a central, upmarket shopping district, assembles a number of exchangeable manicurists, and revolves around its famous products and clients. It is a place where the latest nail polish brands are applied to the mostly immaculate hands of the customers, the famous who know of each other as customers and the less famous who know that the others are customers and hope to be recognized likewise as regulars of this exclusive place.

Eschewing the food and chatting that characterize the Nur hair and beauty salon and other neighborhood salons, even in Nişantaşı, the intimacy at the American nail bar is altogether different. Indeed, signs on the wall ask customers to refrain from using their mobile phones and to keep their voices low. The workers are attentive and polite but refrain from being "chatty" with their customers. Saliha, one of the most senior manicurists, explained this policy in terms of professionalism. To her, talking in an intimate a way with her customers—Saliha employed the term *senli-benli*, literally, to be on familiar terms with someone—signified unprofessional behavior typical of those beauticians who had trained as apprentices rather than in proper beauty schools. Observing Saliha and her colleagues at work, I noted that they made an effort to engage in some small talk with a customer during the first few minutes of the nail treatment, if possible relating to an earlier conversation with him or her ("How was your holiday?" "Has your mother recovered from her flu?"), but then fell silent, to all appearances concentrating on their work. The initial conversation sometimes took the form of customers questioning or mentoring manicurists, then customers shifted attention away from the manicurists, who nevertheless continued to hold customers' hands or feet in their own, clipping nails, pushing back or cutting excess skin, massaging, and finally applying lotions and nail polish. Some customers engaged silently with their smart phones or leafed through the available fashion magazines (*Vogue, Elle, Cosmopolitan*), while others disregarded the notes on the wall and the more tacit rules of the nail bar, making phone calls to family members, friends, and clients or ordering a quick lunch.

Saliha regarded herself not only as professional but as successful, as indicated by the fact that she had many regular customers. These often came for a weekly manicure and an occasional pedicure, eyebrow shaping, massage, or depilation. They were all clearly upper-middle-class, not least due to the nail bar's rather steep prices. In 2014 the cheapest manicure cost TL50 (US$23), more than three times the price in the Nur salon and more than double what Saliha and her colleagues earn per hour. Some of the customers were celebrities or *sosyete* (high-society) people who lived in the neighborhood, among them a famous dietitian who regularly appeared on TV talk shows, a former Miss Turkey, a well-known plastic surgeon, and a blogger whose posts on style and fashion were extremely popular among young Istanbul fashionistas. In the manicurists' imaginations the proximity to power in this topographical center of beauty and the urban elite arguably carries with it a promise of social climbing that makes employment in the nail bar attractive in spite of the long hours working for hardly more than the minimum wage.[12] The intense self-stylization of some manicurists, including in some cases heavy makeup, eyelash and hair extensions, cosmetic surgery, and branded clothes, may be interpreted as the desire for such a rise. In the American nail bar, where customers often encouraged beauty salon workers to "make more of themselves," one could clearly observe a culture of mimicking, with some workers investing so much effort in self-stylization that their colleagues gossiped.

For Saliha too, employment in the nail bar signified a career she had long worked for. Like most of the other manicurists, she started her career early, as an apprentice when she was fifteen years old. She did so out of economic necessity after her mother divorced and took Saliha and her younger sister from Gaziantep in southeastern Turkey to live with relatives in Istanbul. At first Saliha worked in a conservative neighborhood on the outskirts of the city in a small salon that rarely offered manicures. In 2015 she and her husband lived in that neighborhood next to her mother. Applying her ambition and skills, Saliha eventually made it to a more upmarket neighborhood salon in Kadıköy, then to a private beauty school, and finally to the American nail bar.

Power structures in the nail bar, as elsewhere, are temporarily inverted, not least due to the troubling aspects of intimate beauty work itself, that is, the vulnerability and shame related to bodies exposed and the pain of some of the treatments. Saliha was fully aware of the unease customers felt about depilation or even about exposing nails that had been bitten or torn. Calling body hair depilation an example of a service in which intimacy could easily become uncomfortable, Saliha explained that "you see all of her body, all her flaws. I mean she can't trust you not to talk about her with the next customer, because it is common among many people. . . . I realized that people make conversational material out of this among themselves. Disgusting subjects like: 'her [vagina] was like this and the other's was like that.'"[13] It is hardly surprising, then, that some customers seek privacy in the nail bar, coming by appointment during quiet times of the day to avoid encounters with others. Indeed, while weekends, lunch breaks, and early evenings in the nail bar are typically busy with professional women who work in the area, at other times a single manicurist might be alone with a customer while the others wait on their bench. It is on the bench that some of the sociality and chatter often described as typical of beauty salons unfolds. Although manicurists are prohibited from bringing food into the salon, sweets do make the round, as does gossip about customers, photos on smart phones, or babies of friends or former employees. In the manicurists' waiting area, the much-feared abuse of trust that materializes in gossip is accompanied by online searches about prominent customers as a kind of revenge.

In spite of the intimacy between manicurists, Saliha, for example, was reluctant to describe the American nail bar as an intimate social space (*samimi*). This was certainly because the social hierarchies between the owner and the workers and between the customers and the workers were clear-cut but also, I assume, because it was a space accessible to men and women alike. While this did not bother Saliha to the extent that she refused to work there, she described handling male bodies as difficult and affectively uncomfortable, especially when it came to massages. In contrast to her assessment of the salon as a nonintimate space, Saliha removed her head scarf on entry and changed from a more modest attire into pants and shirts. She explained in an interview that she made this strategic decision after consulting a manicurist friend who worked in a nearby salon with her head scarf on. The friend complained that she was continuously forced to explain herself to her secular and ideologically "open" customers, who misunderstood her way of dressing as a sign of oppression. As in neighboring Tesvikiye, where Berna Turam (2013) describes the conflictual encounters between secularists and women in pious dress in high-end clothing stores, coffeehouses, and a hairdresser's, these customers perceive a manicurist with her head covered as an intrusion into "their own" secular space. Moreover, although the fashion-conscious pious women whom Turam describes as visiting and shopping in the neighborhood are still around, none of them is ever seen entering the nail bar.

Sporting carefully manicured nails polished in bright colors is tied to a specific secular middle-class status in Istanbul that, in the atmosphere of political polarization and growing anxieties over the Islamization of Turkish society apparent during my research, turned into a secularist statement. In conversations and interviews with American nail bar regulars and other secular long-term residents of the neighborhood, it became clear that these women saw their stylization and bodywork as part of a personal and increasingly politicized distinction from what they commonly termed the *varoş*, that is, working- or lower-middle-class pious residential areas at the urban margins (Bora 2010; White 2013, 118). In an interview a friend of one customer "explained" the lack of cultural capital that was commonly attributed to the residents of the *varoş*: "these people" are unable "to even match their handbags and shoes." Following Marcia Ochoa's (2014, 231) notion of "spectacular femininities," in this context the female customers of the American nail bar engage in a performance that is "staged, presented before an audience, and subject to interpretation." Stepping out of the American nail bar into Nişantaşı with freshly manicured, colorful nails is a performance of both a specific middle-class position that enables them to afford this kind of beautification and an affective secularist attitude or "internal state" (ibid., 222) of someone seemingly aware of her public moves asserting control over "her own" territorial space while also enjoying the playful and at times spectacular beautification that materialized in her nails. Accordingly, customers often talked about the "joy" they derived from their newly polished nails, a joy that made their days.

To return to Saliha, it can be argued that it was because the salon was so remote from her own intimate daily life and moral world that she did not mind taking off her head scarf to become "professional" in the eyes of her customers. In spite of the sometimes long-standing relations she has with individual customers, the closeness between them, according to Saliha, ends on the doorstep of the nail bar. Creating affective well-being, the "joy" that customers referred to, in spite of the troubling aspects of bodywork, the shame and the pain, the relationships between customers and beauty therapists remain socially distant. Intimate labor here comes across as a devalued, commercialized service that exacerbates existing hierarchies and ideologies rather than instigating reworkings of morals and subjectivities, as in the example of the Nur salon.

The Respectable, Beautiful, Spectacular:
Grooming Istanbul and the Spatialization of Intimate Labor

In spite of their many differences, in both salons intimate labor in the sense of bodily touching, trust between beauty salon workers and customers, and attentiveness to particular bodies takes place in a setting that is removed from the public space and yet functions as a kind of microcosmos of the surrounding neighborhoods. In Nişantaşı women's hair and beauty salons have been part of an elite "secular space" for more than half a century. Indeed, today most of Istanbul's special salons, in Ossman's definition mentioned above, are located in this and similar districts nearby, whereas in recent years the numbers of neighborhood salons in the same areas have dwindled. In contrast, in Fatih beauty salons are a more recent development. Neighborhood salons based on proximate sociability between women who live in the area exist next to an increasing number of what Ossman terms "fast-cut" salons. A specific political economy of middle-class beauty in Istanbul ties the famous beauticians, hairdressers, and stylists to the elite secular spaces of neighborhoods like Nişantaşı, so according to common understanding, one would probably look in vain for a special salon in Fatih. However, with the emergence of a new Islamic middle class that is increasingly concerned with fashion and aesthetics, it is only a matter of time before beauty salons in Fatih and other conservative middle-class districts, like Başakşehir, assume the status of special salons, offering styling of head scarves alongside other aesthetic services with famous stylists, halal brands, and customers of their own.[14] While I chose Fatih and Nişantaşı, neighborhoods typically placed on opposite ends of both the social and the Islamist-secularist axes, to highlight the similarities and differences of intimate concerns and encounters in a polarized political climate, it is important to note that there are elitist salons concerned with Islamic modesty and working-class neighborhoods not so concerned with Islamic modesty.

In the salons described above, distinct types of intimacy and intimate concerns seem to be in place. As a neighborhood salon in a rather conservative district, the Nur hair and beauty salon in Fatih is a space of intimate sociality in the sense of both *samimiyet*, structured by female care and sharing that extends from body-work to other fields of women's daily lives, and *mahremiyet*, an all-female space where treatments are questioned according to their permissibility in Islam. In the American nail bar, a place of exclusive well-being where treatments may assume the status of conspicuous consumption, intimate concerns focus on professionalism, privacy, and exclusivity rather than intimacy per se. Thus the American nail bar more readily brings to mind Viviana Zelizer's (2010, 268) concept of intimate labor as work that is potentially risky, at least for customers, since it exposes personal information that could leave one vulnerable because it is "not widely available to third parties."

In both settings similar services are highly personalized and handled in ways that make a clear distinction between them moot. Customers and beauticians are eager to create long-lasting relationships, and many customers are regulars who return repeatedly to the same beauty therapist. However, in interviews with customers in the American nail bar it became clear that for them the hygiene, concept, and aesthetics of the place are more important than the relationship with a particular manicurist. Similar to what has been analyzed in paid domestic work arrangements, beauty salon workers, at least in the nail bar, may be understood as "marginal insiders and intimate outsiders" (Gamburd 2000, 102) whom one may admit to one's intimate secrets or allow to touch one's body in intimate ways and places, albeit without any further social consequences. Intimacy here is a form of closeness in settings removed from public display, existing not in spite of social distance but because of it.

While both salons are structured by clear divisions of labor and social hierarchies, the extent and rhetoric of inequality between the beauty salon owners and workers and between them and the customers differ. In the Nur hair and beauty salon the owner, who works alongside her employees, and most of the women present share a personal history and aspects of everyday life beyond a remunerated personal service, as expressed in the common saying, "We are like family." Here the long-standing relationships between beauty salon workers and customers and the bodily intimacy of beauty work create a familiarity, despite social hierarchies, that turns the salon experience into a space of bonding for women, where food is shared and strangers are turned into kin.

In spite of their many differences, both the American nail bar and the Nur hair and beauty salon are commercial places that, displaying their branded products, technologies, and diplomas, strive to be recognized as modern, chic, and up-to-date. While Fatih and Nişantaşı are typically placed on opposite ends of the social and the Islamist-secularist axes, they are both rapidly changing urban neighborhoods where a strict division between a secular upper-middle class and a pious lower-middle class makes little sense. In the beauty salons of both Fatih and Nişantaşı, rather pious and more secular women meet just like those of different economic means, even if only, as in the case of the American nail bar, as customers and workers. The development of an Islamic culture industry and a pious middle class that manages to reconcile its desires for fashion and beauty with its belief, as my ethnographic material suggests, has especially strong repercussions in Fatih. Challenging the common assumptions of self-proclaimed cosmopolitans in neighborhoods such as Nişantaşı, beauty salon workers and customers in Fatih and other conservative neighborhoods not only prove well up on the latest styles and fashions but display a striking willingness to establish new intimate relationships and negotiate the boundaries of moral permissiveness and bodily well-being. This resonates with Jenny B. White's (2013, 171) observation of an immense openness to difference among (young) pious women, who are clearly able "to make choices that affect their subjectivity, their sense of who they are in the world," combining "elements of globalism, secularism, Islamic piety, consumerism, work professional engagement, and political activism." In Fatih and other pious neighborhoods, no less than in Nişantaşı, many Turkish women strive to fulfill heatedly debated public ideas of femininity and the latest fashion amid commercialization, negotiating the complex, affective dimensions of intimacy and distance that arise when intimate bodywork turns into a commodity.

This article has examined the subtle ways this is done in a distinct urban space. In particular, I have sought to illuminate how different kinds of beauty cultures and stylizations are inflected by the practices and politics of local life in contemporary Istanbul. Due to the affective nature of beauty work, the process of its commercialization is full of contradictions, with those involved having to negotiate new styles of bodily appearance and forms of intimate relations. In their encounters beauty salon customers and workers not only create strategies to deal with the (bodily) intimacy between them, they also test moral, social, and religious boundaries with regard to what is attractive, respectable, pious, or permissible. Resonating with research on the emergence of *tesettür* as a fashionable choice (see Gökarıksel 2012; Sandıkçı and Ger 2010), the story of the Nur hair and beauty salon and its owner shows that these boundaries have been pushed considerably in recent decades. In the context of heated debates on intimate topics and the right kind of femininity in contemporary Turkey, beauty work and salons are, perhaps more than ever, set in the midst of social and political reproduction. It is here that heteronormative ideals and images of women's bodies become real, incarnated not simply by patriarchy but in a complex array of negotiations and fantasies of who and what are respectable, beautiful, or even spectacular. To sum up, as discussed in the literature on intimate labor, the commercialization of intimate services in the late twentieth century marks an important shift in the relation between the public and the private spheres and in the way seemingly private matters become an arena of intimate politics and public debate. This article has shown that these processes are not the same globally but are highly contingent on space, enfolding in ways, as the examples illustrate, that cannot be routinely anticipated.

CLAUDIA LIEBELT is assistant professor of social anthropology at the University of Bayreuth. She directs a research project on aesthetic body modification, beauty work, and femininity in Istanbul that is supported by the German Research Foundation. Contact: claudia.liebelt@uni-bayreuth.de.

Acknowledgments

This article is based on a larger study supported by the German Research Foundation (No. LI 2357/1-1), the Chair for Social Anthropology at the University of Bayreuth, and the Department of Sociology of Boğaziçi University. An earlier version was presented at the workshop "Probing the Intimate: Cross-Cultural Queries and Beyond" at the University of Cambridge in May 2014. I am grateful to the participants at that workshop; the editors of this special issue, Aslı Zengin and Sertaç Sehlikoglu; the three anonymous reviewers; and Banu Gökarıksel for their stimulating feedback and insightful comments. Thanks to Zeynep Selen Artan-Bayhan for her invaluable research assistance and the staffs and customers of the salons that in this article are called the Nur hair and beauty salon and the American nail bar.

Notes

1. Oktay Erkal, president of the Istanbul Chamber for Women Hairdressers and Manicurists, interview with the author, April 9, 2014.
2. In recent years some of the historical baths have been renovated and are promoted as tourist attractions. In contrast to the baths, which formed part of a neighborhood structure and were affordable for almost everyone, the renovated baths often charge upmarket prices that restrict access to the affluent.
3. See Güzellik ve Bakım, www.guzellikvebakim.com (accessed June 18, 2015).
4. The names of research sites and participants without a public role or function have been replaced with pseudonyms throughout this article.
5. Esra, interview with the author, February 4, 2014; my translation from the Turkish.
6. According to a particular hadith, shaping eyebrows is prohibited, as are tattooing and more generally changing one's features as created by God (cf. Ünal 2013, 138–39).
7. The part to be concealed under all circumstances, according to some Islamic scholars, extends from the knees to the waist. The anxious, present-day inquiries about nakedness in hair and beauty salons by female petitioners and the rulings of a religious authority in the conservative online forum Fetva Meclisi (www.fetva meclisi.com, accessed June 18, 2015) regarding this issue illustrate ongoing concerns and prohibitions.
8. Sibel, interview with the author, January 22, 2014; my translation from the Turkish.
9. The application of nail polish is considered problematic, because, according to prominent rulings in Turkey, it prevents water from entering the body during ablution (*abdest* in Turkish), the ritual washing in preparation for formal prayers, thus rendering it invalid. Insofar as it is considered a form of tattooing, permanent makeup is also prohibited.
10. Stacey, interview with the author, October 10, 2013.
11. Quoted from the nail bar's official website, whose address I do not disclose here for reasons of anonymity (accessed November 7, 2014).
12. In December 2014 the Turkish minimum monthly wage was about US$400.
13. Saliha, interview with the author, January 23, 2014; my translation from Turkish.
14. I am grateful to Banu Gökarıksel for pointing this out.

References

Akşit, Elif Ekin. 2011. "The Women's Quarters in the Historical Hammam." *Gender, Place, and Culture: A Journal of Feminist Geography* 18, no. 2: 277–93.

Arango, Tim. 2013. "After a Break, Turkey's Prime Minister Again Courts Controversy." *New York Times*, November 7. www.nytimes.com/2013/11/08/world/europe/turkey-coed-dormitories-.html?_r =0.

Behar, Cem. 2003. *A Neighborhood in Ottoman Istanbul: Fruit Vendors and Civil Servants in the Kasap Ilyas Mahalle.* Albany: State University of New York Press.

Berlant, Lauren. 1997. *The Queen of America Goes to Washington City.* Durham, NC: Duke University Press.

Black, Paula. 2004. *The Beauty Industry: Gender, Culture, Pleasure.* London: Routledge.

Bora, Tanıl. 2010. "Beyaz Türkler tartışması — kırlı beyaz" ("The White Turk Debate — a Dirty White"). *Birikim*, no. 260: 25–37.

Boris, Eileen, and Rhacel Salazar Parreñas. 2010. Introduction to *Intimate Labors: Cultures, Technologies, and the Politics of Care,* edited by Eileen Boris and Rhacel Salazar Parreñas, 1–12. Stanford, CA: Stanford University Press.

Cichocki, Nina. 2005. "Continuity and Change in Turkish Bathing Culture in Istanbul: The Life Story of the Çemberlitaş *Hamam.*" *Turkish Studies* 6, no. 1: 93–112.

Çınar, Alev. 2005. *Modernity, Islam, and Secularism in Turkey: Bodies, Places, and Time.* Minneapolis: University of Minnesota Press.

Delaney, Carol. 1994. "Untangling the Meanings of Hair in Turkish Society." *Anthropological Quarterly* 67, no. 4: 159–72.

Duben, Alan, and Cem Behar. 2002. *Istanbul Households: Marriage, Family, and Fertility, 1880–1940.* Cambridge: Cambridge University Press.

Furman, Frida Kerner. 1997. *Facing the Mirror: Older Women and Beauty Shop Culture.* New York: Routledge.

Gamburd, Michele Ruth. 2000. *The Kitchen Spoon's Handle: Transnationalism and Sri Lanka's Migrant Housemaids.* Ithaca, NY: Cornell University Press.

Gimlin, Debra L. 2002. *Body Work: Beauty and Self-Image in American Culture.* Berkeley: University of California Press.

Gökarıksel, Banu. 2009. "Beyond the Officially Sacred: Religion, Secularism, and the Body in the Production of Subjectivity." *Social and Cultural Geography* 10, no. 6: 657–74.

———. 2012. "The Intimate Politics of Secularism and the Headscarf: The Mall, the Neighborhood, and the Public Square in Istanbul." *Gender, Place, and Culture: A Journal of Feminist Geography* 19, no. 1: 1–20.

Gökarıksel, Banu, and Anna J. Secor. 2009. "New Transnational Geographies of Islamism, Capitalism, and Subjectivity: The Veiling-Fashion Industry in Turkey." *Area* 41, no. 1: 6–18.

———. 2010. "Between Fashion and *Tesettür*: Marketing and Consuming Islamic Dress." *Journal of Middle East Women's Studies* 6, no. 3: 118–48.

———. 2012. "'Even I Was Tempted': The Moral Ambivalence and Ethical Practice of Veiling-Fashion in Turkey." *Annals of the Association of American Geographers* 102, no. 4: 847–62.

Göle, Nilüfer. 1997. *The Forbidden Modern: Civilization and Veiling.* Ann Arbor: University of Michigan Press.

Habermas, Jürgen. 1989. *The Structural Transformation of the Public Sphere: An Inquiry into a Category of Bourgeois Society,* translated by Thomas Burger and Frederick Lawrence. Cambridge: Polity.

Harris-Lacewell, M. V. 2004. *Barbershops, Bibles, and BET: Everyday Talk and Black Political Thought.* Princeton, NJ: Princeton University Press.

hooks, bell. 2007. "Straightening Our Hair." *Z Magazine,* April 1. zcomm.org/zmagazine/straightening-our-hair-by-bell-hooks.

ISAPS (International Society of Aesthetic Plastic Surgery). 2014. ISAPS International Survey on Aesthetic/Cosmetic Procedures Performed in 2013. www.isaps.org/Media/Default/global-statistics/2014%20ISAPS%20Results%20(3).pdf (accessed December 11, 2014).

Jones, Geoffrey. 2010. *Beauty Imagined: A History of the Global Beauty Industry.* Oxford: Oxford University Press.

Kandiyoti, Deniz. 2014. "No Laughing Matter: Women and the New Populism in Turkey." *Open Democracy,* September 1. www.opendemocracy.net/5050/deniz-kandiyoti/no-laughing-matter-women-and-new-populism-in-turkey.

Kang, Miliann. 2010. *The Managed Hand: Race, Gender, and the Body in Beauty Service Work.* Berkeley: University of California Press.

Korkman, Zeynep Kurtulus, and Salih Can Acıksöz. 2013. "Erdogan's Masculinity and the Language of the Gezi Resistance." *Jadaliyya,* June 22. www.jadaliyya.com/pages/index/12367/erdogan's-masculinity-and-the-language-of-the-gezi.

Mills, Amy. 2007. "Gender and *Mahalle* (Neighborhood) Space in Istanbul." *Gender, Place, and Culture: A Journal of Feminist Geography* 14, no. 3: 335–54.

Navaro-Yashin, Yael. 2002. *Faces of the State: Secularism and Public Life in Turkey.* Princeton, NJ: Princeton University Press.

Ochoa, Marcia. 2014. *Queen for a Day:* Transformistas, *Beauty Queens, and the Performance of Femininity in Venezuela.* Durham, NC: Duke University Press.

Ossman, Susan. 2002. *Three Faces of Beauty: Casablanca, Paris, Cairo.* Durham, NC: Duke University Press.

Özkoçak, Selma A. 2007. "Coffeehouses: Rethinking the Public and Private in Early Modern Istanbul." *Journal of Urban History* 33, no. 6: 965–86.

Özyürek, Esra. 2006. *Nostalgia for the Modern: State Secularism and Everyday Politics in Turkey.* Durham, NC: Duke University Press.

Sandıkçı, Özlem, and Güliz Ger. 2010. "Veiling in Style: How Does a Stigmatized Practice Become Fashionable?" *Journal of Consumer Research* 37, no. 1: 15–36.

Secor, Anna J. 2001. "Toward a Feminist Counter-geopolitics: Gender, Space, and Islamist Politics in Istanbul." *Space and Polity* 5, no. 3: 191–211.

Sehlikoglu, Sertaç. 2015. "The Daring *Mahrem*: Changing Dynamics of Public Sexuality in Turkey." In *Gender and Sexuality in Muslim Cultures*, edited by Gul Ozyegin, 235–52. Farnham: Ashgate.

Semerdjian, Elyse. 2013. "Naked Anxiety: Bathhouses, Nudity, and Muslim/Non-Muslim Relations in Eighteenth-Century Aleppo." *International Journal of Middle Eastern Studies* 45, no. 4: 651–76.

Shissler, A. Holly. 2004. "Beauty Is Nothing to Be Ashamed Of: Beauty Contests as Tools of Women's Liberation in Early Republican Turkey." *Comparative Studies of South Asia, Africa, and the Middle East* 24, no. 1: 107–22.

Tekay, Cihan, and Zeyno Ustun. 2013. "A Short History of Feminism in Turkey and Feminist Resistance in Gezi." Panel transcript of the New School's Historical Studies Department's "Talk Turkey Conference: Rethinking Life since Gezi," October 4–5, 2013. photography.jadaliyya.com/pages /index/15037/rethinking-gezi-through-feminist-and-lgbt-perspect.

Turam, Berna. 2013. "The Primacy of Space in Politics: Bargaining Rights, Freedom, and Power in an İstanbul Neighborhood." *International Journal of Urban and Regional Research* 37, no. 2: 409–29.

Ünal, Arzu. 2013. "Wardrobes of Turkish-Dutch Women: The Multiple Meanings and Aesthetics of Muslim Dress." PhD diss., University of Amsterdam.

White, Jenny B. 2002. *Islamist Mobilization in Turkey: A Study in Vernacular Politics.* Seattle: University of Washington Press.

———. 2013. *Muslim Nationalism and the New Turks.* Princeton, NJ: Princeton University Press.

Yashar, Ahmet. 2003. "The Coffeehouses in Early Modern Istanbul: Public Space, Sociality, and Surveillance." MA thesis, Boğaziçi University.

Zelizer, Viviana. 2005. *The Purchase of Intimacy.* Princeton, NJ: Princeton University Press.

———. 2010. "Caring Everywhere." In *Intimate Labors: Cultures, Technologies, and the Politics of Care*, edited by Eileen Boris and Rhacel Salazar Parreñas, 267–79. Stanford, CA: Stanford University Press.

From Mumbai to Tel Aviv

Distance and Intimacy
in Transnational Surrogacy Arrangements

✧ ✧

SIBYLLE LUSTENBERGER

ABSTRACT This article analyzes the place of intimacy in the encounters between Israeli gay men and Indian surrogates. While transnational surrogacy is often presented either as an act of solidarity or as a contract for mutual benefit, the article complicates this picture. The intended fathers in the study simultaneously negated, expected, feared, and desired intimacy. The emphasis of the surrogates' monetary interests kept the women outside the fathers' families. Yet framing surrogacy as pure work conflicts with the affection and appreciation the men felt toward their surrogates. They felt the need to meet them, even if only once, to bring the relationship to a good end. Their balancing act unveils the asymmetries that structure transnational surrogacy. Gay men rely on distance and proximity to create consistent stories of origin for their children. They do so, however, at the expense of the surrogates, whose possibilities to enact their ideas about these relationships are limited.

KEYWORDS transnational surrogacy, same-sex parenthood, intimacy

In the spring of 2013 I accompanied a couple of Israeli friends to Mumbai for the birth of their daughter Lea.[1] The two men invited me to complement my research on the formation of same-sex parenthood in Israel by studying firsthand the experiences of gay couples with transnational surrogacy. Their agency had arranged for all of its clients to stay in the same hotel, where any time of the year a number of Israeli men and women waited for the births of their children. Staying in that hotel allowed me to accompany six gay couples on a daily basis and to observe the people and procedures that turned their dreams of fatherhood into reality. During my two-month stay I noted how little my interlocutors knew about the women who carried

JMEWS • Journal of Middle East Women's Studies • 12:2 • July 2016
DOI 10.1215/15525864-3507639 • © 2016 by the Association for Middle East Women's Studies

their children. Most of them met their surrogates once or twice, after delivery and for barely longer than an hour. When I interviewed surrogate mothers, the couples were eager to know what they had told me. The couples were concerned about how the women felt, their socioeconomic conditions, and whether the agency treated them well.

In this article the relationships between surrogate mothers and commissioning gay couples are a prism to explore the place of intimacy in reproductive travels from the Middle East to other parts of the world. I ask what place intimacy has in commercial arrangements that are characterized by distance rather than closeness and build on the intervention of agencies. I begin with recent scholarship on the place of intimacy in monetary transactions to show how a focus on intimacy can expand our understanding of the formation of new family constellations in the Middle East. I then provide a short overview of same-sex parenthood in Israel and the constraints same-sex couples experience. In the main sections of this article, I draw on interviews with gay fathers conducted in Israel and my field notes in India. Complementing these data with insights from other scholars, I analyze how same-sex couples evoke and experience intimacy in different moments of time and space. Approaching intimacy as structured by time and space allows for an understanding of commercial surrogacy that reaches beyond the dichotomy between altruism and commodification. My interlocutors shifted the line between economics and intimacy while they assessed and negotiated the boundary between themselves and the surrogates during pregnancy and after delivery. This balancing act between emotional distance and closeness, I argue, reveals the multiple layers of vulnerability in the formation of gay parenthood through surrogacy.

Researching Intimacy: Thinking beyond the Middle East

Reproductive technologies are highly popular in places such as Egypt, Iran, Dubai, Lebanon, and Israel (Birenbaum-Carmeli and Carmeli 2010; Inhorn and Tremayne 2012). The flourishing industry has led to a growing body of scholarship that provides important insights into how "local actors, living their everyday lives at particular historical moments in particular places, mold the very form that global processes take" (Inhorn 2005, 114). Across the Middle East having children is essential to becoming a full-fledged member of society. Infertile women and men often live in fear of divorce and loss of family support and struggle with social isolation (Abbasi-Shavazi et al. 2008, 12–15; Inhorn 2007). Thus childlessness can disrupt those zones of comfort and familiarity—friendship, the couple, and the family—that are usually thought of as intimate (Berlant 1998, 281). In light of this, reproductive technologies are instruments to restore and strengthen relationships between spouses and across generations (Birenbaum-Carmeli and Inhorn 2009; Inhorn 2007).

As these scholars have demonstrated, religious concepts of relatedness and moral codes of sexuality inform medical practices and national laws. Sunni, Shia, and Orthodox Jewish decision makers do not principally oppose reproductive technologies. Rather, they ask which practices may be applied, how, and by whom to generate transgenerational continuities that conform to religious law. Accordingly, the possibilities for women and men who seek fertility treatments depend not only on their countries of citizenship but also on their religious affiliations and traditions. This has caused considerable transnational movement in the region and beyond (Gürtin 2011; Inhorn 2011, 2012).

The intersection between global and local dynamics reflects a central concern of feminist scholars who work on intimacy. Yet an analytic shift from the global and local to the "global intimate" offers an interesting possibility to enrich the scholarship on reproductive technologies in the Middle East. The intimate is not a mere substitute for "local." Rather, it investigates how the global shapes — and is shaped by — the ways bodies and objects meet and touch (Pratt and Rosner 2012). Hence intimacy forces us to carefully study the relationships men and women enter when they travel to other countries to become parents. These relationships are structured by global inequalities and raise important questions pertaining to exploitation and vulnerability and to the relationship between money and intimacy.

Surrogacy is probably the most emotionally and controversially discussed path to parenthood. It is glorified as an altruistic act that puts an end to the suffering of childless couples, condemned as the commodification of women and children, or presented as a freely chosen contract for mutual benefit (Berend 2012; Fixmer-Oraiz 2013). As Viviana A. Zelizer has observed in *The Purchase of Intimacy*, these contrasting understandings of surrogacy ultimately represent different ideas about the relationship between intimacy and money. Reproduction constitutes an epitome of intimacy, and a lot of people — among them also social scientists — struggle with the idea that it can be for sale (Zelizer 2005, 22–26). Framing surrogacy as an act of altruism restores the ideological separation between reproduction and the market but disregards the monetary transactions and the inequalities that are nevertheless involved. Highlighting the contractual dimension in turn follows the idea that "the whole world is nothing but a single big economy" (Zelizer 2006, 36). These narratives too fail to recognize the complicated entanglements between emotions and money, distance and closeness that structure transnational surrogacy arrangements.

Zelizer (2005) has suggested abandoning the dichotomy between market and intimacy. Instead, she has demonstrated that monetary transactions are deeply embedded in people's relational work, as they use different transactions and payment media to distinguish between meaningful social relations (ibid., 27). Thus compensating an escort for her service requires different symbols, rituals, and practices than a gift to a fiancée and establishes a different form of relationship between the one who gives and the one who receives the money. The transfer of money does not necessarily alter relationships or reduce the intimacy of personal ties. When an unmarried man places a diamond ring on the third finger of the left hand of an unmarried woman, the diamond does not cause the couple's relationship to change (ibid., 38). Instead, the couple announces its betrothal by means of the diamond. At the same time, the diamond distinguishes their relationship from dating, friendship, or prostitution. It therefore matters "who pays, how, when, for what, at what time, how much, how often, for how long" (ibid., 57). I argue that the setup of the observed surrogacy arrangements as contractual, the gay couples' payments to the agencies rather than directly to the surrogate mothers, and the emphasis on the women's monetary interests all maintain that the surrogate is not a mother but remains outside the family she helps establish. Yet the framing of surrogacy as pure work relations conflicts with the strong affection, appreciation, and at times also mistrust my research participants felt toward their surrogate mothers.

These paradoxical desires and feelings are not unique to surrogacy but are also observable in the care work of nannies, housekeepers, or nurses. All these labors tend to intimate needs and can therefore be summarized as "intimate labors" (Boris and Parreñas 2010, 4–5). They require knowledge of intimate details about another person and access to the intimate spaces of others. As employment, the intimacy of these encounters creates considerable challenges for an unequivocal definition of the involved relationships. For example, Seemin Qayum and Raka Ray (2010) have observed that when women in New York sought to treat their nannies like employees with well-defined working hours and rights, they still felt personally betrayed when the nannies demanded higher salaries or better working conditions. They thought of their nannies in terms of friendship and loyalty and were disappointed when they did not act accordingly. But while the intimacy of these encounters bears the potential for conflict and disappointment, it also allows for the formation of alliances between care workers and wards. For example, the care workers in María de la Luz Ibarra's (2010) research provided their elderly wards with companionship, affection, a sense of safety, and, with the help of pilgrimage or prayers, even protection of their God. The care workers gained in return the satisfaction of following their moral imperatives.

The care providers in these studies work in the intimate space of the home and family. As Qayum and Ray (2010, 113) have argued, the home is not an emotionally neutral site and thus hampers the development of classic capital-labor relationships in domestic work. Surrogacy crosses the threshold of the apartment and still is all about creating family relations and sustaining homes. Indeed, reproduction is one of the cornerstones of home and family. In surrogacy, then, the intimacy of the home extends at times across oceans and continents. The encounter between geographic distance and the intimacy of the home introduces a particular spatial dynamic into the relationship between commissioning parents and surrogates. When arrangements are purely contractual, they reduce the intended parents' engagement in these relationships and thus expand the emotional distance between the parties. Yet they cannot erase the attachments and emotions the labor of surrogate mothers inevitably forges.

Space in surrogacy is therefore not an independent dimension. Rather, space is dynamic and has to be thought of together with time (Massey 1994). It is constituted through the interplay between physical distance, ever-changing social relations, and the forms of interaction. It matters that my interlocutors were gay and not heterosexual. Gay fatherhood inevitably renders the surrogates visible. At the same time, social expectations about what "the family" is forced my interlocutors to protect the triadic relationship between the spouses and their children. Their vulnerabilities in turn met the global inequalities and the dependencies of surrogate mothers that structure transnational surrogacy. These asymmetries placed the power to define and manage the forms of interaction in the hands of agents and the intended fathers rather than those of the surrogates. The forms of interaction — whether they receive the results of a medical checkup by e-mail or meet the surrogate face-to-face and at what stage of the process — radically alter the proximity between the parties.

The article's focus on the perspective of gay men rather than of surrogate mothers is a result of the strong bonds I developed with the intended fathers during my two-month research stay. My interlocutors were six Israeli gay couples, two heterosexual couples, and a single mother. I accompanied them to the hospital and the embassy or simply sat with them in the dining room, at the pool, and in hotel rooms, sharing their joys and sorrows over parenthood. The intensity of these moments and the intimacy it created stood in strong contrast to my limited interaction with Indian surrogates. While the four women I approached for interviews were very open to talking about their experiences, my unfamiliarity with India and my dependence on a translator made it difficult for me to know which questions to ask and how to analyze their answers. Hence this article cannot provide a balanced picture. Rather, I use the accounts of the interviewed surrogates and the findings of other anthropologists to supplement or to critically question the narratives of the intended fathers. In doing so, I hope to better define the power asymmetries at the core of transnational surrogacy as they protect gay men's desires and aspirations regarding intimacy, thus facilitating the formation of same-sex parenthood.

Same-Sex Parenthood in Israel

Gal and Noa's Daddies (*Ha'abaim shel Gal v'Noa*, 2012) is an Israeli children's book by Shosh Pinkas.[2] It tells the story of her son and his male partner, who had twin girls through surrogacy in India. The book starts with a scene in the girls' kindergarten, where their friends show curiosity over their family constellation. After this the family sits together in the living room, and the two fathers tell Gal and Noa the story of their births. They begin with their love and marriage in Canada, continue with the decision to have children, and then explain what assistance they needed: an egg donor, "compassionate doctors," and a "strong and good woman" who carried the pregnancy (ibid., 17). While the author points to the complications the two men encountered on their path to parenthood, the story's structure clearly locates the generative power in the same-sex couple's intimacy: in their love and their shared aspiration to raise children together.

The understanding that same-sex couples can form families of their own is relatively recent. To be sure, poetry, mystical narratives, songs, and courtly letters tell about homoeroticism and same-sex love in Jewish history (Greenberg 2004). In rabbinic discussions, in turn, homosexuality has long appeared not as an identity but as a transgression of Jewish law. Accordingly, ancient Hebrew has no expression referring to the concept of sexual orientation or identity. However, the terms "gay" (*homo*), "lesbian" (*lesbit*), and "sexual orientation" (*netia minit*) are today widespread in Israel. Thus I use these terms as emic categories, as my research participants employed them either to define a sense of identity or to describe their relationships or status in society. Until 1988 the country's sodomy law impeded the opportunity to fight harassment and discrimination on the basis of sexual orientation (Spivak and Yonai 1999, 271–72). This changed only when the Knesset removed that statute in a major reform of the criminal law (Harel 2000). Since then lesbian and gay activists have fought against discrimination in the Knesset and in civil courts. Lesbian women in particular have put great emphasis on the formation and recognition of same-sex parenthood (Hadar 2005).

When fighting for the right to form families of their own, lesbian and gay activists entered an existing pronatalist discourse that depicted childlessness as suffering and access to reproductive technologies as a legitimate remedy. Indeed, reproductive technologies — including gamete donation and surrogacy — are legal in Israel and are subsidized by the state. The country has one of the world's highest ratios of fertility clinics, and Israeli women are the world's biggest consumers of in vitro fertilization (Birenbaum-Carmeli and Carmeli 2010, 17–21). This institutional and public support goes hand in hand with the state's interest in producing Jewish citizens (ibid.) and the Orthodox rabbinate's favorable approach to medicalized reproduction (Kahn 2000). In this affirmative atmosphere, lesbian women in 1995 successfully petitioned for unrestricted access to anonymous sperm donation (Hadar 2005). Ten years later the Israeli Supreme Court allowed the same lesbian couple to adopt each other's children and recognized that children could have two mothers. And since 2010 gay men have led a legal fight against their exclusion from surrogacy within the national borders. Given the importance of having children in Israel, lesbians and gay men feel that same-sex parenthood provides them with a way to enter mainstream society (Kadish 2005).

This legal trend should not veil, however, the challenges same-sex couples and their children continue to encounter. Same-sex couples have no access to marriage in Israel. While public authorities such as the National Insurance Institute and the tax authorities grant family-related benefits to same-sex couples, without a clear legal status, their recognition of same-sex parenthood often seems inconsistent and unpredictable. Furthermore, the means of lesbians and gay men to protect their family relations are limited. Second-parent adoption cannot replace the all-encompassing recognition provided by marriage (Dalton 2001, 212–16). While Israeli lawyers working in the field assert that, in the end, second-parent adoption orders are usually granted, the couples still depend on the discretion of officials.

Intimacy in Contractual Relations and the Need to Draw Boundaries

Israelis turned to transnational surrogacy in the 1980s, albeit in small numbers. They approached agencies in the United States, where surrogacy soon became a thriving business (Weisberg 2005, 38–58). However, in public debates transnational surrogacy remained largely invisible. This situation changed in 2008 with the establishment of transnationally operating agencies in Israel with significantly lower fees. Since then their activities and the number of clients have increased dramatically. In 2012 alone the Ministry of Foreign Affairs processed 255 requests to register children born abroad through surrogacy (State Comptroller of Israel 2014, 798). By that year India had become the preferred destination for gay men who wanted to have children.[3] India's surrogacy industry was worth over US$445 million per year, serving people from countries as dispersed as the United States, Tanzania, Norway, Ethiopia, and Australia (Deomampo 2013a; Inhorn 2012, 285).

Lacking a legal basis for regulating surrogacy, local hospitals, brokers, and foreign agencies offered a myriad of arrangements and nuances regarding the relationships between clients and surrogates. Most of my research participants decided to contract with an Israeli agency that cooperated with Indian fertility specialists and brokers in Mumbai. In their arrangements, matching between surrogates and intended parents was completely in the hands of the agents. At that early stage of the process, my interlocutors had neither met the women who would carry their children nor learned anything about their lives or how they felt about the pregnancies. Since the eggs came from different women—often white South African donors—the surrogates' identities appeared largely irrelevant.[4]

Parents-to-be signed the contract with the surrogate mother only after they had a confirmed pregnancy. Then they received a copy of her identity card, from which they learned her age and civil status and could speculate about her religious affiliation. During the pregnancy the Israeli agency sent monthly reports of the medical checkups. Through these reports my interlocutors had access to information about the bodily processes of the surrogates. The contract also gave them the power to influence these women's physical conditions and well-being to some extent, for example, when deciding how many embryos to transfer or whether to make an abortion if prenatal tests indicated a high risk for birth defects, chromosome abnormalities, or genetic diseases.

The surrogates only received information about the intended parents if the latter wanted to meet them. They signed the contract before the embryo transfer and without knowing for whom they would carry the child. According to the interviewed surrogates, the contract neither mentioned the names of the intended parents nor fixed the sum of money they would earn. Furthermore, the women got no copy of the signed contracts. One of them, Meera, told me that she once stole a glance at her file, where she saw two names and assumed that they must belong to the intended parents. She would have liked to know more about them but did not dare to ask the doctor. The relations between surrogates and parents-to-be were asymmetrical and lacked the love, comfort, and closeness usually attributed to intimacy. Instead, it was the unilateral flow of bodily information and the surrogate mother's labor that created intimacy.

Interestingly, the asymmetry between surrogate mothers and parents-to-be seems to result from a concern with the prospective parents' vulnerability. Giving birth to the children, surrogates play a substantial role in the procreation process that facilitates parenthood for others. Accordingly, intended parents, agencies, and surrogates have developed ways to explain why the intended mothers and fathers and not the surrogates are the real parents of the children (Ragoné 1996; Teman 2010). In this sense, intimate relations involve, as Zelizer (2005, 34–35) has argued, a constant process of boundary drawing. This is particularly salient when, as in this case, "relations resemble others that have significantly different consequences for the parties" (ibid., 34). Concretely, attributing a family relationship between the surrogate mother and the child would pose delicate material and legal questions. What rights and duties would such a relationship involve? How would it work in practice? And could a couple take the child to a different country and thereby separate him or her from the surrogate mother? But as Elly Teman (2010) has shown, even when the law makes clear that surrogates are not legal mothers to these children, intended parents distance themselves and the newborn from the surrogate after delivery. According to Teman's (ibid., 198) study on the relationship between intended mothers and surrogates in Israel, the former often feel "such a need to encompass in a singular occupancy the role, status, and identity of mother to their child that they engage in rites of integration that end up downplaying or entirely eliminating the surrogate's role." A lot of intended mothers created photo albums that documented their participation in their children's births. These albums did not give any hint that another woman gave birth (ibid., 199–202).

For the gay couples in my study, there was yet another reason to distance themselves from the surrogate mothers. Their choice of surrogacy was at the same time a decision against entering a shared parenthood arrangement (*horut meshutefet*). In such arrangements a gay couple and a woman (or alternatively a gay couple and a lesbian couple) raise together a child without living in the same home. A private contract between the parties usually outlines the principles of these arrangements: the parties' financial responsibilities, the child's living arrangements, and decision-making processes pertaining to the child's upbringing and education. My interlocutors felt that sharing the decisions of their daily family lives with "an outsider," as they expressed it, would be too complicated. But more important, in the view of the Israeli state such arrangements comprise one mother and one father. The same-sex spouses remain legally invisible and outside the family core. My interlocutors therefore feared that *horut meshutefet* would introduce asymmetry into their relationships. They wanted to be recognized as families in their own right and criticized the heteronormative presumption that a child needs a father and a mother. They encountered this presumption in their everyday lives: in their exclusion from surrogacy in Israel; when special offers for baby clothes addressed only mothers; or when a passerby innocently asked, "Where is the mother?" For my research participants, such incidents were disconcerting, as they forced them constantly to explain and defend their family structures.

The thought that the surrogates could be regarded as an additional party in their family was therefore not just a threat to the positions of both men as fathers, it would also question the very concept of same-sex parenthood. When reflecting on surrogacy arrangements that allow for close contact with the surrogate mothers, Avner said, "If I wanted the surrogate to be part of my family, I could also have entered *horut meshutefet* with an Israeli woman" (field note, Mumbai, April 17, 2013). Ben echoed this feeling when he explained that it would feel artificial to him to befriend the surrogate. He said, "Our child should know that she exists, but not who she is" (field note, Mumbai, May 13, 2013). These interlocutors' aspirations for public and legal recognition of same-sex parenthood as a self-sufficient zone of intimacy prompted them to reduce the degree of intimacy they were willing to attach to their relations with the surrogate mothers.

Locating the Surrogates in the Economic Sphere

A number of research participants told me that they would have liked to have contact with their surrogates and were aware that this option exists in other countries. Economic calculation was their main reason to contract with this particular agency. They took out loans and received financial support from their parents to pay the US $50,000 for the process in India. Oded and Gadi were among them. They did everything to keep the costs low and still needed financial help from Oded's father. A month before the scheduled delivery, Oded struggled with not knowing the surrogate mother at all. But somewhat resignedly, he concluded: "This is what we have. It does not matter anymore" (personal interview, Israel, March 9, 2011). These men probably felt that they could not afford another trip to Mumbai during the pregnancy. However, the efforts they had already made to become parents suggest that economic reasons alone cannot explain why meeting the surrogate mothers was not a priority for most of my research participants. Ido Ziv and Yael Freund-Eschar (2015) have suggested that in transnational surrogacy intended fathers play down the role of the surrogate as a way to deal with her geographic remoteness. It is therefore likely that my interlocutors' narratives would have been different had the agency encouraged personal meetings between the parties. Instead, the agency intimated that it was impossible to establish a relationship with Indian surrogates. When I asked the founder and chief executive officer (CEO) about it, he explained: "The Indian surrogates do not really open up and tell us what they think or feel. . . . Whenever I go there I try to talk to them and see how they do. It really matters to me. But there is some kind of a wall. I do not reach them. There is a silence, and it even takes time for a humble smile" (personal interview, Israel, August 16, 2011). When Udi and Yaron started their surrogacy process, Udi was determined to establish a good relationship with their surrogate mother. But after talking with the CEO, he felt that there was no sense in trying. And when I told an employee about my plan to interview surrogates, he replied: "You do not know them. They are very shy to talk about the process, and even for the couples it is very difficult to have a meaningful conversation with them" (field note, Israel, January 31, 2013). Most of my interlocutors accepted the agency's reasoning and explained the lack of communication as due to language differences, the geographic distance, and Indian society itself. Some of the men thought that because of pronounced social hierarchies in India, the women had a hard time interacting with men from a different class background. Others proposed that the women themselves had no interest in establishing relationships, as their only motivation to do surrogacy was to earn money. Accordingly, none of my interlocutors tried to play down the economic inequality that structures surrogacy in India. They accepted it as part of the arrangement and used it to make sense of their relationships with the surrogate mothers.

This line of reasoning stands in stark contrast to the notion that prevails in other countries, according to which pure surrogacy has to be altruistic. US surrogate mothers, for example, risk harsh critique if they emphasize their monetary interest (Berend 2012, 929). My interlocutors, in turn, denied that Indian surrogate mothers could have other motivations at all. David expressed the belief of many when he argued: "They do it because they want to earn money. This is their only reason. We make a contract and pay the money. It is a transaction. They are employed for nine months to carry the child" (personal interview, Israel, January 23, 2012). According to this narrative, the assumed monetary motivation was not a problem. Quite the contrary, for David and many others it made the arrangement cleaner and the relationship clear. They thought of surrogacy as pure work and assumed that the surrogates shared this view.

As Deborah R. Grayson (1998) has reminded us, this narrative requires contextualization in India's history. During the years of British colonialism, sexual relations between colonial servants and native domestic workers were common (Ghosh 2006). But they often remained temporary, and the children of such unions were separated from their mothers so they could become truly British (ibid.). Transnational surrogacy may appear as yet another way of using poor Indian women as laboring bodies without establishing lasting kinship relations. Framing surrogacy as pure work adds to my interlocutors' efforts to draw a boundary between their families and the surrogates. Or to put it in Zelizer's (2005, 35) words, it is another way to distinguish relations that could easily be confused and threaten their claims for exclusive parenthood.

My research participants' emphasis on the Indian women's monetary interest also implied that these arrangements constituted a win-win situation. Nataniel had thought a lot about the difficulties involved in surrogacy and explained:

> Because she is a poor Indian woman she is not stupid, and she knows very well what she wants from her life. She took this decision very consciously in order to improve her life. From what I understand, her situation as a single mother in India is very difficult. And she received money, with which she can buy a house and send her children to school. There is no other work that would have allowed her to make such a big step forward. I do not say that to be a surrogate mother is easy from a psychological or physical perspective. It is also not easy from a moral perspective. But this is the decision you take. And I think it is important to be conscious about it, to recognize that this is the situation. (personal interview, Israel, February 16, 2012)

The agency employs a similar discourse of gendered empowerment when describing its surrogate mothers. According to the website, they are "compassionate women [who] choose to become surrogates in India so they can provide for their families — the same as if they went to work each day. The difference is [that] what they earn from one surrogacy journey can be equivalent to many, many years of hard work."[5] As Susan Markens (2012, 1750) has observed, commentators who emphasize that surrogacy is beneficial for the surrogates often use this argument as a direct reply to the critique that surrogacy is exploitative. But the agency went even farther and claimed, "They are intelligent, informed women and to insinuate otherwise is rather insulting to them" (ibid.). With this argument, the agency implicitly accused feminist critics of being paternalistic. There is of course an important body of profound critique about white European and American feminists' claims to emancipate women in other parts of the world while relying on false assumptions about these women's lives (Pratt and Rosner 2012, 13–16). But at the hands of the agency, the argument only veils the power asymmetries that structure these surrogacy arrangements.

LUSTENBERGER • From Mumbai to Tel Aviv

◊ ◊ ◊ ◊ ◊ ◊ ◊ ◊

Daisy Deomampo (2013b) and Amrita Pande (2010) have demonstrated that surrogacy has become a survival strategy for Indian women and that at times it even enhances their positions in their families. The surrogates with whom I spoke received between 180,000 and 280,000 rupees (at that time roughly between US $3,000 and US$4,600) per pregnancy. For the women, this was indeed a family income of two to five years, albeit not enough for a future without poverty. Meera and her unemployed husband hoped that with the salary and a loan they could finally pay for a rickshaw that would give them a low but steady income. Deomampo (2013b) and Pande (2010) are therefore right to caution against depicting the surrogates as powerless victims. Yet they are also attentive to the structural power relations inherent in surrogacy and the limits they pose to the surrogates' actions. Meera's account about her reluctance to ask the doctor for details about the prospective parents is telling. Deomampo (2013b, 176) has found in her research that surrogates "did not confront doctors and lawyers on crucial issues related to their payment for fear of losing their contract." They received the impression from the agencies that there was a long line of women waiting to become surrogates. As Pande (2010, 977) has demonstrated, this image does not necessarily reflect reality. In the clinic she observed, there were more couples waiting for treatment than women who wanted to become surrogates. Making the surrogates feel disposable appears to be a strategy to curtail their negotiation power (Deomampo 2013b, 176).

Meera was already in the sixth month of her pregnancy and faced no risk of losing the contract. Yet she still felt vulnerable and did not dare to speak up. As I mentioned above, the surrogacy contracts did not determine fixed salaries. The final amount of money surrogates got depended on the local agency's calculations and goodwill. Maryam, for example, gave birth in the thirty-fourth week due to a medical complication, and therefore she got payment for only eight months. Furthermore, the agent sometimes reduced the salaries due to traveling costs and hospitalization. In general, Indian surrogate mothers received one-third of the salary after delivery and only after the children had left the country. The agency thereby kept the surrogates under control until the end of the arrangement and made sure that they would not claim legal rights as mothers.

In light of all this, the positions of agencies and brokers appears to be crucial to understanding the place of intimacy in transnational surrogacy. Through their mediation, these intermediaries facilitate and structure the relationship between surrogates and intended fathers. At the same time, they themselves forge intimate ties with the involved parties that revolve around the management and control of money, bodily service, and information. The asymmetries described in this section therefore emerge out of intermeshing intimate relations that bind together diverging interests. They are not merely a result of unequal economic power but are also an integral part of the arrangements' functioning. The lack of contact between surrogates and intended parents, the narratives that locate the women in the economic sphere, and the agency's control over the flow of money all cut off the women from the families they help form. Their scope of action is constantly limited, as they receive no information about the intended parents, have no say in the frequency and form of contact and reciprocity, and run a risk of losing the contract or money if they speak up against their working conditions. The couples I accompanied in Mumbai knew little about this. While some suspected the various agents of exploiting the women's poverty, most of them could not tell how much money the surrogates earned. Many couples were astonished when I told them that not even half of the US$11,000 dollars, which their Israeli agency categorized as "payment for the pregnancy," reached the surrogates.

Transnationally operating agencies have leeway in defining their roles and in shaping the relations between the parties. And while geographic distance certainly limits the physical encounters between intended parents and surrogates, intimacy does not necessarily depend on physical nearness. As Ann Laura Stoler (2006, 15) has argued, nearness can also be measured by the degree of involvement, engagement, and concern. Still, physical distance facilitated forms of social interaction that made it possible for my interlocutors to maintain a sense of emotional detachment toward the surrogates. How, then, did intimacy change when personal encounters were suddenly within reach? To answer this question, I shift the focus to my interlocutors' experiences in Mumbai. In the following section I argue that there was a force in the sudden physical nearness that caused the emotional distance to collapse. As my interlocutors anticipated and prepared their encounters with the surrogates, they were confronted with new desires, fears, and insecurities. Intimacy appears as a process that—even if it does not depend on physical proximity—is shaped by space and temporality.

Meeting the Surrogate Mothers

During their stay in Mumbai, my interlocutors met their surrogate mothers once or twice. How often and where these meetings took place depended on the intended parents' preferences and on ever-changing bureaucratic requirements. After the births of their children, the parents were largely occupied with collecting the documents necessary for their return to Israel. This included several excursions to the Israeli consulate and the local migration office. It is there that most of my interlocutors met the surrogates for the first time.

When Nir and Michael met their surrogate at the consulate, Nir was prepared for an emotional encounter. This woman had carried his daughter Shahar for nine months, and he thought that it was impossible to be pregnant without getting attached. Therefore he expected her to be very emotional about seeing the baby. Accordingly, he was deeply confused and troubled when she seemed reserved and did not even want to hold her:

This felt so wrong to me that I left the room and started to cry. I understand that she has to disconnect in order to be able to give up the child. But somehow it did not feel right to me, this situation. In this moment I felt that it is not right that we see her only once, and it is as if she had not been there for the last nine months. All the arguments against surrogacy, about exploitation, that you use her as an instrument, suddenly I felt it. And I felt a little bit guilty. I do not think that we did anything wrong. We did not force her, and with the money we bought her children education. But at that very moment I felt the critique. (personal interview, Israel, December 30, 2011)

When they met her again in the migration office, she warmed up, and they took pictures together. Relieved, Nir stated, "Then I felt that we closed the circle in a good way" (ibid.). His partner Michael experienced the situation differently. He was glad that the first meeting was not as emotional as he had feared and reasoned: "She and I were there because we made business together. But we did not share any emotions" (personal interview, Israel, December 26, 2011). In contrast to Nir, he felt uncomfortable when in the second meeting the surrogate became emotional and left with tears in her eyes. But then he thought: "We have now many pictures of her and her daughters. I am glad that we have something to show to Shaḥar, pictures that contain emotions and surely will appeal to her" (ibid.). Nir's and Michael's statements express the unease we also encounter in the argument that commercial surrogacy commodifies reproduction and therefore turns women and children into fungible objects (Humbyrd 2009, 113–14). Like almost all the male couples I met, they planned to make a photo album for Shaḥar to help her make sense of her story of origin. For this purpose my interlocutors took a variety of photos: of the hotel, the moment they held the baby for the first time, the obstetrician and the nurses, the other parents in the hotel, and, most important, the surrogate mothers. Deomampo (2013a, 530–31) has already elaborated on how transnational surrogacy clients in Mumbai sought to maintain "an Indian element" in their children's identities. Yet my interlocutors' expectations for the encounters with the surrogates and their hopes to take pictures are about catching not an Indian element but rather a person to whom they and the children could relate emotionally. These photo albums sharply contrast with the attempts of some of Teman's research participants to erase the surrogates' presence in their children's stories of origin.

I want to suggest here that my research participants' need to remember the surrogates reflects the peculiarities of same-sex parenthood. When same-sex couples have children, the involvement of a third party is always already visible. Gay men cannot choose to whom and on what occasion they disclose the involvement of a surrogate mother. In this situation, including the surrogates in their children's photo albums offers a way to create coherent stories of origin. As Teman (2010, 200) reminds us, photography makes connections between people. These encounters therefore express a relational and interactive understanding of human reproduction. I follow Enric Porqueres i Gené and Jérôme Wilgaux (2009, 114), who have compellingly argued, "[New] technologies and new scientific knowledge associated with reproduction [do not] place us in a post-relational world." The encounters and photos help maintain the surrogates in these children's origin stories and family histories. My interlocutors thereby not only acknowledged the women's contributions. They also preserved intimacy as key to human reproduction, placing their children in a web of relations, concrete bodies, and emotions that distinguish their coming into being from production chains.

During my research stay in Mumbai, I witnessed the thoughts and efforts the couples put into these meetings and how they anticipated and feared them at the same time. Avner and Yigal's encounter with their daughter's surrogate Urvashi upset them terribly. The strong emotions they felt toward this woman did not match the atmosphere in the consulate, a state office with heavy surveillance and no room for privacy. Urvashi had arrived with the agency's lawyer, whom the two men neither liked nor trusted. Apart from that, Avner and Yigal simply did not know what to say to Urvashi. Yigal wanted to express their gratefulness but was afraid to do or say something that could be inappropriate in her view. He asked some questions. But since Urvashi hardly responded, he stopped after a while, and they all kept silent.

Many of my interlocutors had similar stories and feelings about their encounters with the surrogate mothers at the consulate. Ehud, for example, was worried when he saw that the surrogate Avani was "ice cold"—as he expressed it (field note, Mumbai, May 10, 2013)—and did not show any feelings toward the baby boy. He feared that this detachment might have affected the child in a negative way during the pregnancy. His partner Itay, in turn, thought that maybe she was still exhausted, in pain from the cesarean section, in a postnatal crisis, simply shy, or intimidated by the situation. I do not know why it was so hard for them to communicate with Avani. But I find it remarkable that in the context of these encounters, the surrogate arrangements did not remain in the economic sphere. Unlike Michael, most of my interlocutors expected some emotional connection, and they searched for reasons when the surrogates did not behave accordingly. They thereby reiterate a double expectation toward surrogate mothers that Pande (2010, 976) also observed in the work of Indian surrogacy agents and clinics:

> The surrogate is expected to be a disciplined contract worker who will give the baby away immediately after delivery without creating a fuss. But she is simultaneously expected to be a nurturing mother attached to the baby and a selfless mother who will not treat surrogacy like a business. This mother-worker combination is produced through a disciplinary project that deploys the power of language along with a meticulous control over the body of the surrogate.

Without the geographic closeness and the basic opportunity for meeting the surrogates, my interlocutors would probably have continued to draw a boundary between themselves and the surrogates. But these emotional boundaries collapsed at the time of the delivery and the couples' knowledge about these women's immediate presence. Now they felt a need to bring these relations to a good end, and since they had ceased to be purely contractual, this required a personal exchange.

Unsatisfied with the encounter at the embassy, Avner and Yigal hoped to meet their surrogate mother again and invited her to their apartment in the hotel. "We are very tense about this meeting," Avner told me shortly before Urvashi arrived (field note, Mumbai, April 18, 2013). They wanted it to be nice, and they tried to create a comfortable atmosphere. They organized soft drinks and cookies and asked a hotel employee they trusted to do the translation. During my research stay in Mumbai, inviting the surrogate mothers to the hotel was a common practice. Those who were less troubled about the meetings allowed me to participate. In these meetings the surrogates held the babies and were often equipped with a cellphone to take pictures. The couples, in turn, showed pictures of their homes and the rooms they had prepared for the babies. They asked the surrogates how they felt, tried to learn a little bit about their families, and talked about the babies. These were meetings between strangers who were just getting to know each other. But while these personal exchanges could have been the beginning of a lasting relationship, they designated the end.

My interlocutors did not plan to stay in contact with the surrogates. But since the geographic and emotional distance collapsed during their stays in Mumbai, the contracting parents found it difficult to end the relationships like a business transaction. Hence they gave the surrogate a present, usually an envelope with money additional to the contractual payment for the pregnancy. My interlocutors sometimes used the English term *tip* for this extra money and sometimes the Hebrew word *matana*, which means "gift." This dual terminology is no coincidence but rather expresses the ambiguity of this money transfer. As Zelizer (1997, 95) has argued, the term *tip* may have various meanings, as it lies "at the boundary of other critically different transfers, not quite payment, not quite a bribe, not quite charity, but not quite a gift either." My interlocutors got the impression from the agency that the extra money was an informal part of the standard procedure and was expected by everyone. Hence it can be understood as a regular payment. The agency recommended that the couples give between 5,000 and 7,000 rupees (at that time between US$80 and US$100) and cautioned them that higher amounts would raise other surrogates' expectations. Yet many couples felt that the recommended amount was not enough to express their gratitude and disregarded the agency's advice.

However, the recipient was a stranger, and this made it difficult to assess the appropriate amount. Ben and Amit thought a long time about this matter. They wanted to make a real change in the woman's life and tried to figure out the best way to do so. They considered donating money to a local women's organization but eventually decided against it. For them and for others, this money transfer was highly personalized, a way to acknowledge the surrogate mother's gift and to restore reciprocity. Hence they gave her 50,000 rupees, albeit with hesitations. Ben thought that perhaps her husband had forced her to be a surrogate and feared that a high tip would encourage him to do it again. "We do not know anything about her," Ben explained. "It would be good to visit her home to better understand the family dynamic" (field note, Mumbai, May 13, 2013). When they finally met, Ben accompanied the surrogate and her husband to their home outside the metropolis. He was shocked to see how poor the village and the house were. He did not dare to enter even though they invited him. "I was afraid of what I would see and that it would make me feel bad," he confessed. "But now I feel bad that I refused their invitation" (personal conversation, Israel, July 20, 2013).

When my interlocutors tried to make sense of the kind of relationship surrogacy created between themselves and the Indian women, they encountered not only doubts and insecurities but also mistrust. The agency warned its clients not to give their Israeli phone numbers to the surrogates, as they would ask for more money and create emotional pressure. Several men indeed told me about attempts by their surrogate mothers to elicit more money. Pande's (2011) research suggests that for the surrogates, these requests expressed their expectations that surrogacy constructs lasting relationships of reciprocity. Her surrogate interlocutors often emphasized their sisterly ties with the intended mothers and forged real or imaginary ties with the parents-to-be (ibid., 622). Using kinship terms, these women hoped these relationships would secure their children's futures (ibid.). The agency's warning, in contrast, implies that pleas from the surrogate mothers for additional money are at best unjustified and that the intended parents' obligations toward these women ends with the delivery. This rationale encouraged my interlocutors' cautious attitudes. During my stay in Mumbai, my interlocutors had the impression that locals tried to fleece them and each other. When it came to money, my interlocutors found it difficult to trust anyone involved in surrogacy. As for their encounters with the surrogates, this mistrust meant that they not only struggled to bridge the strangeness between them but also were keen to keep some distance.

Conclusion

Intimacy is, as Stoler (2006, 15–16) has argued, a site of constant query and usually is associated with affection, love, bodily closeness, proximity of personhood, and nearness of others. *Gal and Noa's Daddies* tells a story about intimacy in the family. It not only locates love at the beginning of the family formation. It also depicts the home as a place of affection and bodily closeness, illustrated most beautifully in the last picture, which shows the two fathers carrying the girls to bed (Pinkas 2012, 20–21). The story therefore does not escape the tie between the grids of genealogy and intimacy (Povinelli 2002, 234). To be sure, in a cultural context in which the genealogical imaginary is first and foremost heterosexual, the formation of same-sex fatherhood is unsettling. Yet love still culminates in a family and is thereby built into the grammar of genealogy (ibid., 234–35). The surrogate mother and the egg donor, in turn, remain outside the family. They are helpers who appear on the scene to contribute their parts and then disappear.

I have brought the surrogates back into the picture not to restore the heterosexual grid but to shed light on the encounters that are nevertheless intrinsic to the creation of these families and to the vulnerabilities, power relations, and ambiguities they bring. This article is not an attempt to rebut or devalue the intimacy that stands in the foreground of Pinkas's children's book. Pinkas's story is incomplete, but so is mine, and many more encounters and actors need to be analyzed. Yet I hope to complicate the story of pink love with the underlying differences of class and gender. Gay men in Israel are vulnerable to exclusion and everyday incidents that question the concept of same-sex parenthood. At the same time, my interlocutors mobilized enough capital to circumvent their exclusion and to use global asymmetries. They entered the surrogacy arrangements from a position in which their interests were protected through the agency and often at the expense of the surrogates.

To conclude, I want to come back to space and time as they appear in the intimate encounters here described. If intimacy refers to nearness as "something that can be measured by . . . the degree of involvement, engagement, concern, and attention one gives to it" (Stoler 2006, 15), transnational surrogacy provides an interesting opportunity for comparison. Geographic distance limits the possibilities for close encounters but still allows for various degrees of engagement and attention. While I focused here on Israeli same-sex couples, increasing numbers of people engage in reproductive travels in the Middle East and from the Middle East to other regions (Gürtin 2011; Inhorn 2011, 2012). Intimate bonds between spouses and across generations are thereby strengthened, and new relationships are forged through intimate encounters with strangers. A look at "intimacy in the Middle East"—to paraphrase this special issue's title—should therefore not block the view of those encounters that cross regional boundaries while shaping local relationships and social structures. The emotions, disillusions, and anxieties my research participants experienced when meeting the surrogate mothers tell of the force of physical nearness. In the context of immediate encounters, my interlocutors had to reassess the relationships between the surrogate mothers, the children, and themselves. And still, the face-to-face encounters did not create lasting relationships but rather laid bare the dynamics between intimacy, distance, and commercial exchange. Indeed, Pinkas's idealistic portrayal of queer intimacies diverges from the messy relationships Israeli gay men enter with Indian surrogates. Their queer identities render the surrogates visible, thus creating a tension between distance and intimacy. Distance appears as a necessary answer to the everyday incidents that question the concept of same-sex parenthood. But as the surrogates never disappear completely from the children's stories of origin, the intimacy of these encounters has to be restored. How far this is different for heterosexuals who fulfill their reproductive goals abroad remains an open question. While the latter are in a position that allows them not to disclose the involvement of a third party to others, one day their children will probably want to see pictures and hear the stories of their births. Hence it appears that intimacy remains an intrinsic part of reproduction when national borders are crossed.

SIBYLLE LUSTENBERGER holds a PhD in social anthropology from the University of Bern. In her dissertation she explores how Israeli same-sex couples have circumvented their exclusion from marriage to form families of their own and how these same processes bring into being new forms of Jewish continuities. Contact: sib.lustenberger@gmail.com.

Acknowledgments

I want to thank the Wenner-Gren Foundation (grant no. 8061) and the Swiss National Science Foundation for their generous financial assistance. I am much indebted to Édouard Conte for his warm support and guidance.

Notes

1. All the names are pseudonyms to protect the privacy of my research participants and their children.
2. All transliterations in this article follow the recommendations of the Academy of the Hebrew Language (2011).
3. This situation changed in December 2012, when the Ministry of Home Affairs called surrogacy pregnancies for gay and unmarried foreigners to a halt (Rajadhyaksha 2013). The gay men I accompanied to Mumbai in the spring of 2013 were therefore among the last to use the observed surrogacy arrangements.
4. Combining white donors with Indian surrogates is not an invention of Israeli agencies. Rather, this arrangement follows a widespread pattern, as racialized categories and class hierarchies are reproduced in the intimate encounters of surrogacy (Winddance 2011).
5. Tammuz International Surrogacy, "Egg Donation in India with Tammuz," www.tammuz.com /main.php?lang=eng&action=donorsinindia (accessed March 27, 2013).

References

Abbasi-Shavazi, Mohammad Jalal, Marcia C. Inhorn, Hajiieh Bibi Razeghi-Nasrabad, and Ghasem Toloo. 2008. "The 'Iranian ART Revolution': Infertility, Assisted Reproductive Technology, and Third-Party Donation in the Islamic Republic of Iran." *Journal of Middle East Women's Studies* 4, no. 2: 1–28.

Academy of the Hebrew Language. 2011. "Hata'tik m'ivrit l'otiot latiniot" ("Transliteration from Hebrew to Latin Letters"). hebrew-academy.org.il/wp-content/uploads/Transcription2_1.pdf (accessed March 29, 2016).

Berend, Zsuzsa. 2012. "The Romance of Surrogacy." *Sociological Forum* 27, no. 4: 913–36.

Berlant, Lauren. 1998. "Intimacy: A Special Issue." *Critical Inquiry* 24, no. 2: 281–88.

Birenbaum-Carmeli, Daphna, and Yoram S. Carmeli. 2010. Introduction to *Kin, Gene, Community: Reproductive Technologies among Jewish Israelis*, edited by Daphna Birenbaum-Carmeli and Yoram Carmeli, 1–48. New York: Berghahn.

Birenbaum-Carmeli, Daphna, and Marcia C. Inhorn. 2009. "Masculinity and Marginality: Palestinian Men's Struggles with Infertility in Israel and Lebanon." *Journal of Middle East Women's Studies* 5, no. 2: 23–52.

Boris, Eileen, and Rhacel Salazar Parreñas. 2010. Introduction to *Intimate Labors: Cultures, Technologies, and the Politics of Care*, edited by Eileen Boris and Rhacel Salazar Parreñas, 1–13. Stanford, CA: Stanford University Press.

Dalton, Susan E. 2001. "Protecting Our Parent-Child Relationships: Understanding the Strengths and Weaknesses of Second-Parent Adoption." In *Queer Families, Queer Politics: Challenging Culture and the State*, edited by Mary Bernstein and Renate Reimann, 201–20. New York: Columbia University Press.

Deomampo, Daisy. 2013a. "Gendered Geographies of Reproductive Tourism." *Gender and Society* 27, no. 4: 514–37.

———. 2013b. "Transnational Surrogacy in India: Interrogating Power and Women's Agency." *Frontiers: A Journal of Women Studies* 34, no. 3: 167–88.

Fixmer-Oraiz, Natalie. 2013. "Speaking of Solidarity: Transnational Gestational Surrogacy and the Rhetorics of Reproductive (In)justice." *Frontiers: A Journal of Women Studies* 34, no. 3: 126–63.

Ghosh, Durba. 2006. *Sex and the Family in Colonial India: The Making of Empire*. Cambridge: Cambridge University Press.

Grayson, Deborah R. 1998. "Black Surrogate Mothers and the Law." *Critical Inquiry* 24, no. 2: 525–46.

Greenberg, Steven. 2004. *Wrestling with God and Men: Homosexuality in the Jewish Tradition*. Madison: University of Wisconsin Press.

Gürtin, Zeynep. 2011. "Banning Reproductive Travel: Turkey's ART Legislation and Third-Party Assisted Reproduction." *Reproductive BioMedicine Online* 23, no. 5: 555–64.

Hadar, Ira. 2005. "Lesbians in Israel: A Legal Perspective." In *Sappho in the Holy Land: Lesbian Existence and Dilemmas in Contemporary Israel*, edited by Chava Frankfort-Nachmias and Erella Shadmi, 15–38. Albany: State University of New York Press.

Harel, Alon. 2000. "The Rise and Fall of the Israeli Gay Legal Revolution." *Columbia Human Rights Law Review* 31: 443–71.

Humbyrd, Casey. 2009. "Fair Trade International Surrogacy." *Developing World Bioethics* 9, no. 3: 111–18.

Ibarra, María de la Luz. 2010. "My Reward Is Not Money: Deep Alliances and End-of-Life Care among Mexicana Workers and Their Wards." In *Intimate Labors: Cultures, Technologies, and the Politics of Care*, edited by Eileen Boris and Rhacel Salazar Parreñas, 117–31. Stanford, CA: Stanford University Press.

Inhorn, Marcia C. 2003. "Global Infertility and the Globalization of New Reproductive Technologies: Illustrations from Egypt." *Social Science and Medicine* 56, no. 9: 1837–51.

———. 2005. "Gender, Health, and Globalization in the Middle East: Male Infertility, ICSI, and Men's Resistance." In *Globalization, Women, and Health in the Twenty-First Century*, edited by Ilona Kickbusch, Kari A. Hartwig, and Justin M. List, 113–25. New York: Palgrave Macmillan.

———. 2007. "Masculinity, Reproduction, and Male Infertility Surgery in the Middle East." *Journal of Middle East Women's Studies* 3, no. 3: 1–20.

——. 2011. "Globalization and Gametes: Reproductive 'Tourism,' Islamic Bioethics, and Middle Eastern Modernity." *Anthropology and Medicine* 18, no. 1: 87–103.

——. 2012. "Reproductive Exile in Global Dubai: South Asian Stories." *Cultural Politics* 8, no. 2: 283–306.

Inhorn, Marcia C., and Soraya Tremayne, eds. 2012. *Islam and Assisted Reproductive Technologies: Sunni and Shia Perspectives.* New York: Berghahn.

Kadish, Ruti. 2005. "Israeli Lesbians, National Identity, and Motherhood." In *Sappho in the Holy Land: Lesbian Existence and Dilemmas in Contemporary Israel,* edited by Chava Frankfort-Nachmias and Erella Shadmi, 223–50. Albany: State University of New York Press.

Kahn, Susan Martha. 2000. *Reproducing Jews: A Cultural Account of Assisted Conception in Israel.* Durham, NC: Duke University Press.

Markens, Susan. 2012. "The Global Reproductive Health Market: U.S. Media Framings and Public Discourses about Transnational Surrogacy." *Social Science and Medicine* 74, no. 11: 1745–53.

Massey, Doreen. 1994. *Space, Place, and Gender.* Minneapolis: University of Minnesota Press.

Pande, Amrita. 2010. "Commercial Surrogacy in India: Manufacturing a Perfect Mother-Worker." *Signs: Journal of Women in Culture and Society* 35, no. 4: 969–92.

——. 2011. "Transnational Commercial Surrogacy in India: Gifts for Global Sisters?" *Reproductive BioMedicine Online* 23, no. 5: 618–25.

Pinkas, Shosh. 2012. *Ha'abaim shel Gal v'Noa (Gal and Noa's Daddies).* Givatayim: Rimonim.

Porqueres i Gené, Enric, and Jérôme Wilgaux. 2009. "Incest, Embodiment, Genes, and Kinship." In *European Kinship in the Age of Biotechnology,* edited by Jeanette Edwards and Carles Salazar, 112–27. New York: Berghahn.

Povinelli, Elizabeth A. 2002. "Notes on Gridlock: Genealogy, Intimacy, Sexuality." *Public Culture* 14, no. 1: 215–38.

Pratt, Geraldine, and Victoria Rosner. 2012. Introduction to *The Global and the Intimate: Feminism in Our Time,* edited by Geraldine Pratt and Victoria Rosner, 1–30. New York: Columbia University Press.

Qayum, Seemin, and Raka Ray. 2010. "Traveling Cultures of Servitude: Loyalty and Betrayal in New York and Kolkata." In *Intimate Labors: Cultures, Technologies, and the Politics of Care,* edited by Eileen Boris and Rhacel Salazar Parreñas, 101–16. Stanford, CA: Stanford University Press.

Ragoné, Helena. 1996. "Chasing the Blood Tie: Surrogate Mothers, Adoptive Mothers and Fathers." *American Ethnologist* 23, no. 2: 352–65.

Rajadhyaksha, Madhavi. 2013. "No Surrogacy Visa for Gay Foreigners." *Times of India,* January 18. articles.timesofindia.indiatimes.com/2013-01-18/india/36415052_1_surrogacy-fertility-clinics -home-ministry (accessed March 26, 2013).

Spivak, Dori, and Yuval Yonai. 1999. "Bein shtika l'ginui: Havnaiat hazehut shel hahomoim b'siaḥ hamishpati b'Israel 1948–1988" ("Between Silence and Condemnation: The Structuring of the Identity of Homosexuals in Juridical Discourse in Israel, 1948–1988"). *Soziologia Israelit* 1, no. 2: 257–93.

State Comptroller of Israel. 2014. Duaḥ shnati 64.3 l'shnat 2013 v'l'ḥeshbonot shnat hakaspim 2012 (Annual Report 64.3 for 2013 and the Fiscal Year of 2012). www.mevaker.gov.il/he/Reports /Report_248/9295a9dc-fa05-4b43-b83b-0bdef6e5d309/219-ver-4.pdf (accessed December 31, 2014).

Stoler, Ann Laura. 2006. *Haunted by Empire: Geographies of Intimacy in North American History.* Durham, NC: Duke University Press.

Teman, Elly. 2010. *Birthing a Mother: The Surrogate Body and the Pregnant Self.* Berkeley: University of California Press.

Weisberg, Kelly. 2005. *The Birth of Surrogacy in Israel.* Gainesville: University Press of Florida.

Winddance, Twine. 2011. *Outsourcing the Womb: Race, Class, and Gestational Surrogacy in a Global Market.* New York: Routledge.

Zelizer, Viviana A. 1997. *The Social Meaning of Money: Pin Money, Paychecks, Poor Relief, and Other Currencies.* Princeton, NJ: Princeton University Press.

——. 2005. *The Purchase of Intimacy.* Princeton, NJ: Princeton University Press.

——. 2006. "Do Markets Poison Intimacy?" *Contexts* 5, no. 2: 33–38.

Ziv, Ido, and Yael Freund-Eschar. 2015. "The Pregnancy Experience of Gay Couples Expecting a Child through Overseas Surrogacy." *Family Journal: Counseling and Therapy for Couples and Families* 23, no. 2: 158–66.

Violent Intimacies

Tactile State Power, Sex/Gender Transgression, and the Politics of Touch in Contemporary Turkey

◊ ◊

ASLI ZENGIN

ABSTRACT This article is about how sex, gender, and sexuality are governed in Turkey at the intersection of intimate contact and mandated encounters with medicolegal institutions and the bodies of sex/gender transgressive people. To explore this question, it brings two institutional processes together: trans women's gender reassignment processes in public hospitals and gay men's medical examinations to receive exemptions from compulsory military service. In both sites institutional observation and practice are preoccupied with penile penetration as a tool to eliminate and hence regulate sex/gender transgression. I argue that this institutional fixation develops specific proximities and forms of touch by the state on (and in) the bodies of trans women and gay men, which in turn plays a pivotal role in the institutional production of sexual difference and normative regulation of sexuality, desire, sex, and gender in Turkey.

KEYWORDS state violence, intimacy, sex, gender, sexuality

The relationship between intimacy and state power has attracted significant scholarly attention over the last two decades. From affective and sentimental ties of domesticity to the zones of desire, sex, and sexuality, scholars have drawn widely on the involvement of the state in the so-called private sphere of its subjects, charging this with a political content (Aretxaga 2003; Berlant 1997; Povinelli 2006; Stoler 2002). Areas such as marriage, sexuality, and reproduction, to name a few, tend to be critical sites of state regulation and the focus of persistent state projects. Paying attention to these intimate domains reveals a story of the affective, visceral, corporeal workings of everyday state power.

JMEWS • Journal of Middle East Women's Studies • 12:2 • July 2016
DOI 10.1215/15525864-3507650 • © 2016 by the Association for Middle East Women's Studies

Ann Laura Stoler (2006, 13) has convincingly suggested that "to study the intimate is not to turn away from structures of dominance, but to relocate their conditions of possibility and relations and forces of production." Such a focus on the intimate also encourages appreciation of a host of sensory experiences: "sound, smell, taste; the ways bodies and objects meet and touch . . . zones of contact and the formations they generate" (Pratt and Rosner 2006, 17). Developing a special focus on this sensorial — specifically, tactile — component and organization of state power, this article looks at the relationship between intimacy and the state. I employ the conceptual nexus of taction, corporeality, and sensorium in the study of intimate state power for an analysis of the *politics of tactility and touch* shaped at the knot of *violence, intimacy,* and *sex/gender transgressive lives.* I ask how the sensory apparatus, specifically various forms of violent touch by institutional actors on people's bodies, helps us understand the organization and exercise of intimate state power.

To this end, I look at two institutional sites of state interaction with marginalized gendered and sexual figures in Turkey: trans women undergoing gender reassignment processes in state hospitals and gay men being medically examined to receive exemptions from compulsory military service.[1] In both sites institutional observation and practice are preoccupied with penile penetration as a tool to eliminate and hence regulate sex/gender transgression. I argue that this institutional fixation develops specific proximities and forms of touch by the state on (and in) the bodies of trans women and gay men, which in turn plays a pivotal role in the institutional production of sexual difference and normative regulation of sexuality, desire, sex, and gender in Turkey. I bring these two sites together to consider how the Turkish state invents and rationalizes "technologies of sex" (Foucault 1980) and "technologies of gender" (Lauretis 1987) through a channeling of particular heterosexual fantasies and gendering practices based on penile penetration.

By showing the particularities of touch in the two cases and their commonalities and intersections, I approach each touch as a product of heteronormative assumptions and fantasies of sex and gender. Specifically, I investigate how desire, sex, gender, and sexuality are governed in Turkey at the dense meeting point of violent operations on the bodies of sex/gender transgressive citizens at state institutions through two questions: How does the state (re)produce sexual difference and the dominant categories of sex and gender in Turkey? What kind of sociocultural-specific form and definition does the Turkish state gain in the course of this sexual and gendered ordering?

By answering these questions, this article achieves two goals. First, it contributes to the literature on state, gender, sex, sexuality, and intimacy in the Middle East. The specificity of the Turkish state emanates from its institutional fixation with penetration as a medium to regulate sex and gender nonconformity. Second, this article expands on the theories of intimate state power by developing a novel approach that lays emphasis on sensorium as a tool for the exercise of the state's governmental politics. This sensorium derives largely from gaze and touch, which act together and play a vital role in endowing state power with intimate forms of interaction with bodies that are targeted for normalization and control. Gaze, as a political tool, has been widely discussed to understand the exercise of state power vis-à-vis supervision and observation of bodies in myriad institutional settings (Foucault 1980, 1988, 1995, 2004). Yet touch is still a less examined issue in the formation and operation of state power. Hence I build my discussion of intimate state power mainly on the use of touch and tactility as a political tool in institutional settings.

To do this, I first theorize the state and then illuminate the impact of the Turkish sociocultural context on shaping its specific organization in sexual and gendered ways. To comprehend the exercise of intimate state power via this regime of sex, sexuality, and gender, I develop a theory of the politics of touch and tactility, a theory that elucidates the use of corporeality and sensorium as a technology of sex and gender. Finally, a detailed examination of two distinct yet related medico-legal settings that regulate sex/gender transgression help me put this entire theoretical and analytic framework into perspective.

Conceptualizing the Gendered/Sexual State

The formulation of the state employed here is founded on the body of critical theory that problematizes its conceptualization as a reified, empirical object (Abrams 1988) that is distinct from society (Foucault 1980, 1988, 1991, 1995). This follows recent anthropological studies that approach the state as a form, "the presence and content of which is not taken for granted but is the very object of inquiry" (Aretxaga 2003, 395), which problematizes its understanding as a uniform, autonomous, fixed, or bounded entity (Das and Poole 2004; Navaro-Yashin 2002; Sharma and Gupta 2006).

As Begoña Aretxaga (2003, 395) stresses, subjective dynamics are key to the understanding of the state as a form in its relation to people and movements, and without such subjective experience, states do not exist at all. The lived experience of countless everyday encounters between state actors and people paves the way for the state to come into being and gain particular forms of presence. Hence in this article I am particularly interested in this subjective, embodied experience with "the state" and state power and its gendered/sexual dimension. A close examination of the relationship between the political investments in the body, tactile intimacy, and gendering and sexing practices of the Turkish state enables discussion of the *content* that the state gains — a content that is heteronormative, male, masculinist, intimate, and, most important, penetrative.

In the formation of this content, certain modes of political investment in the body are of great analytic significance. Usually referred to as "biopolitics" (Foucault

1995), this political investment transforms every human practice into a potential object of knowledge, regulation, and discipline that creates "populations" (Foucault 1982). As well as deploying rational technologies, these political investments also take sovereign forms that constantly establish a relationship between violence and its ordering functions (Das and Poole 2004; Dean 2001; Hansen and Stepputat 2005; Mbembe 2005). As the medicolegal projects of the state illustrate in this article, these sovereign forms expose the bodies of sex/gender transgressive citizens to violent "economies of touch" (Ahmed 2000, 49) and at the same time constitute an integral element of state biopolitics. A focus on these medicolegal projects reveals the state's sovereign capacity for transforming trans women's and gay men's bodies into a microphysical domain of power in relation to the symbolic and material production of sexual difference and the dominant gender regime.

In general, the ways states are organized both reflect and reproduce the existing gender and sexual cultures in which they are situated. To give an example from the Turkish context, the state's respective issuance of pink and blue identification (ID) cards to its female and male citizens is a product of a culturally specific organization of a gender/sex dichotomy into institutional and national life. As a result of this inscription, the state not only sustains and bolsters gender dichotomy as a crucial determinant of its citizens' official lives but also constitutes distinctive zones to exercise its power when there is a transgression of this gender dichotomy. This article is specifically about those unique ways of intervention in the zones of sex/gender transgression. Yet to grasp why and how the Turkish state intervenes in such unique ways, one should first have a general comprehension of the dominant gender/sexual culture in Turkey.

The Turkish notions of hegemonic masculinity and dominant femininity are closely tied to heteroreproductive sexuality and thus to the processes, desires, and practices of family making and the state's investments in this intimate domain. While an embrace of active female sexual performance and desire (be it straight or same-sex) is socioculturally devalued and substantially diminished, hegemonic masculinity strictly relies on various public and private performances and practices of active heterosexual male desire. For females growing up, menarche is socially invisible, and even though they may have wide access to education and the world of work, the discourses of chastity, domesticity, reproductivity, and moral purity position them as "women" expected to realize their selves first and foremost as proper wives and mothers (Kandiyoti 1987; Sirman 1989). Tying women's social recognition to their reproductive capacities and the domain of family (Durakbaşa 1998; Sirman 2007), this value system marginalizes other forms of existences and possible lives that lie outside this realm, including same-sex relations among women (see Baba 2011). Even though large urban environments do in fact provide alternative forms of relationships and opportunities for nonmarital sex and same-sex intimacies, the codes of honor pervasively shape the texture of social life and mostly disapprove and prohibit intimate affairs outside the marriage boundaries and the heterosexual framework. Honor codes perceive women's sexuality as the property of men, family, or society rather than women themselves (Koğacıoğlu 2004). As long as women regulate and control their bodies in compliance with the socially accepted codes of honor, their sexuality is publicly recognized and celebrated as a part of heterosexual family-making processes (see Zengin 2011). Hence there is a patriarchal consensus for defining women's sexual intimacy as it relates to procreation and social reproduction rather than individual pleasure.

When it comes to the present hegemonic masculinity in Turkey, it is possible to define it as heterosexual, authoritarian, conservative, culturally Muslim, middle- to high-class, and Turkish (as an ethnic self-identification in relation to primarily the Kurdish identity). An ideal Turkish man is expected to be an obedient son to his father and deeply devoted to his mother (Helvacıoğlu 2006; Kandiyoti 1987) and to prove himself a risk taker, assertive, a warrior, courageous, and fearless. Male bonding is ubiquitous and strongly expressed (e.g., physically). Protectiveness and possessiveness, which can take both financial and cultural forms, are also significant aspects of hegemonic masculinity. A constant play of vigilance and willingness to claim and protect and to sacrifice for family, kin, community, flag, and nation is essential.

Several developmental stages and rites of passage transform a male into a member of the Turkish hegemonic masculine world. He should register the following practices and rituals—circumcision, educational achievement, participation in the soccer culture, and military service—before getting a proper job, marrying, having children, and, most important, having an *active* and directing role in sexual relations (see Bereket and Adam 2006). His performance in these sites shapes the public opinion of his masculinity in private and public environments.

Among these realms, sexual potency and its public affirmation occupy a special role, a trait that indicates a man's capacity for vaginal or anal penetration with his penis.[2] This preoccupation with penile penetration as a definitive element of hegemonic masculinity concerns sexual relations not just with women but also with men. Scholars of gay masculinities in Turkey (ibid.; Gorkemli 2012; Özbay 2010; Öztürk 2011; Tapınç 1992) note that culturally dominant roles of gender dichotomy between men and women inscribe themselves on one's sexuality. Whereas women and "real" gay men are expected to occupy the role of insertee (*pasif*), "real" men are those who take the role of inserter (*aktif*) (Bereket and Adam 2008, 217). Hence the "insertee-inserter" (*pasif-aktif*) dichotomy in sexual interaction defines both gender and sexuality.[3] It is not the engagement in same-sex intercourse but the gender role that one holds in this contact that demarcates one's sexual orientation. In this sense, the cultural distinction between the masculine, "active" penetrator and the feminine, "passive" recipient allows men to enter same-sex relations without challenging their straight sense of self (Tapınç 1992, 41).

Men who participate in vaginal or anal penetration may still pass as straight, thus as "real" men, while the recipient partners of these sexual interactions are dominantly marked as feminine.

In this particular sexual and gender environment the Turkish state gains a specific content, and hence particular institutional observations, practices, and, more important, forms of touch become imaginable, possible, and deployable, as is the case with my medicolegal settings that regulate sex/gender transgression. Fixation with penile penetration (vaginal or anal) in everyday relations of sex and gender registers at the institutional level as part of state projects that aim to disambiguate ambiguous gender identities, bodies, and sexual practices. A close focus on this institutional fixation helps me develop a sensorial approach to understand the workings of intimate state power through the lenses of touch and tactility. An exploration of the state's sexual economy of touch (specifically the penile penetration in my examples) allows me to discuss how the state governs sex, gender, sexuality, and desire in a violently intimate way. Before I detail my ethnographic examples, a brief theory on the politics of touch and tactility is helpful.

Laying Out a Regime of Tactility and the Politics of Touch

Paul Rodaway (1994, 41) argues that touch has the status of the most intimate and direct of all senses, because it is constrained by the grasp of the body and it always relies on reciprocal grounds, for "to touch is always to be touched." When we talk about touch, we should not restrict our understanding only to fingers. Rather, haptic experience concerns the whole body or the whole skin covering the body (Montagu 1971). It is also a constant sensual account of our relationship with the world. Through our haptic relationship with the world, we also make sense of it. Touch, as a form of "dwelling on the surface of the body of the other" (Segal 2009, 6), has a tremendous world-making capacity in marking surfaces with value and meaning, establishing boundaries, and indicating borders. From this point of view, it connotes something beyond merely the physical; it is a corporeal situation charged with emotional, political, social, and cultural processes.

A close analysis of touch requires a differentiation between ways of touching. For example, when we talk about touch, it is not always about an affective map of a tactile world that involves, for instance, rubbing, massaging, stroking, soothing, caressing, fondling, patting. Rather, there is an enormously inimical side to what a touch can do when it takes violent forms, such as beating, slapping, kicking, hitting, punching, and, in some instances, penetrating. In this violent economy of touch, our skins, as collectors and registrars of tactile information, may function as an organ not only of protection but also of exposure (Nancy 1997). If we apprehend violation, appropriation, or exploitation as specific modes of touch, then touching one's skin manifests itself as a means of subjugation.

A touch, in its mutuality, can open one's body to other bodies. It is the most intimate cementing force of embodiment, which Sara Ahmed (2000b, 47) calls us to understand as a lived experience with other bodies or "the social experience of dwelling with other bodies." In this theorization, one's body can no longer be regarded as a private realm; rather, it is a realm of incessant opening to other bodies and thus a realm of vulnerability. Yet bodies cannot be thought of as unitary, as in a single category. A power differential between different bodies is intrinsic to the formation of this cartography of embodiment. Not everybody is deemed capable of touching other bodies the same way. One cannot assume the mutuality of touch to be symmetrical. While at the point of contact touching and being touched coincide, they are quite different—especially, for example, when pain results. Moreover, bodies are conditioned and condition themselves to one another in a set of unequal and uneven relations of power. These asymmetrical relations also shape how "bodies are touched by some bodies differently from other bodies" (ibid., 48). And some people may refuse to touch or be touched by others, or touch may be guided or prevented.

To further clarify, the management and mediation of contact between different social groups and communities has long been an effective political tool to implement projects of modernity, transform urban space, and organize city life (e.g., Davis 2007; Harvey 2012; Stallybrass and White 1986). One can recount these stories of modernization and gentrification also as stories of transformation in contact—and thus touch—between different social groups. For instance, displacement and forced mobility can be thought of as a haptic politics of population management that takes spatial forms through minimizing or at times eliminating the contact between people occupying different orders in the social hierarchy. Close contact with marginalized groups (e.g., sex workers, refugees and asylum seekers, the urban homeless) represents a source of contamination in the everyday discourse of the privileged, leading to manipulation and control of city life through the moral organization of contact (including, and paradigmatically, touch) between these groups. The disenfranchised groups thus find themselves deprived of certain forms of contact with the rest of the society.

Some touches are destructive and communicate power, oppression, and domination. Rape, for instance, is one of them. Hence it is crucial to draw attention once again to what Ahmed calls "economies of touch" to ruminate on how each touch, depending on distinct and complex conditionings of bodies to one another, forms and deforms bodies, lives, and communities. In a nutshell, touch has the power to discipline, and it works as a means of manipulation and control.

The question of who can enact and prevent particular forms of touching thus becomes a critical one. This position of tactility can be both the constituent and the product of specific forms of power, especially state power, taking governmental forms. Establishing more contact with individuals or groups (gays, minority ethnic women, the poor, etc.), for example, could be an emphasis on institutional practice and discourse. Reaching out to those people and making more contact with them could function as a governmental tool to render them more visible and proximate for the state power (Cooper 2013, 52–54).

Alternatively, the state power might regulate different forms of touch (sexual, desirous, etc.), defining normative meanings of touch and conditioning who can touch whom and when and how. One can approach regulations around areas like domestic abuse, child adoption, sex work, and pedophilia from this perspective. In these intimate and sexual domains of life, the state's regime of tactility and touch might be "protective," but it might also take coercive and violent forms. As Davina Cooper (ibid., 51) points out, "While touch can thwart or upset hierarchies, it frequently works to confirm and solidify relations of power."

Finally, the state might not operate its power on the structural grounds of a mutual civic touchability but ensure that the active role of touching is solely ascribed only to its own actors (cf. its monopoly of violence). Ultimately, torture and execution express the sovereign forms of violent touch under state rule. Routinely, this is performed by policing practices from the plain illegal to casual manhandling. Less obviously, it is institutionalized in medicolegal settings. My analysis below of two ethnographic settings, trans women's gender reassignment process and gay men's military exemption process, is particularly concerned with this latter form of institutional touch that is violent yet intimate. These two settings demonstrate at length how state control and regulation can be invested in particular forms of violent touch that are imbued with culturally specific morals; values; norms; and relations about gender, sex, and sexuality. The Turkish state's fixation with penetration as a medicolegal gender/sex corrective should be understood from this perspective.

Setting 1: Trans Women's Gender Reassignment and Public Hospitals

On a cold, rainy winter day, Seval, a twenty-two-year-old transgender woman sex worker, and I were sitting in her long, narrow, and poorly lit living room on the fifth floor of a high-rise building. She had recently had vaginal construction surgery and was telling me about her latest visit to one of the public education and research hospitals in Istanbul to get her vagina checked. Seval looked impatient and excited, because, as she articulated, her two-and-a-half-year-long painful and meticulous medicolegal gender reassignment process was finally coming to an end, and soon she would have her pink ID. The doctor had given Seval an instrument and advised her to use it regularly by pushing it in and out of her vagina so that her vagina could function "normally." She explained how this vaginal exercise was central to her receipt of the pink ID and that she had to undergo one more medical check, during which state medical authorities would put her newly reconstructed genitals under detailed scrutiny. They would insert an instrument into her vagina to ensure that it is "deep enough"—only if it is can she apply for her pink ID. I told Seval I had never heard of this test before and asked what the forensic people meant by a "deep enough" vagina. "A constructed vagina should be a minimum 3.5 inches deep," Seval continued (interview, February 2010). Even though there was no specific explanation about this measure in the legal code on transsexuality, Seval said she had a friend whose pink ID was rejected on the grounds of having a 1.5-inch-deep vagina, which meant that her friend lacked legal recognition as a female. After a few seconds of silence, she cracked a bitter joke with a forced smile: "The state rapes us to make sure we are female enough" (interview, February 2010).

In stressing the formation of "terrifying forms of intimacy" under state rule, Aretxaga (2003, 406) calls attention not only to the management of bodies and populations but also to "the intensification of bodies and intimacies that result from those technologies of management." Seval's narrative of her gender reassignment process is a strong account of one of those terrifying forms of intimacy. She recounts how the state's medicolegal technologies intensify the sex of her body through an institutional violent touch, through penetration, and, in her words, through rape. More precisely, when a trans woman's vagina achieves a desired capacity for penetration, the state grants her the pink ID card and bureaucratically incorporates her into its world of female citizens.

Changing the color of one's ID to either pink or blue is a substantial political concern for trans people in their fight, because it directly affects their everyday lives in various institutions, such as schools, hospitals, police stations, and other public offices. Yet this medicolegal process involves rigorous control and institutional supervision before the final step mentioned above, as the current regulation regarding transsexuality states:

> A person who wants to change her or his sex has to apply to the court and ask for permission for a sex reassignment. For this permission to be given, the applicant must be at the age of 18 and unmarried. Besides he or she must prove with an official health board report issued by an education and research hospital that he/she is of transsexual nature, that the sex reassignment is compulsory for her or his mental health and that he or she is permanently deprived of the capacity of reproduction. If it is confirmed by an official health board report that a sex reassignment operation was effected based on the permission given and in accordance with the purpose and medical methods, the court will decide in favor of the necessary changes being made to the civil status register. (Atamer 2005, 66)[4]

This legislation is rooted in the seven-year-long legal struggle of Bülent Ersoy, a trans woman singer, with the state for recognition as a female citizen. Until her case, transsexuality as a category did not exist in the Turkish legal system. The first "legitimate" transsexual woman in Turkey, Ersoy entered the music scene with a male body in 1971, and when she revealed her "true" sex as female and gender identity as a woman, she was banned from performing as a singer (with the coup d'état in 1981). This ban was enacted along with many other regulations inhibiting individual freedoms and rights in society at large that also targeted other trans people, including cross-dressers and drag queens. These measures caused Ersoy to flee the country for nine months. When she came back, she was a post-op trans woman, but official records still displayed her sex as male. Despite her persistent struggle to change her legal sex status to female, it took seven years for the state to recognize her status as a woman and issue her a pink ID.[5]

Ersoy is a key figure in trans people's history in Turkey, since she became the first trans woman whose sex was officially approved by the state. In 1988 her case led to the introduction of the first legal regulations regarding transsexual identity by attaching a new article to the Twenty-Ninth Clause of the Civil Code of 1926. The new article states, "In cases where there has been a change of sex after birth documented by a report from a committee of medical experts, the necessary amendments are made to the birth certificate" (Kandiyoti 1998, 22).[6] This article remained valid until 2002 and made it possible for trans people to apply for a new ID once they had their gender reassignment surgeries (GRSs). In other words, subsequent to their surgeries, if trans people proved their operations with medical reports, they could bring their reports to the court and easily obtain their new pink or blue IDs. The process was not strictly tied to institutional procedures, as it is by the current regulation, an amended version of the Fortieth Clause of the Civil Code, of 2002. Prior to this regulation, trans people did not need official reports of their GRSs. Nor was marital status an issue in changing one's official sex. If the person was married, her or his marriage automatically ceased on the receipt of a new ID, since the Turkish state did not (and still does not) recognize same-sex marriages. Also with this 2002 clause trans people are prevented from biologically reproducing.[7]

With this new article, a multi-institutional space has been constructed to evaluate what constitutes the transsexual "nature," because before, during, and after gender reassignment processes, the Turkish state insists that trans people modify their bodies and explore ways to prove their "true" gender identities. Gathering evidence of one's transsexual identity, which guarantees a pink or a blue ID card, is an arena in which the Turkish state actively and forcibly "materializes" sex "within the productive constraints of certain highly gendered regulatory schemas" (Butler 1993, xi). During my fieldwork in Istanbul in 2009–10, I spoke with numerous trans people who had struggled or who were struggling with this intricate medicolegal process to have their GRSs in public hospitals.[8] Part of this complicated and painstaking medicolegal process involves a medical report by psychiatrists that legally permits GRS. Generally, state psychiatrists in public hospitals manage these therapies, as private psychiatrists demand extreme amounts of money for therapy sessions. The state psychiatrists observe the applicant's transsexual identity to authorize GRS and state in his or her medical report that GRS is necessary for his or her psychological health. This report requires approximately two years of group therapy, during which trans people are evaluated in terms of their gender role performances (see Zengin 2014).[9]

Sometimes the final medical report of the board of doctors is not given any credibility in a courtroom. On receipt of their medical reports, trans people take them to the court and wait to hear the final verdict. In some cases judges simply dismiss the reports and make their own decisions. In addition to the final medical reports, judges also look at circumstances, including age and marital status. That is, the applicant must be a minimum of eighteen years old and must neither be married nor have any children. There are two important consequences to these regulations. First, the state renders the GRS a matter of age or adulthood. Second, it makes sure the family, as the heteronormative space of intimacy, is "untainted" by disorderly subjects. In other words, the law delineates the familial space as an arena that should be devoid of trans subjects, whose anatomy and sex changes break with culturally configured alliances of sex and gender, thus posing a threat to the normative organization of the intimate order.

Part of the dynamics that sustain this normative intimate order depends strictly on circulation and cultivation of particular orientations and desires. For example, "becoming straight" is the most prominent of those orientations and desires, and it can also be understood as a familial inheritance that necessitates that a child track a heterosexual life (Ahmed 2006). Ahmed (ibid., 85) says that "subjects are *required* to 'tend toward' some objects and not others as a condition of familial as well as social love" and explains "how heterosexuality can function as the most intimate and deadly of parental gifts," especially given those with queer desires who shy away from and refuse to carry the heterosexual heritage. Yet there is more to that. In addition to sexual orientation, gender identity is also a focus of family and social inheritance, and I want to stress that the conditions for transference of morals, values, codes, and norms through family ties are correspondingly fortified by law. It is not only about how people are required to orient themselves toward particular objects of love but also how they are expected to pay their debts to their families and the state by both inhabiting and inheriting ascribed sexual identities at birth. Otherwise they lose their right to reproduce, since family cannot be a space of transmitting these "undue" sexual orientations or identifications to younger generations.

Practices regarding juridical expulsion of trans people from the familial line make their way even further into trans people's bodies, exposing them to another violent touch by the state. In addition to controlling marital status and age, the law demands that trans people are permanently deprived of their reproductive capacities prior to their GRSs, and medical authorities at an education and research hospital must document their infertility. Hence reproducibility or biological continuation of the family, so to speak, becomes a privileged right of the nation's proper sexual and gendered subjects. In this way gender reassignment regulations strictly demarcate what an intimate trajectory for a trans life should be. In other words, the intimate forms that a trans life should and should not embrace become a prominent concern for the state, which forecloses the recognition and legitimacy of certain intimacies that have shaped or continue to shape its subjective investments in those lives.

Even when trans people get their official permissions and have their GRSs, they are not immediately delivered blue or pink IDs. They have to undergo one more medical examination before the court decides to change their sexual designations in census records. This last step involves Seval's account of "rape" at the beginning of this section. This particular violent touch, or penetration, is overwhelmingly concerned with the "law's phallocentric imperative" (Sharpe 2006, 621). It highlights how the success of gender reassignment is tied to patriarchal, phallocentric, and heterosexual assumptions about the female body. The female body is defined by its capacity to be sexually penetrated and is in large part equated with the presence of a vagina, which in turn merely functions as a site of male heterosexual desire. In that sense, the law does more than subject trans women to genital reconstruction for the purpose of approving their female identities. Charged with libidinal energies and heterosexual male fantasies, legal regulations aspire to assure that a trans woman's postsurgical genitals form an adequately penetrable vagina and that her desire is a heterosexual one. Andres Sharpe's (ibid., 623) analysis of this situation is illuminating: "Not only is heterosexual functioning scripted as a prerequisite to legal recognition. Rather, sexual function is understood as the end to be realized through the means of GRS. Here the value and meaning of surgery lies in the male to female body's capacity to be sexually penetrated." Heterosexual desire and fantasy condition these surgeries and hence checkpoints of sex, and penetration becomes the ultimate production of sex and thereby sexual difference at the state level.

This preoccupation with penetration as a regulatory measure can be observed in another institutional setting, that is, the Turkish military. Now turning to gay men's medical examinations for exemptions from obligatory military service, I will discuss how military medical personnel use penetration as an eliminatory tool to filter the due members of the military, namely, the "real" men from the "rotten" ones, namely, gay men. In this elimination process, the "inserter-insertee" (*aktif-pasif*) dichotomy in sexual intercourse becomes the criterion according to which the state reaffirms its share of sovereignty among only those men who perform hegemonic masculinity with a penetrative capacity.

Setting 2: Gay Men and the Military

In 2011 a two-page official document became one of the trendiest art pieces in the Twelfth İstanbul Biennale (see fig. 1). The gay artist, Kutluğ Ataman, exhibited his

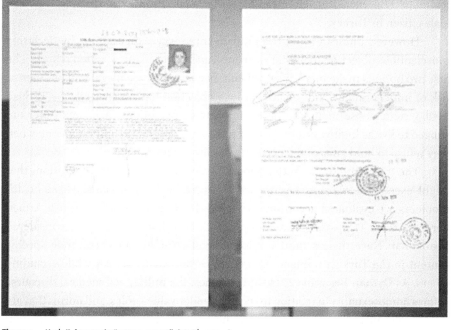

Figure 1. Kutluğ Ataman's "rotten report" (*çürük raporu*)

medical report, which was issued by a military hospital to authorize his exemption from obligatory military service, as a work of art in the section called İsimsiz (Ross). The document reads:

> Psychiatric Examination: His physical appearance fits his actual age. Not handicapped. His attention to his environment is normal. His self-care is fine. He is of quiet nature. His sociability is respectful. His speech is feminine. His tone of voice is feminine. His manners and gestures are feminine. His movements are feminine. He travels and walks around in his leisure times. His sleep is normal. His eating is normal. His urination is normal. (my translations here and below)[10]

On the second page the diagnosis section states, "Sexual behavior disorder (homosexuality [*homoseksüalite*])." The document concludes with the decision: "He is not eligible for military service at peace and war times" ("Barışta ve seferde askerliğe elverişli değildir"). This report, popularly known as a "rotten report" (*çürük raporu*) or "pink discharge paper" (*pembe tezkere*),[11] was issued to Ataman in 2010 after he underwent a medical examination to receive his exemption from military service. Military service in Turkey is obligatory for men, and as I mentioned earlier, it is one of the most prominent sites for the production of gendered life, particularly that of hegemonic masculinity (Açıksöz 2012). Along with the first heterosexual intercourse and marriage, military service epitomizes a rite of passage for "becoming a real man" (Biricik 2009; Helvacıoğlu 2006; Selek 2008), constructing the ideal male citizen in Turkey.

However, one can avoid the draft in three ways: by evading, by declaring conscientious objection to military violence, and by receiving a "rotten report." The first two options make men's lives difficult, because they are illegal and put men at risk of imprisonment. Since conscientious objection has no space in the Turkish legal system, those men who proclaim their conscientious objection either are obliged to live as fugitives from the criminal law or are sent to military prison when they refuse to hold guns and participate in military training.

The third option, the "rotten report," is tied to men's medical conditions that might excuse them from service due to severe health problems. These health problems are evaluated according to the Health Regulations for Turkish Armed Forces (Article 17, "psycho-sexual disorders"), and "homosexuality" is considered one of them. Nevertheless, the definition of homosexuality gains a culturally specific content in the Turkish military, embracing certain gay practices while excluding others. As Oyman Başaran (2014) aptly argues, the militarized medical discourse defines homosexuality in relation to specific gender values, roles, and norms that are socially and culturally considered "feminine" in Turkey, and it serves the production of "homosexuality" as an effeminate institutional category. While feminine gay men or male-bodied trans people obtain "rotten reports" relatively easily, gay men who deviate from effeminate appearance, characteristics, and roles, that is, the military's imagination of homosexuals, are subjected to a meticulous and difficult process. This will become clearer when I explain the medical inspections of men's gay identities step-by-step.

To request exemption from military service, a gay man first reports to the local military office in his district and gets a reference for the psychiatry division of the military hospital, where his stated health condition will be checked. He is not required to declare himself "homosexual" at the local office to obtain the reference; he can declare his status in the hospital. At the hospital he undergoes certain pro-cedures and medical inspections to prove himself "homosexual." His consultation with the psychiatry department is of great significance in shaping the next steps in his sexual orientation exemption (Biricik 2011). The psychiatry sessions include psychological tests, oral interviews, and observations of the applicant's behaviors and body language. The candidate can also be required to stay in the hospital for constant medical inspection for three days to two weeks until a final decision is made about his sexual orientation (Söyle 2012). During his stay in the hospital, he is observed in terms of his use of his body. For example, by looking at how he talks, walks, eats, sits, stands, and so forth, the military medical board assesses his level of "effeminacy."

However, in an interview with Fırat Söyle (2012), a lawyer struggling for the rights of lesbian, gay, bisexual, and transgender people in Istanbul and gay men who have undergone these inspections, he declared that the medical process is arbitrary and heavily dependent on doctors and military hospitals, since there is no clear regulation on the matter. For instance, until recently, gay men who were not found to be "homosexual" (or effeminate) enough by the doctors were asked to submit to the military medical committee visual material (photographs and videos) that revealed them as passive partners during copulation. This practice has been largely abandoned since 2009, as Söyle noted. Nevertheless, recently the committees have started to demand meetings with candidates' families. In these meetings the committee members ask parents about their children's sexuality and general manners to make their final assessments about candidates' sexual orientations. This has placed gay men in difficult situations, since not all of them are open with their families.

In a journal interview a gay man who had to submit pictures to the committee stated that these visuals had to be produced following specific rules to suffice as reliable evidence (*Turk Gay Club* 2011). For example, the pictures should be taken at the moment of sexual intercourse and clearly expose the candidate's face and the bodily area of sexual intercourse. In addition, the candidate should be portrayed as the passive partner and express obvious signs of taking pleasure in copulation. In other words, he is expected to display himself and his sexual desire pornographically. Meanwhile, the other partner, who is either active or fails to display feminine attitudes, is not considered ineligible for the draft. Strikingly, the man in the insertive role is peripheral to the scene and is not considered homosexual. Hence for the institutional gaze, neither the sexual activity nor the sex of the partners is the sole determinant of a gay identity, but the activity of a specific gender, that is, an assumed feminine position, marks a man as gay.

This "insertee-inserter" (*pasif-aktif*) dichotomy in sexual interaction greatly informs the military medical practice with regard to gay men in Turkey. The candidate suspected of a "homosexual nature" might also be subjected to tactile inspection by the military doctors, including rectal examination. Alp Biricik (2011, 80) argues that the medical inspection takes a penetrative form as the military medical personnel check the applicant's rectum to test whether the applicant has a loss of anal muscle control due to repeated sexual activity. The implicit assumption underlying this practice is that a man's capacity for penetrability determines whether he is homosexual enough. Occupying the role of the "recipient" partner in sexual intercourse denotes a "passive" position, which in turn demasculinizes and so (ef)feminizes the male body, excluding it from the membership of the masculine military community. This entire process is marked by sexual desires, pornographic leanings, and fantasies that are invested in the selection and militaristic production of "proper" male bodies of the nation, of who should (is permitted to) have access to a share of state power. In other words, the production of the nation's sovereign bodies, as Başaran (2007, 3) argues, is strictly tied to the production of hegemonic masculinity in relation to the production of femininity that is assumed to be embodied not only by the bodies of women but also by those of gay men. This femininity is defined by vulnerability, weakness, oversexuality, and, most significantly, passivity. Passivity, as the main identifier of femininity and as the capacity to be penetrated, is understood through a certain form of tactility that is proved via rectal examination or submitted pornographic visual material.

In sum, we should speak less of a complete institutional denial or foreclosure of same-sex desire or sexual activity and more of a "homosexuality" that functions as a particular category to define gay men who are feminized by being attributed specific gender roles and desires and physical attributes that are assumed to be part of a woman's nature. The military represents an institutional space in which "homosexual" male bodies are produced not only in relation to same-sex desire but also with regard to the production of dichotomous gender identities based on passive-active opposition. Through this production, the military gains a particular masculine, heterosexual, and penetrative content, which in turn defines the state in a similar vein.

Conclusion

The two settings presented here, trans women in public hospitals and gay men in military hospitals, are closely linked by a shared sexual intimacy: the institutional fixation with (penile) penetration (vaginal or anal). Whereas trans women eventually acquire their legal sex status as female on proving their vaginal capacity to receive a penis, military personnel consider men "homosexual" based on the corporeal clues of penetration in their rectums. Penetration thus becomes a medicolegal abstraction for gender identity and sexual orientation. To test its trans and gay citizens' claims on gender and sexuality, the state becomes considerably intimate with the bodies of its citizens. In fact, through its actors — the institution (hospital) and the individuals working for it (personnel) — it takes the active role of penetrator.

Earlier in this article I mentioned Aretxaga's (2003) emphasis on the formation of terrifying forms of intimacy and intensification of bodies under state rule. This intensification and intimacy takes routinized and governed forms of violence, as evidenced by the vaginal and anal checks in the above institutional settings in Turkey. The state's intense anal and vaginal scrutiny makes penetration an integral tool in its regulation of sex, gender, and sexuality and sets the stage for a violent politics of touch and tactility through this fixation with penetration.

An analysis of this taction, that is, the penetration, sheds light on an irrational component, that is, desire and fantasy, at the very heart of the state's rational techniques and regulations of sex and gender, operating as their engine. Each touch — the forensic technician's insertion of an instrument into a trans woman's vagina, the doctor's sterilization of a trans person, the military medical assistant's examination of a gay man's rectum — is a projection of heterosexual drives and desires that permeate the state's regulation of sex, gender, and sexuality. The state transgresses the bodies of its citizens by incorporating sexual and gendering practices derived from particular heterosexual desires and fantasies that ascribe to the institutional actor the position of the penetrator. These intensely felt proximities between the state's institutional actors and the bodies of its citizen are in fact integral to modern disciplinary practices and rational technologies of control. In this context, the state gains a specific content, that is, an active penetrating, masculinist, male, and heteronormative body.

That this occurs in the hospital setting is interesting insofar as hospitals are assumed to be sites of recovery from ill health. In these inspections nothing is healed, since there is no disease to start with other than the social "illness" of transgression. The medical doctors serving as state actors execute specific legislations in a heteronormative framework either to disambiguate gender nonconforming subjects or to eliminate sexually transgressive subjects from the state's male military body. The individuals performing this execution are essentially rendered invisible, but the structural framework in which sex/gender transgression is examined and proved also enables abuse. Not only does the framework itself thus abuse, but this heteronormativity renders the vulnerable trans and gay persons, as feminine, subject to the masculine state.

The above mentioned medical practices and regulations place the bodies of sex/gender nonconforming people in an economy of institutional touch. In that sense, this medium of state power, namely, touch, renders a sensorial approach both useful and necessary, especially when one analyzes the state's governance of sex and gender, sexuality and desire, and intimacy. The politics of touch and tactility allows us to think creatively not only about the organization of intimate state power but also about the production and regulation of sex/gender difference, the normative domain of sexuality and desire, and "properly" sexed bodies. While partly building on the foreclosure of the recognition and legitimacy of certain desires, gendered subjectivities, and intimacies by the modern state (Povinelli 2002, 2006), this analytic framework broadens the discussion in examining how the state itself becomes an actor producing its citizens as intimate subjects and how it uses touch as a political tool to define, categorize, and govern sex, gender, and sexuality. The dominant categories of sex, gender, and sexuality are defined through the formation of the violent intimacies and proximities between state actors and sex/gender nonconforming people, such as in the cases of trans women and gay men in the spaces of Turkish hospitals. And a focus on these violent proximities and forms of contact allows us to understand intimate state politics enabled by the mediation and governance of violence at the intersection of state power, the bodies of sex/gender transgressive people, their senses of self, their sexualities, and the institutional gaze and touch.

ASLI ZENGIN is an anthropologist and postdoctoral fellow in the Women's, Gender, and Sexuality Studies Program at Brandeis University (www.brandeis.edu/facultyguide /department.html?deptid=24700). Zengin has widely published in peer-reviewed journals, including *Anthropologica* and *Transgender Studies Quarterly*, and edited volumes. Contact: a.zengin@gmail.com.

Acknowledgments

I wish to thank those scholars who contributed to the discussions in this article at several workshops at the University of Toronto, the University of Arizona, and the University of Michigan–Ann Arbor. My special thanks go to Tom Boellstorff, Naisargi Dave, Aaron Kappeler, Michael Lambek, Maya Mikdashi, Andrea Muehlebach, Malini Sur, Holly Wardlow, my three anonymous reviewers, and the editors of *JMEWS* for their invaluable feedback on different versions of this article.

Notes

1. Data with regard to the first are derived from ethnographic research conducted in Istanbul in 2009–10 for my doctoral research. I conducted in-depth interviews with fourteen trans women, four trans men, and seven service providers (individual professionals, including social workers, doctors, lawyers, and therapists and counselors). For the second case study, I use secondhand ethnographic material.

2. This understanding is reflected also in the colloquial language and finds a widespread expression for sexual intercourse mainly as an insertion of a penis.

3. The correspondence between the active-passive distinction and gender identification has been widely examined by anthropologists in Latin American, Mediterranean, and Middle Eastern contexts. For further cross-cultural ethnographic studies on the role of sexual acts in constituting gender identity, see Almaguer 1993; Johnson 1997; Kulick 1998; Parker 1986; Wikan 1977.

4. The English translation of the code is taken from Yeşim M. Atamer's (2005) work on the legal status of transsexuals in Turkey.

5. For a more detailed description and analysis of Ersoy's legal struggle, see Rüstem Ertuğ Altınay's (2008) and Başak Ertür and Alisa Lebow's (2012) elaborate pieces on the issue.

6. Amendment to the Twenty-Ninth Clause of Law no. 743, Turkish Civil Code, May 12, 1988. The English translation of the code is taken from Kandiyoti 1998.

7. See Kurtoğlu 2009 for a detailed discussion of the ban on trans people's biological reproductive rights and its role in the imagination of a sexual citizenship in Turkey.

8. GRSs in Turkey include trans people's bottom and top surgeries, ranging from genital reconfiguration to breast implantation for trans women and breast removal for trans men.

9. These medical models are international and were imported to Turkey in the early 2000s. Doctors in Turkey accept the Standards of Care for the Health of Transsexual, Transgender, and Gender-Nonconforming People set by Harry Benjamin (World Professional Association for Transgender Health 2012).

10. "Ruhsal Muayenesi: Dış görünümü yaşında. Ayakta. Çevresine ilgisi normal. Özbakımı iyi. Mizacı sakin. Sosyabilitesi saygılı. Konuşma efemine. Ses tonu efemine. Mimik ve jestleri efemine. Hareketler efemine. Serbest zamanlarında gezer dolaşır. Uyku tabii. Yeme tabii. İşeme tabii."

11. None of these titles are official, yet they are popularly used in public to refer to one's ineligibility for the draft.

References

Abrams, Philip. 1988. "Notes on the Difficulty of Studying the State (1977)." *Journal of Historical Sociology* 1, no. 1: 58–89. DOI:10.1111/j.1467-6443.1988.tb00004.x.

Açıksöz, Salih Can. 2012. "Sacrificial Limbs of Sovereignty: Disabled Veterans, Masculinity, and Nationalist Politics in Turkey." *Medical Anthropology Quarterly* 26, no. 1: 4–25. DOI:10.1111/j.1548-1387.2011.01194.x.

Ahmed, Sara. 2000. *Strange Encounters: Embodied Others in Post-coloniality.* London: Routledge.

———. 2006. *Queer Phenomenology: Orientations, Objects, Others.* Durham, NC: Duke University Press.

Almaguer, Tomas. 1993. "Chicano Men: A Cartography of Homosexual Identity and Behavior." In *The Lesbian and Gay Studies Reader*, edited by Henry Abelove, Michèle Aina Barale, and David M. Halperin, 255–73. New York: Routledge.

Altınay, Rüstem Ertuğ. 2008. "Reconstructing the Transgendered Self as a Muslim, Nationalist, Upper-class Woman: The Case of Bulent Ersoy." *Women's Studies Quarterly* 36, no. 3: 210–29. DOI:10.1353/wsq.0.0090.

Aretxaga, Begoña. 2003. "Maddening States." *Annual Review of Anthropology* 32: 393–410.

Atamer, Yeşim M. 2005. "The Legal Status of Transsexuals in Turkey." *International Journal of Transgenderism* 8, no. 1: 65–71.

Baba, H. Burcu. 2011. "The Construction of Heteropatriarchal Family and Dissident Sexualities in Turkey." *Fe Dergi (Fe Journal)* 3, no. 1: 56–64.

Başaran, Oyman. 2007. "Militarized Medical Discourse on Homosexuality and Hegemonic Masculinity in Turkey." MA thesis, Boğaziçi University.

———. 2014. "'You Are like a Virus': Dangerous Bodies and Military Medical Authority in Turkey." *Gender and Society* 28, no. 4: 562–82. DOI:10.1177/0891243214526467.

Bereket, Tarik, and Barry D. Adam. 2006. "The Emergence of Gay Identities in Contemporary Turkey." *Sexualities* 9, no. 2: 131–51. DOI:10.1177/1363460706063116.

———. 2008. "Navigating Islam and Same-Sex Liaisons among Men in Turkey." *Journal of Homosexuality* 55, no. 2: 204–22. DOI:10.1080/00918360802129428.

Berlant, Lauren. 1997. *The Queen of America Goes to Washington City: Essays on Sex and Citizenship.* Durham, NC: Duke University Press.

Biricik, Alp. 2009. "Rotten Report and Reconstructing Hegemonic Masculinity in Turkey." In *Conscientious Objection Resisting Militarized Society*, edited by Özgür Heval Çınar and Coşkun Üsterci, 112–17. London: Zed.

———. 2011. "The 'Rotten Report' and the Reproduction of Masculinity, Nation, and Security in Turkey." In *Making Gender, Making War: Violence, Military, and Peacekeeping Practices*, edited by Annica Kronsell and Erika Svedberg, 76–89. New York: Routledge.

Butler, Judith. 1993. *Bodies That Matter: On the Discursive Limits of Sex.* New York: Routledge.

Cooper, Davina. 2013. *Everyday Utopias: The Conceptual Life of Promising Spaces.* Durham, NC: Duke University Press.

Das, Veena, and Deborah Poole. 2004. "State and Its Margins: Comparative Ethnographies." In *Anthropology in the Margins of the State*, edited by Veena Das and Deborah Poole, 3–33. Santa Fe, NM: School of American Research Press.

Davis, Mike. 2007. *Planet of Slums.* London: Verso.

Dean, Mitchell. 2001. "'Demonic Societies': Liberalism, Biopolitics, and Sovereignty." In *States of Imagination: Ethnographic Explorations of the Postcolonial State*, edited by Thomas Blom Hansen and Finn Stepputat, 41–64. Durham, NC: Duke University Press.

Durakbaşa, Ayşe. 1998. "Kemalism as Identity Politics in Turkey." In *Deconstructing Images of Turkish Women*, edited by Zehra Arat, 139–57. New York: St. Martin's.

Ertür, Başak, and Alisa Lebow. 2012. "Şöhretin Sonu: Bülent Ersoy'un Kanunla İmtihanı" ("The End of Fame: Bulent Ersoy's Test with the Law"). In *Cinsellik Muamması: Türkiye'de Kültür ve Muhalefet* (*Riddle of Sexuality: Culture and Opposition in Turkey*), edited by Cüneyt Çakılar and Serkan Delice, 391–426. Istanbul: Metis.

Foucault, Michel. 1980. *The History of Sexuality.* Vol. 1, *An Introduction*, translated by Robert Hurley. New York: Vintage.

———. 1982. "The Subject and Power: An Afterword." In *Michel Foucault: Beyond Structuralism and Hermeneutics*, edited by Hubert L. Dreyfus and Paul Rabinow, 214–32. New York: Harvester Wheatsheaf.

———. 1988. *Madness and Civilization: A History of Insanity in the Age of Reason*, translated by Richard Howard. New York: Vintage.

———. 1991. "Governmentality," translated by Pasquale Pasquino. In *The Foucault Effect: Studies in Governmentality*, edited by Graham Burchell, Colin Gordon, and Peter Miller, 87–104. Chicago: University of Chicago Press.

———. 1995. *Discipline and Punish: The Birth of the Prison*, translated by Alan Sheridan. New York: Vintage.

———. 2004. *Abnormal: Lectures at the Collège de France, 1974–1975*, translated by Graham Burchell. New York: Picador.

Gorkemli, Serkan. 2012. " 'Coming Out of the Internet': Lesbian and Gay Activism and the Internet as a 'Digital Closet' in Turkey." *Journal of Middle East Women's Studies* 8, no. 3: 63–88.

Hansen, Thomas Blom, and Finn Stepputat. 2005. *Sovereign Bodies: Citizens, Migrants, and States in the Postcolonial World*. Princeton, NJ: Princeton University Press.

Harvey, David. 2012. *Rebel Cities: From the Right to the City to the Urban Revolution*. New York: Verso.

Helvacıoğlu, Banu. 2006. "The Smile of Death and the Solemncholy of Masculinity." In *Islamic Masculinities*, edited by Lahoucine Ouzgane, 35–56. New York: Zed.

Johnson, Mark. 1997. *Beauty and Power: Transgendering and Cultural Transformation in the Southern Philippines*. Oxford: Berg.

Kandiyoti, Deniz A. 1987. "Emancipated but Unliberated? Reflections on the Turkish Case." *Feminist Studies* 13, no. 2: 317–38.

———. 1998. "Transsexuals and the Urban Landscape in Istanbul." *Middle East Report*, no. 206: 20–25.

Koğacıoğlu, Dicle. 2004. "The Tradition Effect: Framing Honor Crimes in Turkey." *differences: A Journal of Feminist Cultural Studies* 15, no. 2: 119–51.

Kulick, Don. 1998. *Travesti: Sex, Gender, and Culture among Brazilian Transgendered Prostitutes*. Chicago: University of Chicago Press.

Kurtoğlu, Ayca. 2009. "Sex Reassignment, Biological Reproduction, and Sexual Citizenship in Turkey." *Fe Dergi* (*Fe Journal*) 1, no. 2: 79–88.

Lauretis, Teresa de. 1987. *Technologies of Gender: Essays on Theory, Film, and Fiction*. Bloomington: Indiana University Press.

Mbembe, Achille. 2005. "Necropolitics." *Public Culture* 15, no. 1: 11–40.

Montagu, Ashley. 1971. *Touching: The Human Significance of the Skin*. New York: Harper and Row.

Nancy, Jean-Luc. 1997. *The Sense of the World*. Minneapolis: University of Minnesota Press.

Navaro-Yashin, Yael. 2002. *Faces of the State: Secularism and Public Life in Turkey*. Princeton, NJ: Princeton University Press.

Özbay, Cenk. 2010. "Nocturnal Queers: Rent Boys' Masculinity in Istanbul." *Sexualities* 13, no. 5: 645–63.

Öztürk, Mustafa Bilgehan. 2011. "Sexual Orientation Discrimination: Exploring the Experiences of Lesbian, Gay, and Bisexual Employees in Turkey." *Human Relations* 64, no. 8: 1099–1118.

Parker, Richard. 1986. "Masculinity, Femininity, and Homosexuality: On the Anthropological Inter-pretation of Sexual Meanings in Brazil." *Journal of Homosexuality* 11, nos. 3–4: 155–63.

Povinelli, Elizabeth A. 2002. "Notes on Gridlock: Genealogy, Intimacy, Sexuality." *Public Culture* 14, no. 1: 215–38.

———. 2006. *The Empire of Love: Toward a Theory of Intimacy, Genealogy, and Carnality*. Durham, NC: Duke University Press.

Pratt, Geraldine, and Victoria Rosner. 2006. "Introduction: The Global and the Intimate." *Women's Studies Quarterly* 34, nos. 1–2: 13–24.

Rodaway, Paul. 1994. *Sensuous Geographies: Body, Sense, and Place*. London: Routledge.

Segal, Naomi. 2009. *Consensuality: Didier Anzieu, Gender, and the Sense of Touch*. Amsterdam: Rodopi.

Selek, Pınar. 2008. *Sürüne Sürüne Erkek Olmak* (*Struggle to Become a Man*). Istanbul: Iletisim Yayinlari.

Sharma, Aradhana, and Akhil Gupta. 2006. Introduction to *The Anthropology of the State*, edited by Aradhana Sharma and Akhil Gupta, 1–42. Malden, MA: Blackwell.

Sharpe, Andrew. 2006. "From Functionality to Aesthetics: The Architecture of Transgender Jur-isprudence." In *The Transgender Studies Reader*, edited by Susan Stryker and Stephen Whittle, 621–32. London: Routledge.

Sirman, Nukhet. 1989. "Feminism in Turkey: A Short History." *New Perspectives on Turkey* 3, no. 1: 1–34.

———. 2007. "Constituting the Modern Family as the Social in the Transition from Empire to Nation-State." In *Ways to Modernity in Greece and Turkey: Encounters with Europe, 1850–1950*, edited by Anna Frangoudaki and Caglar Keyder, 176–90. London: Tauris.

Söyle, Fırat. 2012. "'Pembe tezkere'ye koğuş işkencesi" ("Torture in Ward for Pink Certificate"). Interview by Elif Ince. *Radikal*, April 15. www.radikal.com.tr/turkiye/pembe-tezkereye-kogus-iskencesi-1084969.

Stallybrass, Peter, and Allon White. 1986. *The Politics and Poetics of Transgression*. Ithaca, NY: Cornell University Press.

Stoler, Ann Laura. 2002. *Carnal Knowledge and Imperial Power: Race and the Intimate in Colonial Rule*. Berkeley: University of California Press.

———. 2006. "Intimidations of Empire: Predicaments of the Tactile and Unseen." In *Haunted by Empire: Geographies of Intimacy in North American History*, edited by Ann Laura Stoler, 1–22. Durham, NC: Duke University Press.

Tapınç, Hüseyin. 1992. "Masculinity, Femininity, and Turkish Male Homosexuality." In *Modern Homosexualities: Fragments of Lesbian and Gay Experiences*, edited by Ken Plummer, 39–49. London: Routledge.

Turk Gay Club. 2011. "Pembe Teskere ve Çürük Raporu Alan Eşcinsel Askerler Konuşuyor!" ("Those Soldiers with Pink Certificate and Rotten Report Talk!"). December 23. news.turkgayclub.com /yasam/3929-pembe-tezkere-curuk-raporu-alan-askerler-konusuyor.html.

Wikan, Unni. 1977. "Man Becomes Woman: Transsexualism in Oman as a Key to Gender Roles." *Man*, n.s., 12, no. 2: 304–19.

World Professional Association for Transgender Health. 2012. "Standards of Care for the Health of Transsexual, Transgender, and Gender-Nonconforming People." 7th version. www.wpath.org /uploaded_files/140/files/Standards%20of%20Care,%20V7%20Full%20Book.pdf.

Zengin, Aslı. 2011. *Iktidarin Mahremiyeti: Istanbul'da Hayat Kadinlari, Seks Isciligi ve Siddet* (*Intimacy of Power: Prostitutes, Sex Work, and Violence in Istanbul*). Istanbul: Metis.

———. 2014. "Sex for Law, Sex for Psychiatry: Pre–Sex Reassignment Surgical Psychotherapy in Turkey." *Anthropologica* 56, no. 1: 55–68.

REVIEW ESSAY

Women's Worlds in Qajar Iran
Digital Archive and Website
A Report

AFSANEH NAJMABADI

Women's Worlds in Qajar Iran (WWQI) is a digital archive of nineteenth-century Iranian culture that focuses on the lives of women and issues of gender. The initial inspiration for the project arose more than a decade ago from a coming together of intellectual frustration and technological possibility.

The 1970s through the 1990s witnessed an explosion of women's history and the gendering of historical research and writing, but this development had a highly uneven global scope. The unevenness was not only geographic. While certain sub-fields of history proved more open to revisionary explorations, their broader integration into "doing history" remained marginal. In Middle Eastern historiography, for instance, gendering histories of the nation has produced important works on Egypt, Syria, Iran, the Ottoman Empire, and modern Turkey, but these works often remain at the margins of the field. Histories of Iran's Qajar dynasty (1796–1925) continue to be produced in the dominant mode of political history. Social and cultural history in general and histories inclusive of women and gender analysis more particularly remain all but nonexistent.

The exclusion of women from histories of the Qajar period was all the more troubling because many Qajar women lived culturally rich and active lives, including as writers and poets, calligraphers and painters, religious leaders, and, in the final decades, as social critics and activists. Yet gendered analysis in historiographies of the period remained sparse. The main reason historians of Qajar Iran offered for this situation was that sources for doing Qajar history differently did not exist. It is true that historians of Qajar Iran do not have institutional records and state archives comparable to those of historians of the neighboring Ottoman Empire or South

JMEWS • Journal of Middle East Women's Studies • 12:2 • July 2016
DOI 10.1215/15525864-3507661 • © 2016 by the Association for Middle East Women's Studies

Asia. Nonetheless, the apparent lack of archival sources is also an artifact of the predominant state-centered focus of political history. This intellectual tunnel vision has virtually precluded the possibility of asking some rather obvious questions. If the state did not preserve statistics, legal records, and other documents in an archival style ready for our research, where might we locate alternative memory traces? Where and how, for instance, did people preserve necessary contractual information and life registers?

The paucity of sources then becomes not a question of absence but of inaccessibility. For instance, prior to the late 1920s, when the law began to require registration of births and other life events and recording of commercial transactions, families recorded such information on the first pages of the family Quran or other cherished books and objects. Marriage contracts, endowments, wills, and other legal papers were kept at home or entrusted to local village headmen or neighborhood religious notables. In other words, these documents did exist, but not in state or national archives or in any recognized private libraries.

But how could any researcher be expected to spend a lifetime going from family to family, from one local notable to another, from one cemetery to the next, to assemble a usable archive? The emerging Internet technologies offered a perfect tool for consolidation of these materials into a globally accessible virtual archive.

Begun in 2002–3, the WWQI was not a neat and cleanly conceived idea, and many years of slow incubation and maturation and failed grant applications passed before a team of five Qajar-era scholars (Dominic Brookshaw, Manoutchehr Eskandari-Qajar, Nahid Mozaffari, Naghmeh Sohrabi, and myself) received its first major grant from the National Endowment for the Humanities in 2009. The early failed attempts reflect the challenge we faced in articulating persuasively an imagined project that did not have any obvious prior model and that offered possibilities for historical preservation and research beyond its own domain of Qajar women's history.

Unlike most digitized archives, the WWQI did not begin with a discrete collection or even collections. Instead, the writings, photographs, and other primary source materials that the WWQI is digitizing are dispersed across myriad locations and among numerous owners. It is extremely unlikely that these materials would or could ever be released to research institutions en masse in part because of their dispersed ownership but also because of the personal value many of these items hold for their present owners. Captured in digital form, they have *become* an archive.

Initially imagined as a modest project — we had anticipated generating some three thousand images over the first two years — the WWQI has grown beyond our wildest dreams thanks to the overwhelmingly positive responses of families and institutions in Iran and elsewhere. As of October 2015 we had 114 family and institutional collections comprised of 4,360 items and over 35,000 images.

The initial selection of collections depended on availability — on the collaboration of families our team members happened to know. Once the project took shape and became known, we had the opportunity to discuss in our periodic workshops how we could more proactively overcome emerging limitations of the social, geographic, and cultural diversity of the archive. For instance, we have addressed the issue of how not to be limited to the urban elite by reaching out to families with a line of local religious leadership and digitizing the voluminous books of neighborhood registries they hold. More recently, local historians in Iran have made available to us the results of their own archival work — a collaboration that has enabled us to extend the geographic domain of the archive to remote areas that our own resources could never reach. The archive now holds material located in Tehran, Qazvin, Yazd, Kurdistan, Isfahan, Azerbaijan, Mashhad, and several cities in the United States, Europe, Canada, and Australia and material made available to us from major archival institutions, including Majlis Library and Document Center (in Tehran), Malek Library and Museum (in Tehran), National Library and Archives of the Islamic Republic of Iran (in Tehran, Tabriz, and Yazd), Tabriz Central Library, Tehran University Central Library, Center for the Great Islamic Encyclopedia (in Tehran), Institute for Iranian Contemporary Historical Studies (in Tehran), Mossadegh Foundation (in Geneva), International Institute for Social History (in Amsterdam), Astan-i Quds Razavi (in Mashhad), Qajar Museum (in Tabriz), Center for Media Studies (in Isfahan), and Center for Iranian Jewish Oral History (in Beverly Hills).

The project has depended on teams of trained and dedicated assistants in Tehran and Cambridge, Massachusetts, including skilled readers of nineteenth-century handwriting, photographers, data-generating staff, and dedicated project managers. Digital images are preserved in perpetuity as part of the Harvard University Library's digital collections but are architecturally built in interaction with a public website that makes deployment of the latest smart search features possible, even on your smart phone. The process of digitization and data creation, from our first meetings with a family all the way to the material's delivery to the Harvard University Library, has recently been captured in a video essay by Nicole Legnani (2015).

The archive includes poetry, essays and treatises, travelogues, letters, marriage contracts and other legal documents, photographs, works of art, images of everyday objects, and a small collection of oral histories. The website is fully bilingual (Persian and English), and its search function includes filters for major categories, like genre, collection, people, subject, place, and period, allowing users to drill down into the archive and narrow their search results. Digitized images provide detailed views of each object with additional descriptive content.

One recently developed feature is a research platform that offers three distinct threads: Questions and Discussions, Research-in-Progress, and Contributions. All these features can easily link to and draw items from the main archival site. Modifications of the main site now enable users to go from any item display page to the platform. Another innovation contributing to the recovery of microhistories of women's lives is that every person in our database now has a page displaying all the information we have on that person. Dynamic visual time lines of relevant events, biographies in both short and long versions, and hyperlinks to related people and items offer scholars a clearer view of the world inhabited by the individuals in our archive. In a link to our research platform, users can contribute to the biographical information on each person.

As we continue to identify, digitize, and preserve additional materials, we will also add new website features to facilitate researchers' and teachers' use of the archives. For instance, we plan interactive family genealogies and maps that will streamline by many factors researchers' ability to establish connection between the disparate tidbits of data embedded in the archive's primary source materials. This kind of "data connectivity" will make possible a level of research and writing that is virtually unthinkable at the present time. We will also add guided tours with audio, curated by experts in the field, that will take the viewer through a thematic selection of the WWQI holdings.

As exciting as the project of fabricating the archive has been, the question remains: What could we do with it that was not possible or even imaginable without it?

First, at the most obvious level, it is our hope that the issue of nonexistent archival sources can now be put to rest. Second, the sheer mass of some of the documents makes it possible to pursue new kinds of historical research with ease. For example, we currently have close to four hundred marriage contracts ranging from those of the daughters of Fath 'Ali Shah (r. 1797–1834) to those of more modest families, including servants whose marriage contracts were held by the families where they lived and served. While a single marriage contract in one's own family would hardly lend itself to historical analysis, a large number of them make it possible to study the details of class and status among spouses, comparing amounts and kinds of bridal gifts recorded and conditions embedded in different contracts. Moreover, since these contracts come from Muslim, Jewish, and Armenian families, it is now possible to compare the textual and illustrational details of these contracts across various communities.

The more exciting possibility, however, is that by uniting multiple genres of sources—textual documents, visual materials, everyday objects, recorded memories, and so forth—in one virtual place, the WWQI will make it easier to do history differently.

People in the past, as today, did not just write letters, books, newspaper articles—all the usual textual material that comprises the vast majority of archival sources that most historians use. These texts were intimately bound up with and acquired their meaning from the practices of everyday life. Even when we cannot witness these practices firsthand, we can find traces of them in objects, photographs, oral histories, and so forth. Reading a text through related objects and spaces in connection with sounds and memories, we can gain new insights that would be impossible to reach by reading the text alone. Recent works by cultural historians and interdisciplinary scholars have shown how fruitful this multigenre approach can be.

Several features of the WWQI archive enable us to build on these gains. As we meet with families and work through their holdings to choose what is relevant for our digitization, we listen and digitally record their small and large stories about these objects. We tag these recordings and preserve them in our archives as audio clippings linked with the objects, thus preserving something of the memory-context of the objects, which is usually not possible with regular archives. Digital technologies have made it possible for the WWQI not only to virtually consolidate otherwise inaccessible sources but also to provide online tools that allow users to explore and analyze these sources across genres. We hope it will inspire researchers to pursue new ways of thinking and writing about history.

AFSANEH NAJMABADI is Francis Lee Higginson Professor of History and of Studies of Women, Gender, and Sexuality at Harvard University. Contact: najmabad@fas.harvard.edu.

Acknowledgments

This report is based on earlier presentations of Women's Worlds in Qajar Iran at the Massachusetts Institute of Technology in October 2012, Brown University in October 2013, and New York University in October 2015 and on Najmabadi 2013.

References

Legnani, Nicole. 2015. *Workflows: Women's World in Qajar Iran*, November 24. www.youtube.com /watch?v=N9BdK_OYRGI&feature=share.

Najmabadi, Afsaneh. 2013. "Women's Worlds in Qajar Iran Digital Archive and Website: What Could Writing History Look like in a Digital Age?" *Perspectives on History*, November, 32–34.

Unraveling the Bindings of Muslim Women
Agency, Politics, Piety, and Performance

AFIYA S. ZIA and SHAHRZAD MOJAB

Performing Piety: Singers and Actors in Egypt's Islamic Revival. Karin Van Nieuwkerk.
Austin: University of Texas Press, 2013. 320 pages. ISBN 9781477302255 paper

The Veil in Kuwait: Gender, Fashion, Identity. Thorsten Botz-Bornstein and
Noreen Abdullah-Khan. New York: Palgrave Macmillan, 2014. 89 pages.
ISBN 9781137487414 cloth

Women in the Mosque: A History of Legal Thought and Social Practice.
Marion Holmes Katz. New York: Columbia University Press, 2014. 417 pages.
ISBN 9780231162661 cloth

Soft Force: Women in Egypt's Islamic Awakening. Ellen Anne McLarney. Princeton, NJ:
Princeton University Press, 2015. 312 pages. ISBN 9780691158495 paper

These books are recent contributions to the continuing debate about Arab women and their affective engagement with Islam. The two overlapping themes in these publications are, first, the appeal and perspective of a post-Islamist political society in Muslim majority contexts, primarily using Egypt as an example, and, second, probing the older theme of *fitna,* the distracting potential of women's sexuality and bodies and the ways it has been reclaimed and co-opted in the new millennium, often in collusion with neoliberal patriarchal capitalism. In the context of this broad framing, one should also note that, with the exception of *Soft Force,* the books in this review demonstrate an excitement about a supposed post–Arab Spring. However, the post-Islamist wave carried on the back of pietist and/or Islamist women offered in these texts is not entirely convincing.

Performing Piety documents the lives of several famous Egyptian female singers, dancers, and actresses who left the entertainment business in the wake of the Islamic revival of the 1990s and devoted themselves to religious studies and worship. Karin Van Nieuwkerk documents the life stories of these "repentant" veiled artists, crediting this turn in the history of the entertainment trade as a "history-in-miniature of Egypt more generally" (5). The author summarizes and takes as her base the redefinition and exploration (arguably, subversion) of the notion of "agency" as offered by Saba Mahmood (2005) and Sherine Hafez (2011) in their studies on women's piety in the mosque movement in Egypt. Rather than empowerment, the significance of "moral agency" as expressed through piety is confirmed by the self-transformation and moral worth described by "repentant" women artists.

Nieuwkerk's thesis springs from this theoretical spiral, where agency uncoils itself from limited readings of power relations and daily realities and leaps into the self-presentations and "staged presentations and constructed narratives" of ideals and imagined perfection of and by the pious subject (9). The author acknowledges the powerful influence of the celebrities who became the "moral touchstones" of religious and nationalist worldviews for millions of adulating fans. Recognizing the class-based character of her case study of middle- and upper-middle-class "repentant" performers, Nieuwkerk argues that their impact on millions of consumers should not be underestimated and is "warmly embraced by the Islamists" (5). The (less) popular performers simply could not afford the same choice as the stars. The author argues that this spread of piety in the 1990s enabled the development of "pious markets" for leisure and art. The author weaves in sociopolitical debates in the polemics of public spaces where secularists and Islamists debated art and gender in the 1990s (probably the most interesting part of the book) and argues that this mission of popularizing Islam through aesthetics has created a genre in itself. One of the central arguments in the book is how Islamists in Egypt have consciously carried this project through deliberate contradistinction from liberal-secular artistic sensibilities. It qualifies too how among themselves Islamists disagreed on the limits of artistic infiltration into the larger moral-ethical project and how this created tensions between Salafists and *al-wasatiyya* (a moderate Islamist trend) (37).

Divided into three parts, *Performing Piety* begins with the spiritual biographies of the retired performers Nieuwkerk interviewed to illustrate the trajectory of these artists toward piety. The artists include the actress (Shams al-Barudi), the dancer (Hala al-Safi), and the singer (Yasmin al-Khiyyam). Their corresponding paths to spiritual journeys in the 1980s include dreams and visions, *Da'wah* (Islamic outreach/instruction), and charity, respectively. Nieuwkerk analyzes each interview and reveals her broader interest in reviewing the transformation of the Islamist movements through the lens of the performing arts.

The second part explores the public debates between secularists and Islamists on the changing discourses on art and gender. The third part situates contemporary and competing discussions on concepts of post-Islamism, religious markets, and

Islamic aesthetics. The discussion in the last three chapters raises key questions about the impact and consequences of piety movements. Contestations over art with a mission (*fann al-hadif*) were not just offered by way of secular criticism. The older and more orthodox Islamists are deeply critical of what they mock as "air-conditioned Islam" or "market Islam." They apply these pejorative labels to the populist preaching of new Islamists, who hold that piety and prestige can coexist and that wealth is a sign of being chosen by God (202). Nieuwkerk offers a comparative discussion of Oliver Roy and Asef Bayat's different understandings of this transformation and whether it qualifies as "post-Islamism." This last section also opens the debate on whether Islamic consumption has led to genuine transformation or the Islamist movement has just been (willingly?) co-opted by global capitalism (231).

While *Performing Piety* documents artists' efforts to fashion Islamic piety as a contradictory vehicle for promoting the arts (and vice versa), *The Veil in Kuwait* surveys Islamic veiling at the Gulf University for Science and Technology (GUST) as a fashion phenomenon. This book is an interview-based study examining the hypothesis that veiling fashion and reveiling are bridges between religious veiling and nonreligious cultural fashion. Thorsten Botz-Bornstein and Noreen Abdullah-Khan argue that women's morality can be adjusted through veiling, since the concept of *fitna* is linked to the economy of guilt, which implies that women are permanently guilty of causing potential sexual shame in society. The study concludes that the veil is at best an ambiguous signifier and contradicts the notion of a post-Islamist society just because of some performative proof of the veil coexisting with seemingly contradictory fashion. In fact, the authors argue that rather than proving a comfortable Kuwaiti moderate religious consciousness, the apparent fusion of religion and fashion actually reinforces both (71).

The Veil in Kuwait is a slim publication (eighty pages) based on the findings of a survey of women's observation of the veil at GUST in one of the richest Gulf countries. The authors found that 60 percent of the students at GUST are female and that "radical gender segregation" is practiced across the national education institutes, which permit only a quarter of the classes to be mixed genders. The findings show that 66 percent of the female students observe some form of the veil (*hijab* or head scarf, *abaya* or full cloak, *niqab* or face cover), compared with 34 percent uncovered women (24).

The results are discussed in light of the motivations of women who veil. The survey found that most of the respondents (71 percent) who observed the veil stated that they did so out of a sense of obedience to this Islamic requirement, while only 6 percent did so due to parental direction. The survey tabulates perceptions and includes those of the "uncovered" respondents and the male students. About 68 percent of the latter reported that they were very supportive of the veil practice at the university and cited their preferences for their future wives to be women who observe the veil.

As expected of a survey study, multiple divisions in the text discuss the findings yielded through the questionnaires (included as appendixes). Chapter 4, "The Guilt/ Shame Paradigm," unpacks the emotions associated with the concept of the veil as shielding men from the *fitna* (social disorder, chaos, sexual temptation) potential of Muslim women. It sets up the concluding chapter, which threads through the overlapping themes in the other books reviewed here having to do with veiling, fashion, beauty, cultural consumption, and consumer habits.

The authors find a paradox in that Kuwait's religious consciousness does not reside comfortably between religion and modernity. Rather than reconciling and fusing fashion as or through the veil, the analysis shows that respondents continue to view religion and fashion as opposites (71). According to the authors, this "palpable" tension (72) that arises in the combination of *hijab* and fashion seems to remain irresoluble in the veiling environment of Kuwait. This, they argue, is different from other Middle Eastern countries where the veil is no longer *only* an expression of religious belief. According to the authors, this need to interpret and reduce everything cultural and aesthetic into religious and spiritual terms is prompted by the respondents' guilt and unwillingness to take a critical or detached view of religion.

Women in the Mosque is not primarily about Muslim women's ritual practices. Rather, it traces male Islamic (Sunni) legal scholarly arguments about the legitimacy of women's attendance and participation in public worship. The study explores two key questions of whether women were historically encouraged to access mosques or not and what they did while in attendance.

Marion Holmes Katz's chronological and geographic inquiry in *Women in the Mosque* spans the original resistance to the ban on women from the Great Mosque in Mecca in 1530 CE to the twenty-first-century examples of their prolific activism in places of worship. Hers is not a project that suggests that there has been a linear progression from freedom to oppression for mosque-attending Muslim women. Rather, Katz wishes to explore through Sunni legal and nonlegal sources (predominantly Maliki ibn Anas [796 CE] sources) how women sought religious fellowship and fulfillment in other venues because of their political and societal marginalization (4). The central arguments of the book are that women's mosque usage differs from that of men (7), that a longitudinal survey of legal opinions on women's access to mosques found a high degree of negotiability regarding legal norms, and that the basic models of gender underlying these norms have changed significantly over the centuries (99).

Katz connects legal prescription over women's mosque attendance to the paradigmatic case of women's mobility and visibility outside the home (3) and outlines jurists' debates over the authority structure of the family and the limits of governmental power. Who was to set the standards of conduct? At the same time, Katz concurs with earlier studies that found that women's mosque access does not reflect "a linear progression from freedom to oppression for Muslim women" (4). Making the case that mosques are themselves not exclusive venues of Islamic religious instruction, she suggests that women's religious lives are separate and autonomous from those of men.

The significance of *fitna* as a characterization of Muslim women's sexuality in Islamic legal and sociological history is woven throughout Katz's study. She argues that this tool made women's mosque usage dissonant from male ritual models. She notes the progressive ascent of this "multivalent term" (3) and points out that although the centrality of *fitna* has been recognized, the history of the concept has not been written. This is perhaps the key subtheme of *Women in the Mosque*, albeit with reference to legal, or *fiqh*, discourses.

The (nonlinear) chronological span and citations of hadith, fatwas (religious edicts), and legal sources are referenced in impressive detail in this study. Equally relevant are the detailed comparative differences of opinion that Katz mines from the Sunni Islamic schools of jurisprudence on the issue of women's participation in public worship.

The sources (including primary ones) are exhaustive and fill thirty-two pages, but, comparatively, the index is thin, and there is no glossary. It is important to point out that the sources and the study pertain to the Middle East (which is understandable, given that original Islamic jurisprudence is sourced in Arabic). However, the interpretative praxis for and by Muslim women in South Asia and non-Maghreb Africa are absent from this study, and the lack of mention of this in the text gives the impression that the experience of mosque politics for and by women is limited to the Arab world.

Similarly, the book does not examine Jafari, and any comparative discussion of Shia women's historically vibrant role and participation in public worship is therefore not possible. Another omission is how men's and women's seminaries have historically emerged in complementarity or even as alternatives to mosques with their own dynamics, challenges, and consequences for gender politics in the Muslim world.

Ellen Anne McLarney builds a detailed analysis of the concept of her title, *Soft Force*, a term borrowed from the activist Heba Raouf Ezzat to denote "women's jihad" (1). McLarney uses the term to speak of women's nonviolent protest in Egypt against the secular dictatorship of Hosni Mubarak. "Soft force," she writes, "is a keyword used for imagining and creating a just society rooted in the grace of the right path" and "is the gradual institutional change—and the war of ideas—that has been one of Islamic organizations' most powerful tools in Egypt" (2). This is an interdisciplinary study employing cultural studies, sociology, political science, women's studies, religion, and history to read and "chronicle" the writings and activism of diverse and prolific "public intellectuals" (4). McLarney traces the role of these authors and activists in the "awakening of Islamic sentiments, sensibilities, and senses" and articulates it as "biopower from the ground up" (5). These public intellectuals are Bint al-Shati' (professor), Ni'mat Sidqi (preacher), Iman Mustafa (journalist), Safinaz Kazim (theater critic), Muhammad 'Imara and Muhammad Jalal Kishk (polemicists), Heba Raouf Ezzat and Zaynab al-Ghazali (activists), 'Abd al-Wahid Wafi (scholar), 'Atiyya Saqr (mufti), Shamas al-Barudi (actress), and Kariman Hamza (television personality) (4).

This book suggests that Islamist women activists retreated into religion to survive the oppressive secular state. In the process of this revival, the family became the sacred base (100) and site for inaugurating an Islamist rights-based discourse, as seen in the arguments of the scholars discussed in chapter 3, "Senses of Self: Ni'mat Sidqi's Theology of Motherhood." The book is arranged around the sections "Women's Liberation in Islam," "Gendering Islamic Subjectivities," and "Politics of the Islamic Family" and discusses the nexus of community, society, self, women's labor and market reform, and family. To probe the praxis of Islam in these sites, McLarney creatively uses a diverse range of sources, including "fatwas, sermons, lectures, theses, biographies, political essays, newspaper articles, scholarly essays, and exegeses of the Qur'an, as well as websites, Facebook postings, Tweets, and YouTube videos" (4).

Soft Force undoubtedly offers wide-ranging evidence to think through the reawakening of contemporary debates on gender, Islam, and the construction of self, community, and family in Egypt. Though the book covers the role of Muslim women in building a viable Islamist movement in Egypt during decades of resistance against Mubarak's authoritarian regime, we still would have benefited from more debate on the nature, challenges, and continuing struggle of the Arab Spring.

Reading these four books together and noting the persistence of debates on such notions as secularism, piety, agency, subjectivity, body, sexuality, and gender performativity in women and gender studies, we are left with the lingering problem of how to make sense of the lives of women throughout the Middle East and North Africa entangled with incongruities, ambiguities, and conflicts. The books reviewed here attempt to work through these tensions but mainly remain limited to the articulation of Muslim women's capacity and agency as imagined and defined by an Islamist polity — current or futuristic. The experiences of women as defined in these texts implies that the only alternative to secular authoritarianism seems to be a tryst with an undefined democratic Islamism. The academic focus on Islamist women's political movements in Muslim-majority contexts often comes at the cost of a broader and more intuitive understanding of the tensions and challenges not just between the state, men, and women but in women's movements in general. None of these texts discusses those tensions, and therefore a reader may believe that there is nothing more to the Middle Eastern Muslim woman than a desire to examine her divine historical context and harmonize it with her current pietist aspirations.

AFIYA S. ZIA is a PhD candidate at the Women and Gender Studies Institute at the University of Toronto. Contact: afiya.zia@mail.utoronto.ca.

SHAHRZAD MOJAB is professor in the Department of Leadership, Higher and Adult Education and at the Women and Gender Studies Institute at the University of Toronto. Contact: shahrzad.mojab@utoronto.ca.

References

Hafez, Sherine. 2011. *An Islam of Her Own: Reconsidering Religion and Secularism in Women's Islamic Movements*. New York: New York University Press.

Mahmood, Saba. 2005. *Politics of Piety: The Islamic Revival and the Feminist Subject*. Princeton, NJ: Princeton University Press.

BOOK REVIEW

Agency and Gender in Gaza:
Masculinity, Femininity, and Family during the Second Intifada
Aitemad Muhanna
Farnham: Ashgate, 2013
222 pages. ISBN 9781409454533

Reviewed by SARAH IRVING

As Nicola Pratt notes in the foreword to this book, "Paradoxically, the increased international attention to the impacts of conflict on women has been accompanied by an increased silencing of voices of ordinary women living in conflict zones, except where they conform with liberal notions of agency or are victims of violence and patriarchy" (vii). Aitemad Muhanna's exploration of how Palestinian women in poor and vulnerable families in Gaza adapt to "the masculinizing of their enactment and the feminizing of their selfhood" (163) is a major contribution to making such voices heard and to challenging many of the liberal West's assumptions about them.

Muhanna's study covering the period from the start of the Second Intifada in 2000 until 2009 is based on interviews, life stories, and focus group material collected mainly in 2007 and 2008 in the neighborhood of El-Shujae'ya and in Beach Refugee Camp. As she lays out, these years saw a huge shift in gender relations and roles in Gaza caused primarily by the economic impacts of Israeli closures and a 75 percent drop in average family income. Majority unemployment among men is set against increasing roles for women as breadwinners for their families either through paid work or as aid recipients. This in turn has influenced the decisions and choices men and women and their families make around marriage, education, places of residence, and work.

As Muhanna's interlocutors make clear, however, the liberal assumptions of international donor agencies about women's work and mobility constituting empowerment do not apply in this setting. Indeed, it seems that for many women the priorities imposed by such donors, by emphasizing female poverty and helplessness as criteria for receiving aid, create systems in which women are forced to humiliate themselves in return for aid, actually "create another layer of violence that operates in tandem with the violence of

JMEWS • Journal of Middle East Women's Studies • 12:2 • July 2016
DOI 10.1215/15525864-3507683 • © 2016 by the Association for Middle East Women's Studies

Israel's occupation and blockade" (viii). Although women apparently have more "freedom" to act outside the home and the family, Muhanna sees them as having to highlight their subordinate feminine subjectivity both to their families, so that they do not find themselves objects of suspicion, and to charitable groups, who measure their entitlement to aid according to essentialized ideas of gender. Ultimately, very few — if any — of these women are seen to aspire to greater public roles. Their main aspirations are to be properly supported by strong, working husbands confident and powerful in their own masculinity and therefore capable of both giving and bringing them proper respect as women, wives, and mothers.

In tandem with this reorientation of women's work and feminine attributes comes a crisis of masculinity that derives from men's inability to support their families in an environment in which many are also unable to assert their gendered power through public involvement in the resistance. In this complex, nuanced account, educated young men and those who had well-paid jobs in Israel are seen to be most likely to react to the situation with domestic violence and/or extreme apathy toward their children. Unable to meet the duties society assigns to them as men, those seen as having (or thinking they have) more to lose than men in lower-status jobs then adopt extreme measures of enacting their supposed masculinity while almost completely abdicating the associated responsibilities.

In analyzing the complexities of her interlocutors' accounts of their lives and desires with their apparently essentialized notions of male and female roles, Muhanna insists on nonessentializing ideas of gender and gender identities. She draws particularly on R. W. Connell's emphasis on the potential for subordinate masculinities and ideas from Andrea Cornwall (based on Michel de Certeau) of tactical versus strategic choices. In so doing, she acknowledges that rather than creating a single hegemonic masculinity, gendered values and roles may subordinate and constrain men as much as they do women and that both genders may be forced to take options that meet immediate needs even if they erode their long-term positions. Muhanna therefore reaches conclusions that stress the contingency of gender roles, the intersectionality of women's experiences, and the possibility that women may, according to the situation, choose to "not resist their subordination, but question and evaluate it" (172). In laying out her theoretical positions, Muhanna is also deeply critical of much liberal Western scholarship on women in the Middle East, which she sees as "largely empirical and descriptive" (30), relying on Islam and nationalism as explanations and tending to reduce questions of women's agency to whether or not they resist patriarchy rather than engaging with the many other factors that affect their lives.

Consequently, while Muhanna's empirical data are important for anyone seeking an in-depth understanding of the dynamics of economy and gender in Gaza, the lessons she draws from them and the theoretical critiques and insights she derives are particularly significant. In some respects, Muhanna's own position is a vital part of this. Raised in El-Shujae'ya and married in Beach Camp, she inserts — without overlaboring — the extent to which her identity as a mother and as the wife of a political prisoner (later martyr) gave her privileged access and to some extent insights into the lives of her subjects. The balancing act provides some of the lighter moments in what is often a somewhat dry writing style.

I have just two criticisms of any weight. First, although the Israeli occupation and then blockade of Gaza are a constant presence, only late in the book and very briefly does Muhanna engage the extent to which the political situation impacts the choices her subjects make. To what extent, one wonders, might the strength of their nostalgic desire for a stable, traditional gender order be governed by the ideological restraints of the conflict and the claims of an "authentic" set of "Palestinian" gendered identities? Second, and more prosaic, are the terrible copyediting and proofreading of this book—part of a sad trend of cost cutting among academic publishers. Especially in the early chapters, it is bad enough to make some sentences incomprehensible, which is a great pity.

SARAH IRVING is a PhD candidate in Islamic and Middle Eastern studies at the University of Edinburgh. Contact: Sarah.irving@ed.ac.uk.

Security Theology, Surveillance, and the Politics of Fear

Nadera Shalhoub-Kevorkian

Cambridge: Cambridge University Press, 2015

208 pages. ISBN 9781107097353

Reviewed by SARAH IHMOUD

In the summer of 2014 Israel waged a fifty-day military assault on Gaza that claimed the lives of 2,205 Palestinians, leaving in its wake a scale of destruction and displacement human rights groups deemed unprecedented since the beginning of Israel's 1967 occupation. Israel rationalized its assault on the occupied territory as a matter of national security. Yet how could such a scale of human devastation against a captive population (under siege, no less) be justified in the name of security? Completed in the midst of the assault, the renowned Palestinian feminist scholar and activist Nadera Shalhoub-Kevorkian's *Security Theology, Surveillance, and the Politics of Fear* provides an urgently needed analysis of Israel's security paradigm embedded in a settler colonial logic. Of central concern to the author are the ways matters of security for the "Jewish state" enable deployment of a violent, quotidian surveillance over racialized bodies and lives, producing Israel's "political economy of fear" (10) — an ideology that obscures and perpetuates violence and power inequities between colonizer and colonized, settler and native, sacred and profane.

Shalhoub-Kevorkian pursues her theorization not through a distant analysis of the discourse and structures of those in power (though she attentively historicizes a number of contemporary surveillance policies in relation to the structure of colonial dispossession) or through attention to the hypervisible aspects of Israeli violence. Rather, she follows the expansive tentacles of Israeli governance as they reach into the intimate domains of Palestinian life and death in the settler colony, where the terrorizing effects of what she terms the state's "security theology" (14–15) creep into the veins and capillaries of the everyday. "It is the obsession of the occupiers and their bureaucracies," she writes, "with the intimate details of who is sleeping with whom, who is marrying whom, who is giving birth, and whose children are to be recognized" (155). By examining the Tag Mehir (Price

JMEWS • Journal of Middle East Women's Studies • 12:2 • July 2016

DOI 10.1215/15525864-3507694 • © 2016 by the Association for Middle East Women's Studies

Tag) movement's violent writings on the walls of Palestinian communities, state control over Palestinians' legal status and restrictions on family reunification, home demolitions, violation of pregnant women's bodily safety, and denial of a right to a dignified burial for the dead, Shalhoub-Kevorkian's feminist analytics centers the "intimate politics of the everyday" (2), drawing the reader's attention to mundane and private sites where settler colonial power is both reproduced and contested, among them the Palestinian body, psyche, home space, familial relationships, birth, and death.

In the chapter "Israel in the Bedroom" the author examines Israel's biopolitical governance of Palestinian family life and marital and sexual relations through the Citizenship and Entry Law, which she posits as a racializing technology of colonial power. The law prohibits the Palestinian spouses or children of Israeli citizens (approximately 20 percent of whom are Palestinian) from obtaining permanent residency status or citizenship and grants the state power to strip spouses of temporary status based on perceived national security concerns, effectively depriving Palestinian citizens of their right to have a family in Israel based solely on the race or ethnicity of their spouses (52). Barring Palestinians from a path to citizenship, the author argues, is but one of the legal mechanisms employed by the state to "transfer" Palestinians from their native lands and maintain a Jewish racial majority (52). Native eviction, she illustrates, is accomplished not simply through overtly violent means of the state and its military apparatus but also through the state's ability to "keep individuals in a state of uncertainty, sitting in an eternal waiting room in a Kafkaesque labyrinth of administrative processes" (65), where Palestinians are forced to live as illegal entities, permanent refugees "in fear of Israel's surveillance and threat of deportation" in their own native lands (65). In "Hunted Homeplaces" Shalhoub-Kevorkian centers the connection between dispossessions of the home space and memory of home, paying particular attention to gendered effects of Israeli attacks on the Palestinian home/land and its policy of house demolitions deemed a "military necessity" (87) and analyzing the Nakba Law as a technology of colonial surveillance over memory. A particularly poignant chapter, "Birth in Jerusalem," examines the exercise of settler colonial power over the body and psyche of the pregnant woman. Israel's demographically driven policies in occupied East Jerusalem, which aim to maintain a permanent Jewish majority as a mode of solidifying claims to Palestinian land, she argues, rely on a colonial imaginary of a threatening other and its population increase. It is thus that Palestinian women's bodies become reconstituted as security threats to the Zionist state and their children are conceived as already potential terrorists, justifying surveillance and control over their bodies and lives. For pregnant women in occupied East Jerusalem, navigating militarized spaces during the time of birth and encountering various forms of violence by colonial authorities instills an intense feeling of isolation and persecution and a viscerally embodied sense of being surveilled, to the extent of infiltrating colonized women's most intimate spaces. Yet while women's birthing narratives give voice to the ways the state's security ideology invades the most intimate space of the womb, transforming the body into a territory of colonial dispossession, the author reads not only suffering but also resistance in such geographies of entrapment. Despite severe restrictions on pregnant women's freedom of movement, access to medical care, and safe home spaces, she notes that "the willful act of deciding to continue surviving and giving birth is itself perceived as political — as subversion, revolt and agency — by the women themselves" (160).

Each chapter probes a different aspect of the penetration of Israel's security paradigm into the intimate and often invisibilized spaces of Palestinian life and death, serving Shalhoub-Kevorkian's central argument that Israel's security has been "transformed into a religion," a theology that, combined with Zionist biblical claims of a Jewish "birthright" to historical Palestine, naturalizes all manner of Israeli violence against Palestinians as a "security necessity" (14–15), validated by a global geopolitical denial of Palestinian rights and suffering. In bringing together such accounts from various segments of the occupied territories and within the Israeli state, Shalhoub-Kevorkian analytically situates Palestinians as one indigenous collectivity and demonstrates that the complex machinery of settler colonial power works in different modes across space and time. Yet where too often theorization of settler colonialism appears bound by the horizon it sets for itself as a permanent structure of settler invasion and native elimination, foreclosing possibility for native futurity, Shalhoub-Kevorkian's work is a key contribution to this reemergent field of study. Through careful attention to an "epistemology of the details" (181–84), it demonstrates that despite the overwhelming magnitude of the colonial project, possibilities for native survival and life can be found in the microspaces of resistance to state power.

While her theoretical breadth is both novel and insightful, one might have hoped the author would do more to engage contemporary contributions in the fields of critical race and settler colonial studies. Her theorization of the intimate as a quotidian space for the production of racialized subjectivities in the Israeli settler colony could have led to a deeper engagement with contemporary debates surrounding the global dynamics of race, racism, and the politics of indigeneity. Nevertheless, the power of this work lies in its attentiveness to the voices and experiences of those who "keep on existing" (Frantz Fanon, quoted on 1) in and despite the ravages of Israeli settler colonialism as a pathway to understanding the often invisibilized, intimate domains of power and resistance, making it a critically relevant study in multiple fields — from the writer's own province in criminology and law to women and gender studies to those interested in race and power whether from anthropology or Middle East studies. This is a welcome contribution to Middle East gender studies that addresses the nexus of race, gender, and power in a sustained ethnographic way through focusing on the politics of intimacy and the everyday and one of the first to draw on the analytic paradigms of settler colonial and critical race studies.

SARAH IHMOUD is a PhD candidate in social and activist anthropology at the University of Texas at Austin. Contact: sihmoud@utexas.edu.

BOOK REVIEW

Wrapped in the Flag of Israel:
Mizrahi Single Mothers and Bureaucratic Torture
Smadar Lavie
New York: Berghahn, 2014
216 pages. ISBN 9781782382225

Reviewed by ADI KUNTSMAN

Smadar Lavie's *Wrapped in the Flag of Israel* brings together several foundational principles that are detrimental to the lives of many poor, disenfranchised, marginalized women
in the Middle East and beyond and yet are not explored systematically: gender and race
are intertwined deeply and powerfully and cannot be understood separately; poverty
destroys bodies, minds, and spirits, its effects long-lasting and often deadly; the state can
be ruthless in its mundane management of its most vulnerable citizens while still enjoying
their wholehearted loyalty. First and foremost, it is a book about understanding the grip
of state violence on its defenseless subjects — poor women of color — through the notion
of bureaucracy as a form of torture: from everyday humiliation and powerlessness to the
paralyzing impact of all-encompassing webs of procedures to debilitating and long-term
scarring of women's bodies, minds, and souls.

At the center of the book is the 2003 protest of a group of disenfranchised Mizrahi
single mothers, whose lives depended on welfare that had been severely cut by the economic reforms of the early 2000s. At the moment of utter desperation, one of the mothers,
Vicky Knafo, decided to march from the periphery where she lived to Jerusalem, setting
up a protest camp over the summer. Her protest was sporadically and conditionally supported, judged, ignored, co-opted, and eventually abandoned in a moment of a perceived
national crisis when violence erupted once again between Israel and the Palestinians.

Following the protest and its many actors, Lavie, as a Mizrahi feminist activist, a
scholar, and a welfare-dependent single mother herself, uses the protest as a case study
through which matters of poverty and ruthless neoliberal economy, Israeli intra-Jewish
racism, Jewish Ashkenazi domination, nationalism, and the occupation of Palestinian
territories intertwine. It is the first ethnography of the day-to-day experiences of Mizrahi

JMEWS • Journal of Middle East Women's Studies • 12:2 • July 2016
DOI 10.1215/15525864-3507705 • © 2016 by the Association for Middle East Women's Studies

women living at the mercy of the Israeli welfare state. It is also a highly innovative theorization of state power as divine — a theorization that opens new directions in thinking about women and religion and in explaining the state's grip and the failure of antistate social protest by faithful disenfranchised citizens. Last, *Wrapped* is among the very few works that tie Israeli colonization and military occupation of Palestine with internal colonization of non-European Jews, intra-Jewish racism, and Ashkenazi rule.

Wrapped challenges two key assumptions that still dominate both the academic knowledge and the political discourse with regard to Israel/Palestine. The first assumption deals with the presumably monolithic category of gender and "women" and the related expectation of joint women's experiences and (potential for) solidarity. Instead, *Wrapped* demonstrates both the persistent Ashkenazi domination of most Israeli women's nongovernmental organizations *and* the ways Ashkenazi Zionism and its deadly racial and national logic divide between groups of marginalized women (the Mizrahi, the Bedouin, the Russian immigrants), preventing solidarity and alliances among disenfranchised minorities.

The second assumption concerns the simplified distinction between Jews and Palestinians, which also leads to a simplified understanding of the Israeli occupation and military rule as concerning solely the relations between Israel and Palestine. Instead, Lavie draws the complex interrelations between the occupation of Palestine and the internal colonization of the Mizrahi Jews, or Arab Jews, whose "border zone" position makes them hostages to Israeli colonial nationalism twice, both times through the divine logic of Jewish unity, "one state, one people." First, the myth of such unity is used to sustain Mizrahi women's (and men's) love for the "Jewish state," no matter how harsh the dispossession, how poisonous the racism, and how debilitating the economic precariousness. Lavie shows us the impossibility of resisting the violence of the state due to both the state's divine nature and the survival mechanisms inflicted institutionally and psychically by the bureaucratic torture. Second, the state uses the myth of "one people" repeatedly and effectively to shut down the social Mizrahi protest, turning each time to yet another political crisis that demands national unity and that is usually followed by a military intervention.

In cutting across lines of nation, gender, class, race, and religion — something many cultural studies and feminist theory scholars overlook — Lavie builds on and continues her long-standing intervention into the anthropology of border zones and decolonial anthropology as "homework." Homework here is about questioning both the power relations that shape the "field" *and* the analytic tools used to capture it. Lavie writes as both an observer and a survivor, and her book is neither a raw testimony nor a detached, objective theorizing enforced by the Anglo-American academic canon. Informed but not constrained by the discipline's rich tradition of doing fieldwork, *Wrapped* is based on scrupulous research and participant observations. Yet it is simultaneously an account of Lavie's own journey enduring the gendered and racist violence of both the Israeli academy and the Israeli welfare state: a world-renowned anthropologist and California-based professor fleeing domestic violence and finding herself in Israel as an hourly paid adjunct and a "welfare

◊ ◊ ◊ ◊ ◊ ◊ ◊ ◊

mama," neither her pioneering scholarship on border zones nor her partly Ashkenazi and partly middle-class parentage saving her from the bureaucratic torture of the Israeli welfare machine whose logic, as Lavie poignantly notes, has no border zones (100).

Wrapped is incredibly insightful conceptually but also powerful politically. It does not merely challenge conceptual frameworks and academic canons but actively undoes them through shifting and diverse modes of writing, moving from theory to feelings, memories, diaries, academic writing, field notes, thick descriptions with comments, fragments of conversations, and silences — all to "overcome the elusiveness of bureaucratic torture" and "attempt to attain mimetic redemption from non-discursive suffering" (87).

The book is a must for anyone wishing to understand what Lavie calls the "Gender-Race" fabric (80) of Israeli intra-Jewish racism but also, more crucially, of the deepest connections between Ashkenazi internal colonization, racialized social deprivation, and the murderous war machine of the Israeli military rule in the West Bank and Gaza. Beyond that, *Wrapped* is key reading for all of us doing feminist, decolonial, antiracist, and intersectional work, especially in contexts where the torture of oppression is not obvious or is constantly explained away, for all of us needing and wanting to learn how to be an academic survivor and how to write a scholarship of the disenfranchised making the pain of others (or one's own) into a consumable fetish, devoid of political work.

ADI KUNTSMAN is lecturer in the Department of Languages, Information, and Communications at Manchester Metropolitan University. Contact: A.Kuntsman@mmu.ac.uk.

Editorial Cover Art Concept

◇ ◇

The Palestinian-British artist Mona Hatoum's *No Way III* (2000) perfectly articulates the complicated relationship of intimacy and the domestic that the authors of "Everyday Intimacies of the Middle East" explore in their articles. Hatoum's work was part of *Domestic Disturbance*, an exhibition of fifteen works shown at the Massachusetts Museum of Contemporary Art from March 17, 2001, through February 4, 2002. In 2005 Hatoum wrote that, far from evoking the calm safety of home, the spiked colander that is *No Way III* "makes you think about all the possible unpleasant things to do with home, whether it's like the housewife or the woman feeling entrapped by domesticity, or whether it's to do with a condemned environment where the inhabitants have to flee, or an environment that is to do with incarceration as in being under house arrest, or the notion of the home denied."

JMEWS • Journal of Middle East Women's Studies • 12:2 • July 2016
DOI 10.1215/15525864-3507716 • © 2016 by the Association for Middle East Women's Studies

Trauma, Collective Memory, Creative and Performative Embodied Practices as Sites of Resistance

❖ ❖

DENA AL-ADEEB

I returned to Iraq in March 2004 during 'Ashura, the commemoration rituals of the martyrdom of the grandson of the Prophet Muhammad, Imam Husayn, in the seventh century. It was a year after the US invasion and occupation of Iraq, and it was the first time 'Ashura was publicly celebrated because it had been banned during Saddam Hussein's regime for over thirty years. In the face of random violence and repression, I became preoccupied with the concept of trauma and bereavement, memory and witnessing, and performative embodied and creative practices as sites for the intervention, reinterpretation, and transformation of the dystopian reality in Iraq. My encounters during 'Ashura with the women in my family and community in Baghdad and Karbala brought me closer to an embodied practice for coping with the violence and day-to-day reality in Iraq. 'Ashura's ritual practices manufactured a community of witnessing and remembrance across time that is now confronting radical political and social transformation.[1] These creative and performative embodied rituals provide a structural framework to commemorate the past, a methodology to survive a chaotic present, and the means to create a resistance movement.

The Second Room of the *Sacred Spaces* Art Installation
Two years later I constructed a four-room art installation, *Sacred Spaces*, in the Falaki Gallery at the American University in Cairo, Egypt, that experimentally

JMEWS • Journal of Middle East Women's Studies • 12:2 • July 2016
DOI 10.1215/15525864-3507727 • © 2016 by the Association for Middle East Women's Studies

decoded 'Ashura commemorations and the journeys pilgrims undertook to Karbala in 2004.[2] In this article I focus on the second room.

The art installation brought into play an experiential approach to remembrance and memory, archiving and repertoire, and embodiment and performance. My work is informed by Diana Taylor's (2003, 192–93) work, which sheds light on the different ways of arranging, conveying, and disseminating memory: "The archives . . . can contain the grisly record of criminal violence—the documents, photographs, and remains that tell of disappearances. . . . The repertoire . . . holds the tales of the survivors, their gestures, the traumatic flashbacks, repeats, and hallucinations—in short, all those acts usually thought of as ephemeral and invalid forms of knowledge and evidence." The art installation and written work are also informed by interviews with women in my family and community and participants and bystanders in the rituals and performances.

The installation simulated 'Ashura rituals and pilgrimage to Karbala, inviting the audience to walk through the space as a multilayered interpretation of 'Ashura, exploring new relations between performative embodied practices and witnessing and the possibility for reparation. Replicating the pilgrim's journey, audience members navigated the multiple objects, such as the black silhouettes, until they reached the shrine (figs. 1–2). Such navigation between space and matter is meant to assist pilgrims in transcending their specific realities, to create a rupture in their everyday lives, and to encourage them to enter a liminal space. This in-between space represents the experience pilgrims undergo. Um 'Ali, my aunt, affirms that these performances allow the community to transcend their predicaments by projecting their pain and suffering into the calamity of the Karbala narratives. She

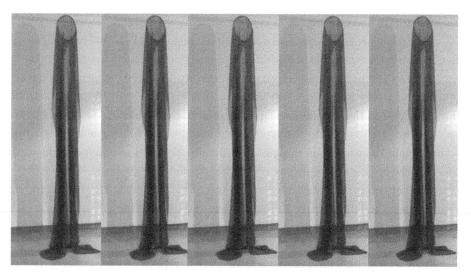

Figure 1. *Black Silhouettes*

Figure 2. *The Shrine*

claims that the shrine and the rituals are portals for pilgrims to cross time and space to connect to a higher plane that provides comfort and minimizes their own pain and suffering compared to this catastrophe. The Karbala narratives epitomize Shi'i history of martyrdom, which must be placed in a universal narrative of redemption. Performative rituals are not merely cathartic and a quest for deliverance; they also symbolize unequivocal devotion and a pledge to their imam to continue his revolutionary message for justice.

The tension between the fixedness of the centripetal art installation of Husayn's shrine as opposed to the marginal, fluid, and disembodied black silhouettes hanging across each corner of the shrine was evident in the second room. On the other side of the shrine, I placed a black mantelpiece against a dividing wall. The black box supports a bowl filled with green ribbons of various sizes.

Reconstruction of the Shrine

The second room of the art installation reconstructed the shrine, which represents and embodies symbolic, cultural, and religious ideals sought by pilgrims. The pilgrims travel to the shrine to renew their covenant with their imam while seeking his intercession and blessings.

The reconstructed shrine was a massive rectangular, three-dimensional black tomb. The shrine was made of wood to the dimensions of approximately 1.9×1.9× 0.75 meters. The bottom quarter was solid, in contrast to the balance, which was porous. On closer inspection, you would notice that the pores were in fact an intricate construction of arabesque panels (*shansheel* or *mashrabiya*)[3] that provided a restricted view into the sepulcher. The lighting in this room was set up to illuminate the arabesque designs. The illumination of the arabesque designs reflected elaborate star-like shapes, enhancing the shrine's stateliness. These reflections further enhanced the themes of this room that represent the marginal and unseen (the silhouettes) versus the central and seen (the shrine).

Peering through the arabesque holes into the encasement, you would become aware of Husayn's simulated martyred corpse covered in black cloth and impaled by silver arrows (fig. 3). I pierced the arrows into the replicated corpse to represent Husayn's slaying in Shi'a imagery. The shrine provided a symbolic aperture into these visual and performative expressions, histories, and narratives.

Um ʿAli cries every time she visits Husayn's shrine in Karbala, since it recalls the calamity that befell the house of the Prophet. The shrine becomes a channel between the sacred and the human realms, a conduit to a transcendent entity, the imams and the Prophet. For her, weeping for the imam is the only solace for the pain she has endured throughout the wars and the loss of her husband and her children, who have fled Iraq. Mahmoud M. Ayoub (1978, 147) addresses the merits of weeping for the imam and the sacralization of space and time in his chapter "The Sigh of the Sorrowful": "Sorrow and weeping for the martyrdom of *Imam* Husayn

Figure 3. *Arrows Piercing the Corpse*

and the suffering of the Holy Family became a source of salvation for those who chose to participate in this unending flow of tears. . . . The rest of creation, however, is by divine decree the stage, as it were, upon which this drama of martyrdom is forever enacted." The pursuit of Shi'a ideals revolves around commemorating the martyrdom of Imam Husayn and embodying his and the rest of *ahl-al-bayt*'s (the Prophet's family) characters. Husayn's martyrdom incites political mobilization (through the visual representation of the shrine in the installation), and his sister Zaynab's role (through hanging black silhouettes around the shrine in the installation) stages a commemorative movement to endure the tumultuously violent contemporary realities in Iraq.

Disembodied Black Silhouettes

The larger-than-life elongated silhouettes were made of gauzy, almost transparent black fabric, representing female figures wearing black ʿ*abayas*.[4] Draped from the ceiling to the ground across each angle of the shrine, they hovered across each corner of the shrine, generating a tension between their fluidity and the shrine's solid fixedness.

The black silhouettes represent the main female figures in the Karbala stories (such as Fatemeh, Zaynab, Zaynab's sister Omm Kalthoum, Husayn's daughter Sokayneh, and Kalthoum, among others) dressed in 'abayas. I hung these figures at the corners of the shrine to symbolize their roles as key pillars of the commemorative movement. The black silhouettes also represent Zaynab's moving and expressive narrations at Umayyad caliph Yazid Bin Mu'awiya's[5] court, since the narration and performative rituals marked the evolution of Shi'ite rituals.

By representing the black silhouettes as disembodied, I wanted to suggest that while women have been visible symbols in the debates on the war and current events in Iraq, they have also been invisible victims of the US invasion and occupation. The depiction of the disembodied figures as larger than life signifies how women have been exploited by the US war campaign to rally support for its continuous war on Iraq. The transparent silhouettes symbolize this visible-invisible tension employed by the US media, military, and government. For example, the Abu Ghraib prison scandal exposed American soldiers' abuse of Iraqi men but did not publicly mention the soldiers' consistent sexualized violence against and sadistic torture of the female inmates. In a briefing paper presented to the UN Commission on Human Rights, Kristen McNutt (2005) maintains:

> Attorney Amal Kadham Swadi, one of seven female lawyers now representing women detainees in Abu Ghraib, began to piece together a picture of systemic abuse and torture by US guards against Iraqi women held in detention without charge. This was not only true of Abu Ghraib . . . but was . . . "happening all across Iraq.". . . "Sexualized violence and abuse committed by US troops goes far beyond a few isolated cases.". . .
>
> . . . A fifty-three-page report . . . written by Major General Antonio M. Taguba . . . points to complicity to sexual torture by the entire Army prison system. . . . Taguba found that . . . there were numerous instances of "sadistic, blatant, and wanton criminal abuses" at Abu Ghraib.

As a response to such stories and other incidents of sexual assault on women by both American soldiers and Iraqi men, many women were forced to become marginal spectators and invisible phantoms, relegated to the private sphere. The installation represents the marginalization of Iraqi women in the public realm and those who have died and disappeared.

Green Ribbons as Nadhr (Vowing)

I placed the green ribbons in a bowl on the black mantelpiece across the shrine. Before the opening night, I tied a green ribbon around one of the star-shaped pores of the arabesque panel of the shrine just as pilgrims do in the shrines in Karbala. A descriptive note on the wall above the bowl encouraged the audience to participate

JMEWS • Journal of Middle East Women's Studies • 12:2 July 2016 in this specific ritual. During the opening night, participants walked up to the black mantelpiece, picked a green ribbon, and tied it around a star-shaped pore of the arabesque panels. By the end of the exhibit, numerous green ribbons adorned the black shrine.

I used the color green — the color of Islam, the Prophet Muhammad, and the Prophet's descendants — since this is the color pilgrims use. Green is the dominant color throughout Shi'ite iconography and imagery. Pilgrims customarily purchase the green ribbons from sayyids, descendants of the Prophet who work as shrine keepers. Pilgrims rub the green ribbons against the shrine while making their vows to their imam, seeking blessings from him. After their vows, pilgrims tie the green ribbons around the shrine grating or their own wrists. Lubna, my cousin, suggests that while vowing, repenting, and pleading for their imam, the intercessor between them and God, the faithful trust that the green ribbon can serve as a medium to salvation. They hope that in his love for their imams, who are the legatees of his Prophet, God will grant them their wishes. A plea is customarily expressed through vowing (*nadhr*) that if their wishes are granted, they will make an offering in return.

My aunt Um 'Ali vowed and pleaded with Imam Husayn to rescue her brother, who was severely wounded by shrapnel from a bomb explosion in Basra during the Iraq-Iran War in the 1980s. A fellow soldier dragged him from the battlefield to a hospital in Basra. My aunt found his blackened body rotting on the hospital bed. She was forced to leave her work, home, and family and drive from Baghdad to Basra (during the war a very risky endeavor) to nurse him until he miraculously recovered. My aunt is still fulfilling her promise to the imam. Vowing can take many forms, such as distributing water to pilgrims on foot, donating money to the poor, and cooking *kemma* (a dish customarily cooked during 'Ashura as a *nadhr* and distributed to the community), among others.

The Karbala tragedy continues to unfold in the present day. My cousins recently said that their main concern is related to the expansion of the Islamic State of Iraq and Syria (ISIS), especially to Karbala. Displaced women who fled the violence in the north of Iraq have resettled in shelters near Karbala. The Organization of Women's Freedom in Iraq (OWFI) founded Women's Peace Farm shelters near Karbala and throughout Iraq. The OWFI shelters provide safe housing, education, and training; support women farmers; and create support networks and community. These women farmers reassert their agency while providing for their families. It is evident that women have had to carry the brunt of the violence inflicted by the old regime, the Iraqi state, the US occupation, military forces, various extremist militias, and armed forces that cross sectarian lines. My interest in crafting the art installation and simulation of the pilgrimage was to provide an alternative historiography situated at the intersections of memory, trauma, and resistance.

DENA AL-ADEEB is an artist and scholar-activist born in Baghdad and now based in New York. She is a PhD candidate in the Middle Eastern and Islamic Studies Department at New York University. She is also a visiting instructor in the Humanities and Media Studies Department and in the School of Architecture at the Pratt Institute. Contact: daa317@nyu.edu.

Notes

1. Since 2004 the new governing bodies and ruling elites have co-opted 'Ashura's meaning, practices, and rituals to advance their own political agendas.
2. I have published articles related to the first and third rooms of the *Sacred Spaces* art installation. See Al-Adeeb 2008, 2012.
3. A traditional Arabic architectural feature projecting oriel windows enclosed with carved-wood latticework usually located on the second story of a building and sometimes used internally in a courtyard. Its main social function is to conceal or create a visual boundary between the private domain and the public, including ensuring segregation of the sexes.
4. Black clothing that covers the entire body.
5. Yazid sent his troops to Karbala, Iraq, to eliminate Imam Husayn and his seventy-two followers in AD 680. Zaynab and the other women were taken as *sabaya* (captives) to his court in Damascus.

References

Al-Adeeb, Dena. 2008. "From Sacred Ritual to Installation Art: A Personal Testimony." *Alif: Journal of Comparative Poetics*, no. 28: 7–40.

———. 2012. "Migratory Sacred Spaces: Re(creating) 'Ashura." In *We Are Iraqis: Aesthetics and Politics in a Time of War*, edited by Nadje Al-Ali and Deborah Al-Najjar, 127–43. Syracuse, NY: Syracuse University Press.

Ayoub, Mahmoud M. 1978. *Redemptive Suffering in Islam: A Study of the Devotional Aspects of 'Ashura in Twelver Shi'ism*. The Hague: Mouton.

McNutt, Kristen. 2005. "Sexualized Violence against Iraqi Women by US Occupying Forces." Briefing paper of International Educational Development presented to the United Nations Commission on Human Rights, 2005 Session, Geneva, March. psychoanalystsopposewar.org/resources_files/SVIW-1.doc.

Taylor, Diana. 2003. *The Archive and the Repertoire: Performing Cultural Memory in the Americas*. Durham, NC: Duke University Press.

Bad Dolls/Reappropriating Badness

Performing the Feminine with Reference to
Arab Muslim Dolls and Tiqqun's Young-Girl

◇ ◇

RIMA DUNN and ADAM GEORGE DUNN

Some Islamic countries, such as Saudi Arabia and Iran, prohibit sales of the Barbie doll, because she promotes "degenerate values," leaving them to the black market. The Saudi religious police (the Committee for the Propagation of Virtue and Prevention of Vice) denounced the doll as a blasphemous object, a threat to Islamic teachings, a "Jewish doll." The religious police headquarters in Al-Madina hung posters in public places, including schools, that display a photo of a Barbie doll in a pink minidress with the following text warning of the enemies of Islam: "A strange request. A little girl asks her mother: Mother, I want jeans, a low-cut shirt, and a swimsuit like Barbie. . . . Jewish Barbie dolls, with their revealing clothes and shameful postures, accessories and tools are a symbol of decadence to the perverted West. Let us beware of her dangers and be careful" (*Sydney Morning Herald* 2003). The permanent collection of confiscated items that violate Islamic law at the Exhibit of Violations section on the religious police website displays images of Barbie dolls and warns that "the enemies of Islam want to invade us with all possible means, and therefore they have circulated among us this doll, which spreads deterioration of values and moral degeneracy among our girls" (Middle East Media Research Institute 2003).

Sheikh Abdulla al Merdas issued a fatwa banning Barbie and locating the problem in her unrestrained physical form: "It is no problem that little girls play with dolls. But these dolls should not have the developed body of a woman and wear revealing clothes" (Associated Press 2003). The doll is also referred to as a blasphemous object on the same grounds. Although human figuration is forbidden

Figure 1. Islamic dolls, 2014. Private collection

according to Islam as practiced in Saudi Arabia, the representation of the human body was not the main reason for banning Barbie. According to Merdas, Barbie's "revealing clothes will be imprinted in [children's] minds and they will refuse to wear the clothes we are used to as Muslims." Merdas preaches against playing with Barbie dolls. He explains that the religious police "take their anti-Barbie campaign to the shops, confiscating dolls from sellers and imposing a fine" (ibid.).

Iran took positive action as well. In 2002 the Institute for the Intellectual Development of Children and Young Adults produced Sara and her brother Dara to replace Barbie and Ken. Sara and Dara wear modest clothing to display "traditional Islamic values." "I think Barbie is more harmful than an American missile," explains the Iranian toy seller Masoumeh Rahimi, stressing that the significance of Barbie's danger is that the doll is "foreign to Iran's culture" (BBC News 2002). The Fatima doll is a recent Islamic doll created in Iran and is designed to fight "the enemy's cultural invasion," as its creator Hossein Homay Seresht explains: "The Westerners, by creating Barbie and marketing it, are encouraging bad veiling and not wearing the hijab; all of these factors led us to take it as our duty to present Islamic dolls to the market" (Venezia 2010). In Indonesia, Sukmawati Suryaman described the process of creating the Salma Islamic doll for the Indonesian market. She was inspired by watching her niece play with a Barbie and her concern that her niece would lose connection to the Indonesian culture. Suryaman explained: "I was thinking I wish we have these dolls in traditional garb that fits our tradition. As we all know, children are easily influenced and often imitate their toys." Suryaman said she ordered a large quantity of Barbie dolls from China and hired seamstresses to sew Islamic outfits for them. They thus became Salma Islamic dolls (Dhoundial 2007) (fig. 1).

Islamic Barbies, as the *Guardian* describes these dolls (Tatchell 2004), are products commodifying Islamic identity. Although their clothes, a *hijab* and an *abaya*, fit their presentations as Islamic dolls, their origins as blonde and cosmopolitan copies of Barbie dolls do not. While the Fulla doll created in 2003 asserts an Arab Muslim identity, she does so from a global and secular embodiment. The asymmetry between the Fulla doll and her predecessor Barbie locates Fulla at the tense border of two opposing cultural systems. Fulla ultimately presents a distorted identity, being both Islamic and Western at the same time.

Ann duCille (1994, 50) describes ethnic Barbie dolls as a Western stereotyping of the ethnic: "Regardless of what color dyes the dolls are dipped in or what costumes they are adorned with, the image they present is of the same mythically thin, long-legged, luxurious haired, buxom beauty." Ultimately, Arab Muslim dolls are Barbie dolls made from a mold almost exactly the same as Barbie's. So a Barbie with an Arab Muslim identity presents stereotyped expressions of an Arab Muslim girl, with subtle differences and slight variables between what is considered by the masses to belong to Western or Islamic cultural identities.

Body: Performing Arab Muslim Identity

The 2007 special edition of the *Market News Reports of the Middle East* promoted the Jamila doll for the toy fair held at the Dubai International Exhibition Centre (May 13–15, 2007) as follows: "Starting off as a single but truly Arabic doll, Jamila was launched in 2006 wearing a traditional black Abaya. Accompanied by her two best female friends and her soon-to-be husband Jamil, she truly hit the market" (*Market News Middle East* 2007). But what makes Jamila a "truly Arabic" plastic doll? Her marketing as a stereotyped image of an Arab girl.

Jamil, the soon-to-be husband of Jamila and the male version of the Jamila doll, was described as Jamila's friend on the box of the first edition of the Jamila doll in 2006. The mere existence of the Jamil doll as a friend is problematic in relation to the actual existence of male friends of Arab Muslim girls. This led Chris Becker, the head of operations and marketing at Simba Toys Middle East—the branch of the American company responsible for Jamila (Simba Toys Inc.)—to begin marketing Jamila and Jamil as a married couple soon after they were released in the Middle Eastern market.

Jamil, Ahmad, and Dara are not significant in themselves, as the Arab Muslim female dolls are. The male dolls are accessories to the female dolls, just as the Islamic outfits and the promotional narratives are. The Islamic branding of Arab Muslim dolls is not complete without an Islamic male figure. Male Arab Muslim dolls have the simple and clear functions of brothers or husbands. Remaining true to the actuality of Arab Muslim girls, especially in Saudi Arabia, where the law requires a female to be escorted by a male *mahram* (male one cannot marry because of kinship) in the majority of public situations, the male dolls highlight the Islamic identities of female dolls.

The narrative descriptions advertising Arab Muslim dolls imply a "true Arab-Muslim Identity." In her essay "Toy Theory: Black Barbie and the Deep Play of Difference," duCille (1996, 45) explains the "captions contributing to the museum of cultural effects" on the boxes of multicultural Barbie dolls: "The cultural captions on the boxes help to sell the impression that what we see isn't all we get with these dolls." Consumers are assured that this purchased doll is specifically Arab Muslim. Even though the dolls are copies of the Barbie doll, with the same blue eyes and blonde hair, they maintain an Arab Muslim identity.

The Fulla website calls her "Arab, body and soul," yet each of these dolls presents a different version of this true Arab Muslim (fig. 2). The arbiters of which counts as the "true" version are ultimately the parents who decide for one doll or another. In addition to demonstrating en masse the difficulty of agreeing on the "essence" of the "Arab Muslim girl," the origin of each doll as a copy and a repudiation of Barbie makes each a contradiction in herself. The clothing choices for the doll, asserted as properly "Islamic," layer over a plastic chassis corresponding to the very object that is forbidden.

The Arab Muslim doll sometimes asserts an Islamic identity by wearing the *hijab* and the full "Muslim" outfit; at other times she aligns instead with global secular elements, sometimes even going unveiled, like the Jamila doll. While some Islamic dolls, like Sara, are presented as girls less than nine years old (the age at which the *hijab* is mandated), others, like Fulla and Jamila, are portrayed as fourteen to sixteen years old. For the latter, the veil becomes a live issue.

The dolls perform Arab Islamic identity in other ways. For example, the songs in Fulla's marketing campaign stress her cultural background. "Al Salat" ("The Prayer") is a song about waking up early to attend prayer; "Al Watan Al Arabi" ("The Arab Homeland") is about preserving "Arabic values" and calls for Arab unity. Leen, a cheap replica of Fulla created by a Syrian company, is promoted as the "first speaking Islamic doll" (according to the doll's packaging). Leen comes in two versions: one dressed in a black Islamic outfit (the *abaya*) and the other in a white prayer outfit. Both versions are blonde with blue eyes and full makeup, but they speak different recorded phrases. Dressed in white, Leen recites Surat al-Fatiha from the Quran; in black she states what is described on the box as the "mother's anthem" in Arabic (fig. 3).

These features of Islamic dolls aim to resist Western stereotypes by offering alternative models for young girls. In *Framing Muslims* Peter Morey and Amina Yaqin (2011, 182) write that Islamic dolls and Barbie dolls are instances of the same marketing ideologies: both "operate to define available spaces for Western and Muslim femininities." Positioned as an alternative to Barbie, Fulla enters into the same discourse on femininity that she purportedly stands against.

This close link between the dolls and what they oppose is seen in the comments of one of the creators of the Razanne doll: "It's no surprise that they'd try to portray a

Figure 2.　Screenshot from www.fulla.com (accessed on December 13, 2015)

Middle Eastern Barbie either as a belly dancer or a concubine" (Associated Press 2015). Razanne explicitly stands as an alternative to the supposed Western stereotyping of Muslims (or at least the stereotypes of the exotic and implicitly erotic Middle East Barbie). Although Mattel did not produce an Arab Islamic doll with the specific cultural properties of today's Arab Muslim dolls, in 2013 the company added a Moroccan Barbie doll to its Dolls of the World collection. The description on her box says, "Strolling through the colorful souks, vibrantly colored spice bazaars, Barbie doll wears a pair of stunning golden earrings and an ornately stitched kaftan trimmed in sequins and golden brocade." However, the Traditions Moroccan Style version of Fulla also wears a colorful caftan. This Traditions series includes Fulla in Kingdom of Saudi Arabia Style, United Arab Emirates Style, Egypt Style, and Indian Touch. These dolls are specifically copies of Barbie's World Collection Moroccan Princess. Notably, the Fulla dolls differentiate between national versions rather than present a singular Arab Barbie as a Moroccan princess, but the

Figure 3.　Fulla prayer set at www.fulla.com (accessed December 13, 2015)

Morocco Barbie® Doll

$16.95

Product Code: X8425
Ages: For ages 6 and over.

DESCRIPTION ▼

Pink Label®

Designer: Linda Kyaw

Release Date: 5/23/2013

Salaam! Greetings from the kingdom of Morocco, an ancient land of kasbahs and camels. Strolling through the colorful "souks, " vibrantly colored spice bazaars, Barbie® doll wears a pair of stunning golden earrings and an ornately stitched kaftan trimmed in sequins and golden brocade. Includes "passport" and country stickers.

DETAILS ▶

Figure 4. Morocco Barbie at www.thebarbiecollection.com (accessed December 13, 2015)

basic approach of a feminine figure made culturally specific by adding certain clothes and accessories remains. Underneath is the same abject and unaltered plastic body, with the "goodness" of the vestments covering the "badness" of the feminine.

Sexuality as Badness as Power

Islamic dolls are promoted as alternatives that combat the "cultural invasion" of Western values through the Barbie doll. But they are appropriations of Barbie dolls. Given this hostility to the feminine and distrust of the female body, leading to repression of (certain kinds of) representations, the temptation might be to see the opposite as a kind of liberation. If the distrustful covering up of the feminine is the problem, then the purest alternative might well be the full display and performance of femininity. The specific alteration is a response to the "badness" of the feminine, an attempt to convert it from flaw to power. This section briefly sketches such an alternative from the point of view of the French critics collective Tiqqun (2012).

Given the system, in which the badness of the doll is the cause of inferiority or of corruption, the alternative is the idea that badness can be a source of power and a form of liberation. Tiqqun calls this alternative the system of the Young-Girl. The collective's members assure us that their description of the Young-Girl is not misogynist, because in their view we are all Young-Girls now (Tiqqun 2012, ii) as part of the functioning of late capitalism (ibid., i). The key feature of the Young-Girl is artificiality, the need to constantly *perform*: "The Young-Girl carries the mask of her face" (ibid., 9). This performance is so thoroughgoing that "what she loves is 'her' image, that is, something that's not just foreign and external, but which, in the full sense of the term possesses her" (ibid., 22). Ultimately, nothing remains but the performance. According to Tiqqun, the Young-Girl is reduced to a self-commodifying identity that holds no other value. She is product and consumer at the same time. The body of the Young-Girl functions purely in its appearance: "The Young-Girl is the commodity that at every moment demands to be consumed because with each passing moment she is getting closer to her expiration date" (ibid., 30). Tiqqun's Young-Girl is a living prosthesis of youth and femininity, as is the Arab Muslim doll (figs. 5–6).

This act of producing identity makes the parallels between the Young-Girl and the Arab Muslim doll obvious. In both cases, the per-

Figures 5–6. Images from Tiqqun 2012

formance is for the sake of another and is also intimately related to a stereotyped preexisting social role. The Young-Girl, no less than the doll, is a deliberate and purposeful performance of the feminine. Both are commodities. But these systems differ in terms of how badness can relate to the value of the commodity. For the doll, badness is what must be tamed or avoided; this is one-half of the liminal status of the female. It must be excluded—though it can never be dispelled—even though femininity is also the source of the doll's value, for example, Fulla's painted-on underwear. But this is a repressed femininity, a form of power that must be tamed to become useful or good. Most often Fulla gets to be a mother, though she is allowed to be a teacher, a doctor, a reader of the Quran, and a follower of fashion. The props sold with the dolls (all the dolls, Barbie as often as Fulla) are the means of funneling the energies of the doll—and therefore the girl playing with her—into specific and manageable roles. In Fulla's case, the props include schoolbags, prayer outfits, magazines, perfumes, handbags, veils, and prayer mats.

Key to both is the nature of their sexuality, repressed in the doll and expressed maximally in the Young-Girl. The necessity of repression is what turns the feminine, the doll, into the abject. But what happens to sexuality in the modern self-commodifying Young-Girl? It is brought out of the zone of repression by converting it into something that can be used, can be made useful and tradable. This is not to say that sexuality is not part of the doll but that there are two ways of dealing with it. The Arab Muslim doll's implicit sexuality is the model for the girl who plays with her. It has power and value only insofar as it remains implicit, suppressed, untainted by use, and unattached to a doll or a girl's own agency.

Conclusion

The Tiqqun alternative might be seen as a form of liberation, and in some sense it is. However, what is liberated is not the agent but a certain set of expressions. The Young-Girl, lacking the painted-on underwear of Fulla, is not punished but rewarded for expressing sexuality as badness. But this reward comes from conforming to a different system of self-presentation. Sexuality becomes part of what *must* be displayed; it is liberated at the cost of the underlying agent, for whom it simply becomes a tool of a different kind. The Jamila doll has her own pink Mercedes SLK; women in Saudi Arabia are not yet legally allowed to drive.

RIMA DUNN is a visiting researcher in the Games Design Hub, Winchester School of Art, and the School of Electronics and Computer Science, University of Southampton. Contact: rima.dunn@gmail.com.

ADAM GEORGE DUNN is a teaching fellow at the Winchester School of Art, University of Southampton. Contact: a.g.dunn@soton.ac.uk.

References

Associated Press. 2003. "Saudi Religious Police Say Barbie Is a Moral Threat." Fox News, September 10. www.foxnews.com/story/2003/09/10/saudi-religious-police-say-barbie-is-moral-threat.

———. 2015. "Muslim Doll Offers Modest Alternative to Barbie." CNN.com. www.noorartinc.com /newspage/CNN.html (accessed December 12, 2015).

BBC News. 2002. "Muslim Dolls Tackle 'Wanton' Barbie." March 5. news.bbc.co.uk/1/hi/world /middle_east/1856558.stm.

Dhoundial, Shreya. 2007. "Meet Salma, the 'Muslim Barbie Doll.'" Video. CNN-IBN, October 10. ibnlive .in.com/news/meet-salma-the-muslim-barbie-doll/50287-3.html.

duCille, Ann. 1994. "Dyes and Dolls: Multicultural Barbie and the Merchandising of Difference." *differences: A Journal of Feminist Cultural Studies* 6, no. 1: 46–68.

———. 1996. "Toy Theory: Black Barbie and the Deep Play of Difference." In *Skin Trade*, 8–59. Cambridge, MA: Harvard University Press.

Market News Middle East. 2007. "Middle East Toy Fair Dubai." www.toyfairme.com/userfiles/image /pdf/market_news/tf_market_news_dec_2007.pdf (accessed March 2016).

Middle East Media Research Institute. 2003. "Saudi Religious Police Launch a Website." May 13. www .memri.org/report/en/0/0/0/0/0/0/865.htm (accessed March 2016).

Morey, Peter, and Amina Yaqin. 2001. *Framing Muslims: Stereotyping and Representation after 9/11*. Cambridge, MA: Harvard University Press.

Sydney Morning Herald. 2003. "Saudi Police Outlaw Barbie." September 10. www.smh.com.au/articles /2003/09/10/1062902076884.html (accessed March 2016).

Tatchell, Jo. 2004. "Meet the Islamic Barbie." *Guardian*, September 30. www.theguardian.com /lifeandstyle/2004/sep/30/shopping.

Tiqqun. 2012. *Preliminary Materials for a Theory of the Young-Girl*, translated by Ariana Reines. Cambridge, MA: MIT Press.

Venezia, Todd. 2010. "Islamic Rival for Barbie." *New York Post*, November 20. nypost.com/2010/11/20 /islamic-rival-for-barbie.

Jineology
The Kurdish Women's Movement

◊ ◊

MERAL DÜZGÜN

The thirty million Kurds in Turkey, Iraq, Iran, Syria, and Armenia are the largest ethnic group that has not gained its own permanent nation-state (BBC News 2014). Although statelessness generally renders women socioeconomically and politically vulnerable, susceptible to male oppression, gender prejudices, and inequality, the Partiya Karkerên Kurdistan (PKK) includes one of the largest contingents of armed women militants in the world (Yildiz 2013).

Female combatants from the Women's Protection Units (Kurdish, Yekîneyên Parastina Jinê; YPJ) and the women's military wing of the PKK, Yekîneyên Jinên Azad ên Star (YJA-Star), have challenged traditional gender roles and contributed to the idea of "democratic confederalism," a term the PKK leader Abdullah Ocalan coined to highlight a move away from patriarchal nationalism. Kurdish women join the YPJ/YJA-Star ranks because they offer a possibility of achieving freedom and equality. In rejecting the idea of the state and taking up arms on behalf of their nation, the women of the YPJ/YJA-Star units are walking toward liberation. In her testimonial Bejan Ciyayi, a member of the YPJ, writes: "There are ideological, political and sociological reasons behind my desire to fight against ISIS. I have sworn to defend the Kurdish people against all evil" (Platt 2014). Is putting one's life on the line worth the fight for women's liberation? Or is Dilar Dirik (2014) right to argue that "wartime, uprisings, social unrest often provide women with space to assert themselves and to demand representation in ways that normal, civilian life would not permit"?

Many Kurdish women demand gender justice. A member of the pro-Kurdish Peace and Democracy Party, founded in 2008, which mandates that 40 percent of its representatives be women, writes, "When women have freedom to think then the Kurdish question will be solved" (Krajeski 2013). Abdullah Ocalan (2013, 57) reflects this belief:

> The extent to which society can be thoroughly transformed is determined by the extent of the transformation attained by women. Similarly, the level of woman's freedom and equality determines the freedom and equality of all sections of society. . . . For a democratic nation, woman's freedom is of great importance too, as liberated woman constitutes liberated society. Liberated society in turn constitutes democratic nation. Moreover, the need to reverse the role of man is of revolutionary importance.

With its Marxist-Leninist political roots, the PKK abjures capitalism. A combatant of the YPJ/YJA-Star units identified as Desine expresses such a view: "I fight for the enslaved woman, and help her liberation from oppression. I believe capitalism enslaves women. In capitalism men dominate while women are the underdogs. . . . Capitalism first oppressed European women. . . . I want to ask why many European women are still oppressed?" (Ahmad 2014). The women of the YPJ/YJA-Star units who do not require male permission to act in war wonder why European women tolerate their subordination in capitalist systems.

The PKK regards gender inequality as something that must be addressed in the party's "Women's Liberation Ideology" (Nurhak 2014). The party promotes the term *jineology*: "a fundamental scientific term in order to fill the gaps that the current social sciences are incapable of doing. Jineology is built on the principle that without the freedom of women within society and without a real consciousness surrounding women no society can call itself free" (ibid.). Zîlan Diyar (2014) writes:

> The whole world is talking about us, Kurdish women. It has become a common phenomenon to come across news about women fighters in magazines, papers, and news outlets. . . . To them, our rooted tradition is a reality that they only recently started to know. They are impressed with everything. The women's laughter, naturalness, long braids, and the details of their young lives feel like hands extending to those struggling in the waters of despair.

Diyar critiques the Western media's focus on the physical appearance of the Kurdish female fighters that trivializes women's roles in war and distracts "from the fact that the vast majority of Kurdish women join the struggle out of conviction, out of a desire to fight oppression, that they are conscious actors who want to determine their lives autonomously" (Dirik 2014).

This active consciousness is demonstrated in the testimonial of another Kurdish female fighter in her account of a fellow comrade's suicide attack:

One of my comrades, Arin Mirkan, recently blew herself up, and she is not the first female fighter in the Kurdish freedom movement to carry out such an attack. She followed a long line of such martyrs. Whenever there has been a threat of genocide against our people, Kurdish women have resorted to such actions. However, [the suicide attack] is not a tactic of our fight. It is not even approved of by our organisation. This kind of action is completely decided by the person carrying it out. It is not even a type of attack. It is a sacrificial action, the person undertaking such an action is sacrificing her life in order to defend her people from a force wanting to commit genocide. (Platt 2014)

The feminist consciousness of these women is alive and active. The political beliefs of the YPJ/YJA-Star units are consistently foregrounded in the Kurdish movement. For example, Turkey's Kurdish People's Democratic Party political parties "proudly represent at least 40% women." One can argue that "the strength of the resulting women's movement illustrates that the point in establishing structures such as copresidency (one woman and one man sharing the chair) and 50-50 gender splits in committees on all administrative levels is no mere tokenism to make women more visible" (Dirik 2014).

Kurdish female fighters of the YPJ/YJA-Star units challenge the gendered notions of the nation-state paradigm. Gender equality is a key motivator for the YPJ/YJA-Star women and for many people of the Kurdish movement. Kurdish female fighters take up arms and in so doing transgress patriarchal gender hierarchies and subvert traditional gender roles.

MERAL DÜZGÜN received her MA in cultural and critical studies from the University of Westminster, London. Contact: M.Duzgun1@westminster.ac.uk.

References

Ahmad, Rozh. 2014. "YPJ Kurdish Female Fighters: A Day in Syria." Video. *Kurdistan Tribune*, August 23. kurdistantribune.com/2014/ypj-kurdish-women-fighers-day-syria.

BBC News. 2014. "Who Are the Kurds?" October 21. www.bbc.co.uk/news/world-middle-east-29702440.

Dirik, Dilar. 2014. "What Kind of Kurdistan for Women?" Kurdish Question. www.kurdishquestion.com/index.php/woman/what-kind-of-kurdistan-for-women/25-what-kind-of-kurdistan-for-women.html (accessed April 1, 2015).

Diyar, Zîlan. 2014. "Kurdish Women Fighters: The Light of the World." Tendance Coatesy. tendancecoatesy.wordpress.com/2014/12/27/kurdish-women-fighters-the-light-of-the-world (accessed May 1, 2014).

Krajeski, Jenna. 2013. "Kurdistan's Female Fighters." *Atlantic*, January 30. www.theatlantic.com/international/archive/2013/01/kurdistans-female-fighters/272677.

Nurhak, Delal Afsin. 2014. "The Kurdish Woman's Liberation Movement." Partiya Karkerên Kurdistan. www.pkkonline.com/en/index.php?sys=article&artID=180 (accessed December 12, 2014).

Ocalan, Abdullah. 2013. "Democratic Modernity: Era of Woman's Revolution." In *Liberating Life: Woman's Revolution*. Neuss: International Initiative Edition with Mesopotamian Publishers.

Platt, Gareth. 2014. "A Kurdish Female Fighter's War Story: 'I Don't Know How Many I've Killed in Kobani—I Don't See Isis as Human.'" *International Business Times*, October 23. www.ibtimes.co.uk/kurdish-female-fighters-war-story-i-dont-know-how-many-ive-killed-kobani-i-dont-see-1471412.

Yildiz, Yesim Yaprak. 2013. "Turkey and the PKK: The Kurdish Women Who Take Up Arms." BBC News, January 15. www.bbc.co.uk/news/world-europe-21026273.

THIRD SPACE

Third Space Masculinities
Unnamed Sexualities in Turkey

◆◇◆

IKLIM GOKSEL

G rounded in everyday life, the practice of male same-sex relations is neither uncommon nor a dominant trend but rather a renegotiated space for many young men in Turkey today. This unnamed practice creates a "third space" that forms and transforms young men's alternative sexual subject positions. My conversations with young men revealed that in this third space the male body comes to terms with a new form of masculinity and male sexual pleasure that destabilizes both heteronormativity and homosexuality. I conducted fieldwork in Ankara, Turkey, between 2003 and 2005 to study the rhetorical uses of language in the context of virginity examinations. My study was based on participatory action research methods, and my field sites included a squatter settlement, a village, and an upper-class neighborhood. While there is a large literature on homosexuality and same-sex relations in Iran and the Arab world, this essay adds to the emerging scholarship that focuses on Turkey through its identification of a "third space" masculinity and its examination of not only urban but also rural and semiurban areas.

Young men who engage in same-sex practices often seek release from the material conditions of social norms governing premarital sexuality and virginity. Men who have sex with men do not have a language to name the sexual activities they engage in. They neither use terms such as homosexual or gay nor conflate their sexual encounters with homoerotic desire similar to what Huseyin Tapinc's (1992) research revealed in Turkey. Rather, they perform their sexualities in a ritualized manner to prove their maleness or abilities at penetrating. Hence rather than ascribing to a sexual orientation or gender identity, men who have sex with men build an alternative sexual space where they reconfigure masculine sexual behavior.

JMEWS • Journal of Middle East Women's Studies • 12:2 • July 2016
DOI 10.1215/15525864-3507760 • © 2016 by the Association for Middle East Women's Studies

In the newly configured third space of male same-sex practices, where affection and romance mostly do not reside, roles and meanings associated with masculinity, heterosexuality, and homosexuality blur. Contained in spaces reserved for young men, men who have sex with men do not depart from heterosexuality toward homosexuality. Rather, the third spaces they create are sites of response to social codes that prohibit sexual encounters between men and women. Hence men who have sex with men are dissidents renegotiating their sexualities and redrawing the boundaries of what may be possible in a culture of compulsory virginity. The third space is a way to reinscribe sexual behavior and build solidarity in the spaces reserved for men where opposite sex partner relationships are not available. However, this is not to say that male same-sex sexuality is always a direct consequence of norms regarding virginity and women's seclusion. As Afsaneh Najmabadi (2006) points out, it can be reductive and totalizing to always attribute same-sex sexuality to societal practices such as gender segregation and veiling.

The third space masculinity in the Turkish context illuminates modes of sexuality that lack a linguistic space. Situated in a context that legitimates only marital heteronormative sexual behavior and pleasure, men who have sex with men live in a culture of secrecy and silence. Yet, in spite of the lack of a language, this third space masculinity speaks in other ways. First, third space is liberating in its attempt to create a medium through which entry into a sexual subjectivity is sought without privileging a sexual identity or sexual orientation. Second, it is a space of critique and empowerment that makes a potential argument for sexual freedom a possibility. In this nondiscursive space silence seeks to break away from repressed sexualities. Although an everyday language to name it does not exist, this space is a means of coming to terms with societal norms and men's relationships to each other. Without female participation, it is a space where patriarchal economies are reproduced; it is a male-defined marginal space structured around the male body and the phallus.

The presence of this male domain points to the need to develop a new discourse to theorize the unnamed third space and its implications. As an alternative space partly created in response to societal constraints, third space masculinities provide an opportunity to rethink male sexuality and masculinity in the heteronormative order. Instead of totalizing men's and women's experiences with patriarchy, the third space masculinity in Turkey can broaden the possibilities of using a new nuanced language to contextualize and theorize how patriarchal patterns in society shape masculinities and male sexualities as well. Finally, third space masculinities in Turkey have the potential to contribute to the feminist agenda by addressing unnamed but lived sexualities, so that individuals' experiences with sexuality are not totalized but grounded in everyday stories to capture nuanced sexual subjectivities that move beyond the heterosexual versus homosexual dualism.

IKLIM GOKSEL is adjunct lecturer in the Women's Studies Program at Indiana University–Purdue University Fort Wayne. Contact: iklim.goksel@gmail.com.

References

Najmabadi, Afsaneh. 2006. "Gender and Secularism of Modernity: How Can a Muslim Woman Be French?" *Feminist Studies* 32, no. 2: 239–55.

Tapinc, Huseyin. 1992. "Masculinity, Femininity, and Turkish Male Homosexuality." In *Modern Homosexualities: Fragments of Lesbian and Gay Experiences*, edited by Ken Plummer, 39–49. London: Routledge.

We pay tribute to the Algerian historian, filmmaker, and novelist Assia Djebar (née Fatima-Zohra Imalayen), who died on February 6, 2015. She was seventy-nine years old. Author of seventeen novels and short story collections, she published her first novel, *La soif* (*Thirst*), in 1957. Her best-known work is her semiautobiographical *L'amour la fantasia* (1985), which Didem Havlioğlu and Rachel Rothendler analyze in their contributions to this issue. —The Editors

The Writing Subjects

Halide Edip and Assia Djebar

◇ ◇

DIDEM HAVLIOĞLU

Despite their physical distance from each other in terms of time and place, the Turkish Halide Edip (1882–1964) and the Algerian Assia Djebar (1936–2015) wrote in surprisingly similar ways. They share a multicultural and multilingual education and position as writing subjects. As Muslim women writers in the modern literary world, they traverse political, literary, and linguistic borders. This essay explores their autobiographical writings, Djebar's *Fantasia* (1993) and Edip's *Memoirs* (Adıvar 2004), where they contest colonialism, nationalism, and patriarchy.

Who is the Muslim woman writer? The last few decades have witnessed a number of invaluable studies that examine the question, working mainly in a framework of ethnic, national, and linguistic origins (see Badran and cooke 2004; Brookshaw 2013; cooke 2001; Fernea and Bezirgan 1977; Havlioğlu 2010; Malti-Douglas 1991; Mehta 2014). As for Djebar, there has been much thought-provoking research on her writings in the context of postcolonial literature.[1] Studies on Edip, on the contrary, have remained in the domain of national literature, and she is typically read in the context of Turkish literature.[2] This essay reads Djebar and Edip through their Islamicate aesthetic heritages to examine how they challenge orientalist discourse and local patriarchies.

JMEWS • Journal of Middle East Women's Studies • 12:2 • July 2016
DOI 10.1215/15525864-3507771 • © 2016 by the Association for Middle East Women's Studies

Trapped between imperialism, colonialism, and Third World nationalisms, Djebar and Edip might have been doomed to silence.[3] However, their writing liberated them from their prescribed "double prisons." They gave voice to others who had been silenced and forgotten. How did they escape their prisons and rewrite history?

Djebar's and Edip's alternative discourses stem from Islamicate literary aesthetics that contest colonial and national binary constructions, linear and progressive plotlines, and the authoritative narrative voice. Instead, they opt for fragmentation, multiple voices, and alternative uses of language, replacing the native with "foreign" as the original. In their works the difference between self and other or public and private are intentionally blurred, as each is the reflection of the other.

Djebar and Edip wrote outside colonial, national, and patriarchal discourses. Their self-constructions are based on a fine balance between acceptance of and resistance to their literary heritage.

Her Story Is History

Djebar's and Edip's personal stories retell their national histories. The "personal" is not a single self but a combination of self and others. The individual is not dissolved into the collective but rather finds value in the interaction between self and other. They refer to themselves in the third person, replacing the single authoritative voice of the narrator with the voices of silenced women throughout history. These intertwined stories are necessary parts of their identities as Muslim women writers.

One of the builders of modern Turkish history, Edip was a soldier alongside men in the War of Independence against the Western occupation. In *Memoirs* she proposes an alternative narrative to that of the nation's father, Mustafa Kemal Atatürk. His *Nutuk* (*Speech*) deals with the establishment of the Republic of Turkey, with himself as hero (Atatürk 1989). He even calls some individuals who participated in establishing the Republic of Turkey traitors, including Edip for supporting the American colonization of her country.

That her image could change from being the "daughter of the republic," the voice of the War of Independence, to a "traitor" is curious. The friction between Edip and Atatürk dates back to their time in Ankara, when they worked together closely. Edip's expulsion from this core team has been a subject of interest. Some claim that she opposed initiatives such as the language and dress reforms as transgressive.[4] She left the country in 1925 with her husband, Adnan Adıvar, and lived in London and Paris; she also spent some time in the United States and India. The couple returned to their country only after Atatürk's death in 1938.

Edip wrote her autobiography, focused on the silenced voices of the Turkish nation, in English in response to Atatürk's *Nutuk* (see also Adıvar 2007). Coming from a Mevlevi Sufi family, she was sympathetic to the story of the Prophet's cousin Ali, who "is the least successful Islamic hero. Every adversary of his takes advantage of his nobility of heart. . . . No wonder there are so many religious sects that worship him, not only as a great hero but even as the incarnation of Allah" (Adıvar 2004, 120). Edip refers here to the oral traditions and legends about Ali, which are considered the secret knowledge of heterodox communities in Anatolia. Immediately following this section, she writes: "Mustafa Kemal Pasha was studying the epoch-making struggles of the Islamic Republic. . . . I was interested to observe his contempt for what he considered Ali's weakness. 'Ali was a fool,' he used to say" (ibid.). "If only history would refuse to record martial glories, and literature to immortalize them, there might be some semblance of peace and relative human happiness in the world" (ibid., 118–19). Edip took an active part in the struggle for independence, yet she refused to take credit for the victory, as it should belong to the people.

Likewise, Djebar uses other histories to tell her personal narrative. In *Fantasia* she combines her story with those of women who fought the 130-year occupation of Algeria. The structural balance between her own voice and other voices creates her personal narrative of history. The historical documents chronicling the occupation of Algeria are carefully selected to reveal the untold versions of historical events.[5] The voices in Djebar's work had been forgotten or ignored. Like Edip's narrative, Djebar's personal story works to fill in the gaps.

Language of War or Language of Love
Both authors use a foreign language to tell a personal narrative. Djebar wrote *Fantasia* in French, and Edip wrote *Memoirs* in English. In 1926, during her self-imposed exile, Edip published the first volume of *Memoirs*. Two years later the second volume's publication aroused hostility toward her in Turkey, where she was accused of being a Western agent and even of being morally corrupt. She never responded. When she translated her memoirs from English to Turkish in 1962, shortly before her death, she omitted some sections that criticized Atatürk. Was she still afraid of attacks, or did she not want to harm the grand image of Atatürk, the father of the nation that she had worked hard to build?

Djebar's treatment of language is closely related to her self-construction. She addresses the issue of writing in French throughout the novel. French, her "step-mother's tongue," allows her to travel between texts, between French and Arabic, between written and oral (Djebar 1993, 214). "Autobiography practiced in the enemy's language has the texture of fiction. . . . While I thought I was undertaking a journey through myself, I find I am simply choosing another veil. While I intended every step forward to make me more clearly identifiable, I find myself progressively sucked down into the anonymity of those women of old — my ancestors" (ibid., 216–17).

Djebar's choice of "the enemy's language" reflects her strategy to break binary oppositions, such as war and love. She opens *Fantasia* with the chapter title "The Capture of the City or Love Letters." She uses war and love interchangeably as metaphors of a similar desire to make history. With metaphors of love, such as "the impregnable city" (ibid., 6), she renders the occupation of the land as a form of desire to capture and possess. Djebar constructs an alternative space where the two languages complement each other. Similar to Edip's choice to open *Memoirs* with the chapter title "This Is a Story of a Little Girl" (Adıvar 2004, 3), the first story Djebar (1993, 3) tells in *Fantasia* concerns a little Arab girl on her way to school, "hand in hand with her father." This girl will learn how to write, and the implications of her writing will be unexpected. She attends a French school, where she learns not only how to write but also how to speak a foreign language, the enemy's language. Though her father encourages her French education, he has no tolerance for her unanticipated uses of her education, such as love letters. When she receives a love letter from a boy, a classmate, she realizes the significance of language. First, it is written in French; second, her father destroys it. Through this incident she discovers a secret: love is a trespassing action, and its vehicle is the second language. This is the moment of her awakening; she loses her innocence and becomes the subject who can tell or write her own life story. She says, "In these early stages of my sentimental education, our secret correspondence is carried on in French: thus the language that my father had been at pains for me to learn, serves as a go-between, and from now a double, contradictory sign over my initiation" (Djebar 1993, 4). Both for Djebar and for Edip, writing in the enemy's language is not a choice but a necessity to resist local patriarchies.

Conclusion

Both Djebar and Edip were raised in Muslim traditions, received their institutional educations in foreign schools, and became internationally acclaimed intellectuals at a time when their countries were fighting against occupation and undergoing nationalization. Furthermore, they faced similar challenges as Muslim women writers in the global literary world. Both argued that historical narratives always have unspoken stories that, if heard, might give us a version of events that is closer to reality. For Edip and Djebar, writing provides a space where the emancipation of the writer and her characters is possible.

DIDEM HAVLIOĞLU is assistant professor of Turkish language and literature at Istanbul Sehir University and teaching fellow in Asian and Middle Eastern studies at Duke University. Contact: didem.havli@duke.edu.

Notes

1. For an interesting take on Djebar's use of language, see Corbin 2014.
2. Apart from research on Edip in Turkish, for a recent deliberation of her writing in terms of modern Turkish literature, see Göknar 2013 and Seyhan 2008.

3. Hülya Adak (2001, 100) reviews feminist postcolonial theories, in particular those of Deniz Kandiyoti and Meyda Yeğenoğlu, to suggest that they do not acknowledge a possibility for women as speaking subjects, since colonial discourse controls what can be said.

4. In her biography of Edip, İpek Çalışlar (2010, 223–25) chronicles the silent friction between Edip and Atatürk and suggests that Edip decided to write *Memoirs* right after their first argument.

5. For instance, she insinuates French officers, such as Captain Pierre François Bosquet, into the narrative (Djebar 1993, 49).

References

Adak, Hülya. 2001. "Intersubjectivity: Halide Edib (1882–1964) or the 'Ottoman/Turkish (Woman)' as the Subject of Knowledge." PhD diss., University of Chicago.

Adıvar, Halide Edip. 2004. *Memoirs of Halide Edip.* New York: First Georgias Press.

——. 2007. *Türk'ün Ateşle İmtihanı: İstiklal Savaşı Hatıraları.* Istanbul: Can.

Atatürk, Mustafa Kemal. 1989. *Nutuk (Speech).* Ankara: Türk Tarih Kurumu Basımevi.

Badran, Margot, and miriam cooke, eds. 2004. *Opening the Gates: An Anthology of Arab Feminist Writing.* Bloomington: Indiana University Press.

Brookshaw, Dominic. 2013. "Women in Praise of Women: Female Poets and Female Patrons in Qajar Iran." *Iranian Studies: Journal of the International Society for Iranian Studies* 46, no. 1: 17–21.

Çalışlar, İpek. 2010. *Biyografisine Sığmayan Kadın: Halide Edip (The Woman Who Does Not Fit into Her Biography).* Istanbul: Everest.

cooke, miriam. 2001. *Women Claim Islam: Creating Islamic Feminism through Literature.* New York: Routledge.

Corbin, Laurie. 2014. "The Other Language, the Language of the Other in the Work of Assia Djebar and Hélène Cixous." *MLN* 129, no. 4: 812–28.

Djebar, Assia. 1993. *Fantasia: An Algerian Cavalcade,* translated by Dorothy S. Blair. Portsmouth, NH: Heinemann.

Fernea, Elizabeth Warnock, and Basima Qattan Bezirgan, eds. 1977. *Middle Eastern Muslim Women Speak.* Austin: University of Texas Press.

Göknar, Erdağ. 2013. "Halide Edip's Gendering of Ottoman Modernity: *The Clown and His Daughter* (1935)." In *Orhan Pamuk, Secularism, and Blasphemy: The Politics of the Turkish Novel,* 150–58. New York: Routledge.

Havlioğlu, Didem. 2010. "On the Margins and between the Lines: Ottoman Women Poets from the Fifteenth to the Twentieth Centuries." *Turkish Historical Review* 1, no. 1: 25–54.

Malti-Douglas, Fedwa. 1991. *Woman's Body, Woman's Word: Gender and Discourse in Arabo-Islamic Writing.* Princeton, NJ: Princeton University Press.

Mehta, Brinda J. 2014. *Dissident Writings of Arab Women: Voices against Violence.* London: Routledge.

Seyhan, Azade. 2008. "History Conjugated in the First Person." In *Tales of Crossed Destinies: The Modern Turkish Novel in a Comparative Context,* 46–56. New York: Modern Language Association of America.

Languaging Space in Assia Djebar's *L'amour, la fantasia*

◇ ◇

RACHEL ROTHENDLER

This essay examines Assia Djebar's approach to language as a temporal, physical, and imagined space. In *L'amour, la fantasia* (1995), the first volume of her "autobiographical quartet," Djebar intertwines her own stories with those of girls and women living during and after the Algerian War of Independence (1954–62); historical narratives of French soldiers, reporters, and painters during the years of colonization; and fictional anecdotes. She demonstrates that Algerian history is reflected in her own experiences. Appropriating the voices of colonizer and colonized across time, Djebar creates a chronotope, a kind of temporal landscape in which French, the language of the colonizer, becomes her own to the extent that she inhabits it.

Shortly after Algeria's independence, the narrator is walking in Paris with her brother when he calls her *hannouni*, meaning "my dear" or "my love." Thrown back to her childhood, she muses: "My brother . . . reminds me . . . of the local spoken dialect of the mountains where we spent our childhood. I felt a somewhat bittersweet embarrassment. I turned away. I began to reminisce about the past" (Djebar 1993, 80–81).[1] The text subtly switches tenses from the present to the past, a technique employed throughout the book, illustrating the association between the past, tradition, and the languages of Arabic and Berber. The Arabic word *hannouni* evokes nostalgia, regret, and longing, all the more poignant since Djebar is forced to narrate in French, the colonial language that the younger generation speaks fluently and that separates them from their mother tongue, the language of their parents and grandparents.

JMEWS • Journal of Middle East Women's Studies • 12:2 • July 2016
DOI 10.1215/15525864-3507782 • © 2016 by the Association for Middle East Women's Studies

Scholars often refer to the entry of the colonizers' language into Algeria as an *implantation* of French, making language into something physical. The French initiated this implantation with the idea that to unify a region, one had to unify its language. In 1938 Arabic was declared "a foreign language," so that French became associated with citizenship and freedom, especially freedom *of movement* in a space no longer belonging to the indigenous population. In fact, this implantation had the unintended consequence of reinforcing regional language differences such that the regions became increasingly delineated by the languages of their inhabitants: Berber, Arabic, Spanish, Italian, and Turkish. The French policies and attitudes established language as an immense dividing factor among the various indigenous groups and of course between the native Algerians and the European colonists.

Different physical language-spaces are an ever-present element of the narratives of *L'amour, la fantasia*, literally dividing the world inhabited by Arabic from that inhabited by French. In one story from Algeria before the outbreak of the war, the narrator, a young girl at the time, describes a French family living in her neighborhood. She never enters the family's house but watches the goings-on through the windows. One interaction that captures her attention occurs between the eldest daughter and her new fiancé. Contrary to local customs, the two publicly display their affection, touching and exchanging words of endearment. She expresses her sense of removal and distance watching the scenes on the other side of the glass: "I decided that love must necessarily reside elsewhere and not in public words and gestures. . . . The French language could offer me all its inexhaustible treasures, but not a single one of its terms of endearment would be destined for my use" (27). For the narrator, the French language becomes a space of intimacy, of "the couple," and of a different kind of happiness to which she cannot gain access despite learning French in school.

French is also the language that this same narrator uses to write love letters to an anonymous correspondent overseas, her words literally traveling across the oceanic expanse: "When I write and read the foreign language, my body travels far in subversive space" (184). She uses spatial terms to describe her study of Arabic at the Quranic school too: "The learning was absorbed by the fingers, the arms, through the physical effort. The act of cleaning the tablet seemed like ingesting a portion of the Quranic text" (183–84). Yet this physical space of language is perhaps most apparent in the idea of *la langue du corps*, "body language." Body language of course includes the physical act of *l'écrit* (writing), but, more significantly, it encompasses *les cris* (the cries) of the female ancestors, both the cries present in the traditional matrilineal ceremonies and the cries of despair and rage spurred by 132 years of French colonization.

A similar sense of disorientation develops in the imagined spaces of these languages. Due to the extreme regulation of language during colonization and directly following independence with the promotion of Arabization, the younger generation that had grown up under French rule was thrown into a state of language crisis, torn between Arabic and French. The narrator vacillates between the sense that linguistic *métissage* offers her more control and movement and the sense that one language will forever interrupt the other, leading to a mental aphasia. The two languages demarcate distinct physical areas in endless confrontation, engendering feelings of exclusion and isolation. The narrator fears that she will never be able to fully express herself, that there will always exist silences between her words: "The compliments—harmless or respectful—expressed in the foreign language, traversed a no-man's land of silence. . . . The word had simply drowned before reaching its destination" (126).

Legitimacy plays a major role in the imagined space of language. Ordinances related directly to the French language and to the enforcement of French law as a whole turned French into a symbol of freedom, intellect, and citizen status in colonized Algeria. Thus the connection between legitimacy and language was sharpened greatly, a feature mirrored in one of Djebar's narratives describing the fall of Algiers in 1830. A French army captain recounts the event through letters, indicating frustration at the lack of *regard* given to the victorious soldiers by the indigenous population, especially by the women: "The native . . . [d]oes not raise his eyes to gaze on his vanquisher. Does not 'recognize' him. Does not name him. What is a victory if it is not named?" (56). *What is a victory if it is not named?* This question precisely exemplifies the need for recognition through naming, through *language*. By refusing to acknowledge the French soldiers' victory, the women refuse to grant the victory legitimacy.

Despite her use of primarily French words in *L'amour, la fantasia*, the language is Djebar's own. It falls outside the simple characterization of "French," because she constructs it as a space: "I cohabit with the French language" (213). Djebar took words from the physical spaces of the archives and from the locations where she conducted interviews and ethnographic studies and literally placed them on the pages of her book. She recounts events in her own words and manipulates the narrative flow and syntax of the text. One is thus forced to move back and forth between the pages to understand her language. Reading becomes a physical experience.

In creating the imagined linguistic space of her narratives, Djebar may refuse to translate Arabic words. In the final chapter of the book she presents the definitions of the word *tzarl-rit* from two Arabic-French dictionaries. Evidently, neither definition manages to fully capture the meaning and implications of the word, which refers to *les cris* of women. In her choices of where to withhold translation, she actually straddles the boundary between the spoken word (associated with the Arabic oral tradition) and the written one (associated with French text and schooling).

In spite of the limitations and boundaries that each of these languages possesses and in spite of her aphasic *métissage*, Djebar gives voice to Algerian women across generations, an accomplishment she seems to recognize at several moments in the book: "Writing in a foreign language, not in either of the tongues of my native country . . . has brought me . . . to my own true origins. Writing does not silence the voice, but awakens it" (204).

In *Ces voix qui m'assiègent . . . en marge de ma francophonie* (*These Voices That Besiege Me . . . on the Margins of My* Francophonie, 1999) Djebar explores her relationship with languages in even greater depth through poems, short stories, and essays. The work attempts "to 'put into words' [her] writing process, [her] journey, [her] country" (à "rendre compte" de [son] écriture, de [son] trajet, de [son] pays) (ibid., 7).[2] In so doing, she describes what writing means to her, whether her texts can be considered "francophone" texts, and whether she considers herself a francophone writer (ibid., 25). Djebar is privileged in her capacity as an academic to put anything at all into words and to reach an audience, yet writing constitutes a struggle to create a meaningful space that cannot be encompassed by any one language. Moreover, she characterizes this "putting of voice into writing" as a "putting to death of voice" (ibid., 26), emphasizing the somewhat contradictory nature of the writing space. Although she places her writing (*écriture*) in a space *hors-les-langues* (outside languages), she also asks whether it is truly writing (*écrire*): "No, I would say rather that it is 'transmitting, teaching, communicating' and, later, seeking to move beyond the geographic limits of the French language. In this linguistic territory of so-called 'francophonie,' I place myself on the borders" (ibid., 26–27).

Before the act of writing begins, Djebar feels "a movement within, a rhythmic pounding without words" (ibid., 25) that gives birth to the physical inscription of words on pages. Language must initiate the writing process to communicate to her readers, to transmit her message. Yet she makes words into her own space in which she literally and figuratively pushes "the geographic limits" of the French language so that she can inhabit its borders, itself "a linguistic territory" *hors-les-langues.*

Dorothy S. Blair, in her introduction to *Fantasia: An Algerian Cavalcade*, the English translation of *L'amour, la fantasia*, remarks that Djebar, while maneuvering her "love-hate relationship" with the French language, sometimes, "in a conscious effort to escape from the shackles of writing in 'the enemy's language' . . . seems to be colonizing the language of the colonizers. She does violence to it, forcing it to give up its riches and defying it to hand over its hidden hoard" (Djebar 1993, xviii). While I do not agree with Blair's assertion that Djebar "does violence" to the French language, I do believe that she challenges it, pushes its limits with her extensive use of unusual and foreign vocabulary, her shifts in narrative structure and voice, and her manipulation of grammar and syntax. As Jean-Pierre Cuq notes, "Language is the space where the individual's driving internal forces converge" (quoted in Arezki 2010, 166). Thus despite the seemingly isolating and limiting nature of the language-space, it has the potential to be individualized, as Djebar so clearly illustrates in *L'amour, la fantasia*. It presents an opportunity for expression that need not be restricted to our constructed categories of French, English, Arabic, and so forth. Rather than consider Djebar's use of language as a *violent* act then, I view it as a *re*construction. She *re*news language, *re*appropriates its limits, and injects her own driving internal forces, effectively inscribing herself into the language-space and making it her own.

RACHEL ROTHENDLER is a JD student at Duke University School of Law and a PhD student in French in Duke's Department of Romance Studies. Contact: rachel .rothendler@duke.edu.

Notes

1. For quotations from *L'amour, la fantasia*, see the English translation, Djebar 1993.
2. All translations of *Ces voix qui m'assiègent . . . en marge de ma francophonie* are my own.

References

Arezki, Abdenour. 2010. "La planification linguistique en Algérie ou l'effet de boomerang sur les représentations sociolinguistiques." *Le Français en Afrique*, no. 25: 165–71. www.unice.fr/ILF-CNRS/ofcaf/index.html.

Djebar, Assia. 1993. *Fantasia: An Algerian Cavalcade*, translated by Dorothy S. Blair. Portsmouth, NH: Heinemann.

———. 1995. *L'amour, la fantasia*. Paris: Michel.

———. 1999. *Ces voix qui m'assie `gent . . . en marge de ma francophonie*. Montreal: Presses de l'Université de Montréal.

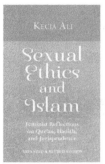

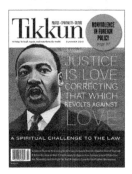

Printed and bound by CPI Group (UK) Ltd, Croydon, CR0 4YY

13/04/2025

14656483-0003